Editing
Across Media

ALSO BY ROSS F. COLLINS

The Rise of Western Journalism, 1815–1914:
Essays on the Press in Australia, Canada, France,
Germany, Great Britain and the United States (2007)

Editing
Across Media

*Content and Process for Print
and Online Publication*

Edited by ROSS F. COLLINS

McFarland & Company, Inc., Publishers
Jefferson, North Carolina, and London

LIBRARY OF CONGRESS CATALOGUING-IN-PUBLICATION DATA

Editing across media : content and process for print and online
publication / Edited by Ross F. Collins.
p.   cm.
Includes bibliographical references and index.

ISBN 978-0-7864-7342-7
softcover : acid free paper ∞

1. Editing.   2. Editing — Data processing.
3. Mass media and literature.   4. Scholarly publishing.
5. Electronic publishing.   I. Collins, Ross F. editor of compilation.
PN162.E19 2013   808.02'7 — dc23   2012048776

BRITISH LIBRARY CATALOGUING DATA ARE AVAILABLE

Manufactured in the United States of America

McFarland & Company, Inc., Publishers
Box 611, Jefferson, North Carolina 28640
www.mcfarlandpub.com

Table of Contents

Introduction

Editors in the new millennium have faced enormous technological change. Duties and routines that lasted a century or more have fallen faster than tight deadlines at big dailies—that is, if those dailies still existed. Some are gone. The rest are surely online, either incidentally or totally. Editors who could do an excellent job of working a written story into a polished showpiece found that this considerable skill was no longer enough.

Today many editors have to do more, know more, be more. They have to master technologies that reach beyond copy editing. They may write headlines for search engine optimization and construct blogs for reader discussion. They may tweet the news and tweak the pictures for presentation in print or on screen. They may design pages and opine in social media. They may even write stories based on material transmitted from reporters, and certainly they will brainstorm the multimedia packages readers expect in a converged media world. Editing, like all journalism, has become a process.

But editors today don't all work in news operations. Editing is critical to all communication, including public relations and advertising. Many writers in these areas also are editors, the roles blurred, but the expectations still high. Writers should know how to edit. Editors must know how to write. And they'll probably do both.

The challenge is to produce in one textbook a series of essays that touches on all jobs listed under the title "editor" in the twenty-first century. We decided it's impossible to do alone. If editing students today are more and more expected to learn it all, textbooks need to draw from many areas of expertise to help them learn it. This text attempts to address the needs of editors both in and out of the newsroom. The writers of these essays acknowledge the continuing power of newsprint, but also consider the growing influence of convergence. They assess the ever-greater significance of visual literacy and the need of editors in public relations to present polished work to their clients. What is an editor? Maybe we should ask what an editor is not. The traditional copy editor is becoming a content editor.

These essays help us to understand those new demands. An editor today may be the classic multitasker. But some tasks haven't changed. An editor is not a professional who takes no pride in careful grammar and considered word usage. She is hardly ignorant of the wide world around her, having soaked up knowledge like a wiki through widespread reading and wide-ranging education. He is not oblivious to the ethics of plagiarism and the law of libel that could damage his operation and destroy his career.

1

These are among the editing skills that haven't changed and still must be part of editing textbooks. You'll find them here.

If an editor's duties today have extended beyond those of the past, however, a single course and a single text cannot hope to cover the entire spectrum. Perhaps such a text never could; thorough coverage of the mechanics of English copy editing alone demands entire books devoted to usage. Writers of this text have tried to address the most common grammar and usage mistakes university students make. They have tried to encourage students to think like an editor, to take a critical and detail-oriented approach to their work. But they have not claimed to cover the complete AP *Stylebook,* or rewrite classic usage guides such as *Fowler's Modern English Usage.* Editing professors would be delighted if students could master the lessons of this text. This knowledge offers the minimum competence a student needs to be an editor in a complicated and rapidly changing world of mass media.

In addition to the chapters, this text offers vocabulary and informal sidebars that should enrich a student's learning, and perhaps even offer an opportunity to chuckle at the craft's quirks and history. Also included are lists of readings and websites for a student interested in knowing more, and exercises designed to build competence. This text can be the basic for students who will edit in many different job capacities, over many platforms, in an unpredictable but exciting future of mass media.

"In my view, it's a great time to be an editor," Teresa Schmedding, president of the American Copy Editors Society, told members at its 2011 conference. "It may be the best time in history if you're a good editor — if you're intelligent and thoughtful and creative and adaptable."

ONE

Editing Across Media

Margot Opdycke Lamme

If you visit the references page of the American Copy Editors Society website you'll find a list of links: grammar, vocabulary, punctuation, time zones, topography, technology, silent movies, disasters, math, stats, the Bible, dictionaries, the weather, Iraq, Zip codes, social security numbers, the Middle East and word games. The message is clear: copy editors need to know a lot about a lot of things to ensure that the news is reported clearly and accurately and that it is presented in a way to drive consumers to the news source.

First, though, the news.

In his 1918 book, *The Profession of Journalism*, Willard Grosvenor Bleyer, a venerated journalism educator at the University of Wisconsin, defined news as timely information in relation to local, state or national concerns that readers would find important. Today, five fundamental news values help guide editors' decisions about news gathering and reporting. Consequence emphasizes topics that educate, affect lifestyle or are of social importance. Timeliness emphasizes topics that are current or present a new angle or trend related to a current topic. Proximity emphasizes topics nearby. Human interest emphasizes topics that are unusual, entertaining or thought-provoking. Prominence favors topics related to or focusing on famous people or on institutions.

While reporters are on the front line, gathering the news, interviewing eyewitnesses and constructing the who, what, when, where, why and how of the story, editors are back at the newsroom, residing in a real or virtual "slot" (copy desk chief) or "rim" (copy editors). Nevertheless, even though reporters may seem to have the glamorous job, it is the copy editor who is often described as the glue that holds the news gathering and news production processes together. The operation requires input from different section editors and their reporters, research librarians, photographers and graphic designers, press operators and circulation staff.

Across time and textbooks, the responsibilities of a copy editor are frequently described in terms of their breadth and depth. Responsibilities include correcting fact errors, language, grammar, and punctuation errors, ensuring stories conform to the appropriate style guide, tightening and enlivening copy, ensuring timeliness, meeting deadlines, eliminating editorializing, writing headlines, verifying numbers and percentages and the conclusions based on them, eliminating potentially defaming material, ensuring the clear, accurate and logical flow in stories, and overseeing the news selection and publication process. In doing these things, editors also attend to the preservation of voice, the authenticity of the writer's own words and tone. Indeed, the advent and proliferation of social media, of online communities and networks, of citizen journalists, global communities and employee-bloggers, to name a few, has only strengthened the importance of authenticity and credibility in writing.

Editors strive for perfection but remain mindful of time constraints, making them pragmatic in approaching their work. They know the difference between a story that is ready for publication, even if it could use more work, and one that is not ready, that *needs* more work. They evaluate the quality of the news gathering and reporting processes not only from a technical perspective but from a legal and ethical one as well, with an eye trained on the "big picture." Editors are constantly on the lookout for new story ideas. They determine not only what constitutes news, but also how it will be framed (what or who will be emphasized, included or omitted) and how it will be presented through images and word choices in the copy, the headlines and the captions. Such characterizations of editors have remained remarkably consistent over time and across mass communications.

The editing function: Beyond the newspaper

Like newspaper copy editors, magazine editors also maintain a big-picture perspective, even as they attend to the details that comprise the production of a single issue, such as the story budget, submission specs, writing assignments, manuscript reviews and editorial calendars. Calendars help freelance writers, public relations professionals and advertisers pair their submissions, pitches and ad buys, respectively, with an issue theme or topic. The result is an issue that stands alone, distinctive in its copy, concept and design, even as it reflects the larger identity of the publication. Similarly, video editors focus on continuity and adherence to the storyline, merging the director's and actors' visions. Design editors construct and adhere to visual identity standards that allow for flexibility in individual page designs (hard copy or electronic) that remain consistent with the overall look and tone of the medium.

In a 1923 book, *Newspaper Writing and Editing,* Bleyer laid out the roles within a newsroom, many of which still hold true. Editors-in-chief and editorial writers determine editorial policy, and managing editors supervise reporters and editors. Additionally, in Bleyer's time, editors handled the city news, as well as the state, national, and global news delivered by the wire services and the newspaper's correspondents. Newsrooms might have included numerous other specialized positions. These might have been labeled telegraph editor and cable editor or sporting editor, society editor, financial and market editor, literary editor, editor of the woman's department, dramatic and musical critics, exchange editor (who reviewed other newspapers and magazines for relevant copy to reprint) and Sunday, or magazine, editor.

THE BIG FIVE NEWS VALUES THAT HAVE SURVIVED

1. Consequence: So What?

Editors know people are less likely to read stories that apparently don't directly affect them. But stories of consequence can help people cope with issues or events. Perhaps an editor encounters a lead like this: "The North Gulch State University Senate met Tuesday." No one will read the second sentence, guaranteed — except the senators themselves, probably, and the writer's mother, possibly. But begin with this lead: "Students who cheat will be named on a university-wide cheaters' list, the North Gulch State University Senate decided Tuesday." The second sentence will probably be read.

2. Timeliness: We Want It Now.

News is the plural of new. Timely stories are those that tap into topics of interest or concern in the national conversation. For example, stories that coincide with Valentine's Day might focus on chocolate sales or trends in dating. By the same token, advertisers and public relations professionals also tap into timeliness to promote and explain products and services in contexts that are currently on the minds of their stakeholders. For example, an environmental group might launch a recycling campaign to coincide with Earth Day.

3. Proximity: We Want It Here.

What do you care if East Gulch property taxes are going up 10 percent? Exactly, say news manufacturers. Let Podunk's media cover Podunk, and we'll cover our town. Stories of proximity are those with a local angle. They build on national or regional stories that touch on people, places or events that are meaningful to a local community.

4. Human Interest: We Need to Feel It.

Human interest stories are those that evoke an emotional response, that engage news consumers with an issue or event on a human level. Editors know a story that touches hearts is likely to be read or listened to. Human interest, in journalism sometimes called "soft news" or "feature," is designed to make you happy, sad, compassionate, angry — in fact, to elicit just about any emotion except boredom, which may be illegal in the media business. It is one thing to consider statistics concerning distracted driving; it is quite another to learn about one person's tragedy caused by distracted driving. Additionally, stories that might be hard to explain on a technical level — how a prosthesis works for an Olympic runner, for example — might be better told by people who use the same prosthesis as part of their daily lives.

5. Prominence: It's Whom You Know.

You go out jogging and it starts to rain, so you go back home. Do you think a dozen news people are following you to write this into a news story? If you're the president of the United States, they are. And they did — a number of years ago just this story about George H. W. Bush was broadcast over national network news. Editors and others outside the media know that these kinds of stories attract interest. This is why, for example, activist groups engage celebrity members to serve as their spokespeople: famous people will attract media coverage for the organization and its cause.

Convergence has created demands for new editorial functions, however. In a 2004 article, "The Cultural Logic of Media Convergence," Massachusetts Institute of Technology Professor Henry Jenkins examined convergence. He defined it as a process that can take place not just across distinct platforms, such as broadcasting and print media, but also within a smaller, single platform, such as a smartphone or a single newspaper. As such, convergence is influencing how traditional media organizations define and shape themselves, their operations and their business plans and how they relate to their consumers. The media are no longer simply delivering news. They are no longer simply telling consumers what to think about, to use the classic phrase of agenda-setting theory. Instead, they are challenged to find ways to engage active and participatory media consumers who are already developing and defining the news on their own terms.

Some media specialists have focused on the process of convergence from an operational standpoint. They explore how electronic and print production can come together within a newsroom and the problems and opportunities therein, including the continued importance of ensuring accuracy and source credibility. Although copy editors have traditionally filled newsroom jobs that are separate and distinct from those of reporters, the age of convergence coupled with a media industry reeling from declines in profits have begun to integrate the editing function into a number of different roles throughout the news-gathering and news-reporting processes.

Copy editors routinely multi-task, simultaneously editing a number of stories at different points of development and working with the writers of those pieces to enhance and enrich their work; however, convergence requires editors to work on stories across multiple platforms. In *Principles of Convergent Journalism*, authors Jeffrey S. Wilkinson, August E. Grant and Douglas J. Fisher explain that editors might now also work in a news-gathering, writing and presentation team, rather than among other editors in the rim. For example, a print editor might oversee a team that collectively gathers the elements for a story that can be told in print, in sound, in film and/or online. In broadcasting, an editor could take on the role of producer as well, shooting footage that can be directly uploaded to the Web or into programming. A newsroom research librarian could combine journalism, editing and news judgment to enrich content across media. And, like the media planning and traffic management duties of advertising, a "newsflow editor" would oversee timing, placement and updates of content across print, broadcast and online media, deciding where and when to file particular stories and related story elements as the work itself develops. As such, convergence demands more editing at more points in a story's development. That function begins when the editor identifies and assigns the story and starts thinking ahead to the elements needed to convey it, such as visuals. The process continues as the editor considers the appropriate and relevant timing and medium for the story's filing. It further extends to the possibility of more media integration as the story develops.

It should be noted, too, that the speed demanded in filing stories on the Web means that editors might now sort through the gathered information, a step normally left to reporters, and begin exercising the editing function even before the story is written. By the same token, new forms of media, particularly online channels such as blogs and microblogs, also have changed the way news is developed and reported, providing media outlets and their reporters more ways to engage and connect with their news publics directly. In a PRWeek/PR Newswire Media Survey findings, journalists reported that this expansion into such online outlets was partly due to budget cutbacks, the need to do more with fewer people and the Web's potential as a revenue source. The upshot is that more reporters are online, blogging, posting video and developing social networking sites to maintain connections with the media audience between issues or broadcasts, essentially developing themselves as individual brands, separate from their media organizations. Indeed, many reporters and the audiences for whom they write increasingly self-identify as individuals interconnected by networks built on common interests and experiences rather than as the "masses" implied in mass communication. This transition was recognized years ago in the Dec. 25, 2006/Jan. 1, 2007, issue of *Time* magazine in which its annual Person of the Year was "You." A year later, Ketchum, an American global public relations firm, and the University of Southern California's Annenberg Strategic Public Relations Center released findings from their international survey, "Media Myths & Realities: A Public of One." It concluded that we were now, each of us, a public of one. One result of this transition from a mass culture to a culture of one-ness is that organizations, media and otherwise, are continuing to learn how to yield control of their messages and their gatekeeping function and embrace the value of authentic voices, even when the message is negative. Another result, and one most important to the subject at hand, is that the immediacy and individual nature of these trends increasingly demand that journalists integrate the editing function into the writing function themselves, rather than rely on a separate copy editor.

In this sense, then, journalism is becoming more like advertising and public relations. Although the latter two focus on research-driven strategic communications, all emphasize editing as a dimension of good writing. Additionally, all three demand writing proficiency for a number of platforms, such as print, radio, television, Web, blogs and microblogs. Writers in these three disciplines must select appropriate features for each platform, such as links, visuals and interactivity. And they all must constantly seek ways to engage and retain their target publics. Unlike journalism, though, the integration of copy editing and writing is nothing new in advertising and public relations. Instead, the standards for effective writing in these disciplines incorporate a number of elements of good copy editing as an integral part of the advertising and public relations writing functions.

In advertising, copywriters are part of the creative side of ad production, providing the words to complement the visuals. Effective ads are built upon creative briefs—strategic plans that feature research and analysis of the target audience, the product, and the appropriate media. Both the copy and the visuals conform to a series of steps that start with attracting the attention and interest of a key audience and, ultimately, driving it to action. Some of the standards for effective copy in advertising are not unlike those in journalism, such as getting to the point, focusing on a single idea, using active voice and writing tightly. Because advertising seeks to persuade the consumer to engage with the brand, however, other standards include writing with flair, using personal pronouns and contractions, and reinforcing the brand throughout. Thus, like other writers in mass communication, ad copywriters do their research before they begin writing, and they have to master a broad range of topics. Additionally, like public relations and more recently in journalism with the advent of convergence, writers have to adapt copy style and emphasis to different communication channels. Ultimately, though, ad copywriting needs to convey meaning in the fewest words possible while preserving emotional appeal.

As in advertising, the editing function is woven into the public relations writing process. With no separate "editor" position within the public relations career ladder, writing is taken as a given, as a core skill, a core requirement, for succeeding in the field. Part of that skill entails editing. As in journalism, effective writing in public relations is based on clarity, variety, simplicity, active voice, grammar, spelling, punctuation, accuracy, rhythm, flow and, to ensure substance over sizzle, a commitment to showing, not telling. Additionally, like news copy editors, public relations writers also have to be concerned with deadlines, tone, accuracy, AP style, cohesion, logical presentation, organizational culture/mission, goodness of fit with intended key publics, and the presentation of the message through layout and design. They, too, have to maintain a big-picture approach to editing, beyond technical and factual accuracy, to consider current and historical context. They have to know when to stop, and they have to know when more information is needed.

Such knowledge, however, does not make public relations writers "in-house journalists," a long-held misconception. Public relations writers seek to build and maintain relationships among internal and external stakeholders based on research-driven strategy, often referred to as the "four-step process." The first of these steps is research, in which the public relations writer conducts a situation analysis to learn as much as possible about, among other things, the client, its product or service, its target stakeholder communities and the environment in which the client operates. The second step of the process is the development of a strategic plan, followed by the communication itself and the evaluation of the effectiveness of the plan. In conforming to this process, public relations writing/editing also entails checking for key messages, connections with key objectives and target stakeholders and the consistent use of symbols and graphic elements. Public relations writers have to consider the purpose of the copy to be written and its shelf life, which will affect the timeliness of the copy and the selection of channels that will be used to disseminate it. As in advertising, the variety of such channels is extensive, compelling public relations writers to master a number of different copy styles to effectively convey their messages. Examples include a CEO's letter, a brochure, a newsletter, a website, a microblog post or a text message. Additionally, public relations writing demands a holistic eye. Simply writing well might open a door or two, but it is just as important to know how different writing styles for different target publics through different channels demand different sets of skills and emphases— especially in today's Web environment.

Public relations is alone among advertising and journalism, however, in its attention to writing for internal target stakeholder groups, specifically employees. In 1920,

Robert E. Ramsey characterized the public relations writer/editor as "a mixture of author, special feature writer, advertising man, investigator, salesman, preacher, teacher, and newspaper reporter." Much remains true today. In-house editors strive to let the publications sell themselves. Editors try to engage employees, balance news and features and address items of particular interest to employees. They remember not to talk down to them or to underestimate their interest in the organization's business plans, challenges and accomplishments. Employee publications that include recipes, horoscopes, birthdays, vacation photos and the like are not serving the needs or interests of one of the organization's most important publics. Employees want to know their organization. They can be an organization's best — and most credible — spokespeople if they are treated as seriously as, say, stockholders, customers or donors.

It should be noted, too, that, unlike in journalism, it is not uncommon in public relations to obtain copy approvals before publication. This process can create new avenues of challenges for the public relations writer/editor, though, such as diplomatically educating colleagues who might reject AP style edits as errors.

The editing mind set

In 1918, Bleyer urged the public and newspaper publishers and editors to protect the integrity of the press from corruption by private ownership. Indeed, newspaper employees were exhorted to serve as public servants, to take seriously their roles as guardians of the Fourth Estate, and to not simply function as business employees. Ultimately, though, the editing function is part of a business, whether it be print, broadcast, online, community, citizen journalism or nonprofit, government, agency, corporate public relations, advertising or commercial, independent or documentary film. The goal is to build and maintain an audience that will read, engage and support the content, product, service and/or that of the sponsors. As such, editors must be concerned with factors outside of the copy at hand. They need to keep an eye on the larger picture to ensure that they will continue to attract more people within a given stakeholder community or across communities, by meeting their needs, interests and changing demands.

It follows, then, that the medium is a product and that it is the copy editing function that oversees the production and promotion of that product through straight news, features, editorials, headlines, layout and images. As such, editors seek to enhance brand loyalty — to create a package through content and design that not only will generate consumer loyalty but draw an increasingly wider circle of news consumers. In doing so, editors need to understand them. To attract them to the product, editors have to know who they are, what they care about and what is most meaningful to them. Editors have to assume their perspective and put themselves in the shoes of their audience. The result is that the audience — the readers, listeners, viewers, consumers and other stakeholders — drive decisions about news, advertising and public relations. In fact, it's not uncommon for reporters and editors to use online tools, such as blogs and social networking sites, to gauge public interest in a story and help prioritize its placement, to

VOCABULARY AND JARGON FOR EDITORS

AP.

Associated Press. A newspaper cooperative that spans the world to gather news for its members and shares news among members. Much of what we know about the world comes from the AP. It was established by New York newspapers in 1849.

AP Style.

Editors developed the AP style to ensure style consistency among the members, and it remains today the standard used by many American newspapers. Journalism student learn AP style to write news copy. Public relations students learn AP style to submit stories to mass media that conform to their standards.

Convergence.

The evolution of editing for a single platform, such as a newspaper, to multiple platforms using print, video and the Internet. Convergence can also mean bringing together multiple platforms into one communication channel, such as a smartphone or website.

Fourth Estate.

The press, or news media. The term dates from 18th-century Britain. In the United States it has evolved to mean an unofficial fourth branch of government power, operating outside of the executive, legislative and judicial branches.

Lead, lede.

The first sentence or two of a story written for mass media. Similar to "nut graf," it distils the story and attracts the reader. Editors consider a compelling lede to be critically important, because it brings readers into a story.

Rim.

Old-style editing desks were shaped like a U. In the center, or slot, sat the city or managing editor, who directed copy to editors sitting around the table, the rim.

Scoop.

Get the information first; a fresh news story. Newspapers can't often beat broadcast and the Web on breaking stories, so they find ways to expand upon the story, such as providing deeper explanation or analysis.

Social networking.

A duty requiring the editor to interact with news consumers by posting blogs, short statements or Tweets—short status updates.

Wire.

News services such as AP provide material for member news organizations. Usually the material is national or international in scope. Subscribing news organizations try to localize these generic stories, if they have enough time and staff. It's a badge of pride for an editor to rely on his or her own staff rather than on the wire. Competing journalists used to judge the value of other local media by counting the number of AP stories the lazybones rely on. Wire material actually used to come through a wire. Now it mostly arrives by Internet.

drive visitors to the media site or to gather and monitor feedback once a story is published. They will also conduct research with their readers, the results of which can inform content, just as *Better Homes* did decades ago.

According to a 1938 case study by Mitchell V. Charnley and Blair Converse, the research department at *Better Homes & Gardens* at that time worked closely with editorial to monitor reader demographics, lifestyle and interests, to conduct reader surveys, to determine reader reactions to new products and to compare the amount of content focusing on certain topics across magazines. The results not only were applied to content decisions, but to advertising and circulation as well. This emphasis on knowing the audience and "fitting news to family" was considered paramount to radio, too, during its golden age of the 1930s and '40s. A contemporary text by Medill School of Journalism Instructor Carl Warren noted that the script editor understood news value, audience listening habits, script-writing, dangers of defamation and the importance of interpersonal communication.

The magazine editor of today also uses research to gauge reader perspectives, trends and interests that in turn drives editorial decisions concerning writing that will attract those readers, balancing growth (for increased ad revenues) with clear product definition. Understanding the stakeholder communities is a cardinal rule of advertising and public relations. It sparks research-based businesses and drives the body of knowledge in both fields, such as consumer attitudes and behavior in advertising, relationships and organizational leadership in public relations, and social media engagement. And with convergence, editors and multi-skilled journalists not only have to convey a story across multiple platforms, but they also must provide relevant information on demand at the point of access on a given platform.

Such demands require that good editors stay plugged in, scanning the environment for news, trends and events that could be relevant to their audiences and to their own industries, including trends in communications and the channels different publics use to access and receive information. Such a broad world view does not mean editors have to know everything, but they do need to be informed enough to judge a story's accuracy and relevance. Part of that perspective derives from a broad exposure to current events, culture, history, politics and business. It also comes from traveling and education, exposure to other places and other ideas, all of which, advised Warren in 1947, help the editor to hone clarity and cohesion in conveying the news.

It also helps, as Ethel Colson Brazelton found as far back as 1927, to be able to identify with the audience, to remember that it is often in part made up of an editor's own community. As community newspaperwomen assumed the editing role in their towns, she found, the same qualities that made them good neighbors made them good editors. They not only could relate to the needs and interests of their audiences, but they shared them, as well. While such connection belies the image of the journalist as a loner, it reinforces the copy editor's function as the glue that holds the news process together. The concept is particularly important because, at the outset, it was thought the challenges of convergence would concern clashes among equipment, news systems and styles of reporting. But they actually lay in clashes of culture, reporting traditions and senses of ownership of the story and the platform — and in the interpersonal relationships between and among the news staffs.

The editing job market

Editors' and journalists' value is increasingly tied to an ability to generate, package and deliver content on deadline and in accordance with the appropriate medium that best fits the story and meets the needs and interests of the audience. Editors add to this their world view, their mastery of language, their commitment to accuracy and credibility, and their knowledge of design to maintain a critical and constructive eye in the whirlwind of convergence. More than ever, then, good editors cannot procrastinate. They have to work even more efficiently and effectively under time pressure, maintaining continuity among a number of stories across a number of media platforms throughout the news-gathering and news-reporting processes. And they have to work fast. Even as copy editors and journalists work against the clock to deliver timely news, they compete against more than other traditional media organizations. They compete against online media, and other individuals and organizations that are posting, uploading, linking, forwarding and commenting upon information as it appears. This competition means that, at times, the immediacy of online access can trump accuracy and source credibility, leaving the "news" gathering process unchecked and unverified and the "news" writing process unexamined and unedited. Although little is mentioned specifically about the copy editing function in discussions of convergence, the implication is that more people will do more across the news-gathering and reporting spectrum, including, presumably, copy editing. While the importance of speed is often mentioned as a key element of convergence — speed in gathering, writing, posting and updating copy — little is said about the *quality* of that posted content from a copy editor's perspective.

Additionally, as the business of journalism struggles with the survival of print newspapers and magazines, the dominance of cable over network news, the proliferation of satellite and syndication in radio, and the explosion of online interconnectedness, the business of copy editing is taking a hit as well. Indeed, John McIntyre, who blogs about writing on "You Don't Say," has written that the loss of a copy editor under budget cuts cannot be remedied by renewed attention to spelling among those who remain in the newsroom; the proofing, the flow, the attention to historical and contextual accuracy are also lost, ultimately "destroying a craft."

Nevertheless, a brief look at copy editor job postings reveals that regardless of medium (e.g., corporate newsletters, small and large dailies, and websites) copy editing skills are still valued and sought after. Applicants are required to be proficient in grammar, AP style, punctuation and spelling. They need to be able to polish stories, enhance flow and clarity, meet deadlines, and shift among diverse story topics, such as corporate earnings, foreign policy, local news and TV reviews. Accessibility also is important via phone, e-mail, and on site at the job, including nine-hour evening shifts with some weekends and holidays. In addition to headline writing, applicants need to know layout and design, and, in the aggregate, these applicants also need to be proficient in web design, pagination, video editing, photo editing and graphic design software. With the exception of software proficiency, the same characteristics required of copy editors today resonate with those offered a decade ago by Ann Auman for ASNE. Her list included versatility, attitude, collaboration, "fresh eyes," attention to deadlines, fast and efficient work habits, "knowledge of current events," problem solving, and drive for self-improvement.

It is still important to gain as much experience as possible as a student, whether through internships, jobs or volunteer work, but the age of social media also provides some excellent platforms to future editors looking for ways to demonstrate their skills— and build professional networks along the way. Microblogs and blogs in particular are good outlets for demonstrating expertise in language, grammar, punctuation, flow, current events and the many other skills copy editors need to master. For example, a University of Alabama law student, Sharon Nichols, started blogging about grammar and then started a Facebook social networking group, which grew to more than 400,000 members and thousands of examples of poor writing. Those projects led to a book, *I Judge You When You Use Poor Grammar* (St. Martin's Griffin, 2009). Most important for prospective copy editors, though, is the ability to demonstrate their skills through perfectly written resumes and cover letters and through an array of clips, print, broadcast and electronic, that cover a broad range of subjects across different media platforms.

Know more

AIGA/The professional Association for Design, http://www.aiga.org.

American Advertising Federation, http://www.aaf.org.

American Copy Editors Society, http://copydesk.org.

Auman, Ann. "Who would want to be a copy editor? The industry and academe should work to raise the value of editing." In "On Copy Editing" (from *The American Editor*, January 2000), http://www.copydesk.org/words/ASNEJanuary.htm.

Bleyer, W.G., ed. (1918). *The profession of journalism*. Boston: The Atlantic Monthly Press.

_____ (1923). *Newspaper writing and editing*. Boston: Houghton Mifflin.

Brazelton, E.M.C. (1927). *Writing and editing for women: A bird's-eye view of the widening opportunities for women in newspaper, magazine and other writing work*. New York: Funk and Wagnalls.

Charnley, M.V., and B. Converse (1938). *Magazine writing and editing*. New York: Cordon.

Evans, M.R. (2004). *The layers of magazine editing*. New York: Columbia University Press.

Fellow, A.R., and T.N. Clanin (2007). *Copy editors handbook for newspapers*, 3d ed. Englewood, CO: Morton.

Fisher, H.A. (2009). "Developing media managers for convergence." In A. E. Grant and J. S. Wilkinson (Eds.), *Understanding media convergence: The state of the field* (135–150). New York: Oxford University Press.

Jenkins, H. (2004). "The cultural logic of media convergence." *International Journal of Cultural Studies* 7(1), 33–43.

Ketchum/University of Southern California's Annenberg Strategic Public Relations Center.

(2007). *Media myths and realities survey.* Retrieved from http://www.ketchum.com/2007 mediasurvey.

LoCicero, G. (2004, May 5). "News resourcer is key information chief." *The Convergence Newsletter* 1. Retrieved from http://www.jour.sc.edu/news/convergence/issue12.html.

McIntyre, John. "You Don't Say." http://johnemcintyre.blogspot.com.

National Association of Broadcasters, http://www.nab.org.

Owen, J., and H. Purdey, eds. (2009). *International news reporting: Frontlines and deadlines.* Malden, MA: Wiley-Blackwell.

Public Relations Society of America, http://www.prsa.org.

Raiteri, C. (2006). *Writing for broadcast news: A storytelling approach to crafting TV and radio news reports.* Lanham, MD: Rowman and Littlefield.

Ramsey, R.E. (1920). *Effective house organs: The principles and practice of editing and publishing successful house organs.* New York: D. Appleton.

Russial, J. (2004). *Strategic copy editing.* New York: Guilford.

Society of Professional Journalists' Journalist's Toolbox, http://www.journaliststoolbox.org.

Sugarman, J. (2007). *The Adweek Copywriting Handbook.* Hoboken, NJ: John Wiley and Sons.

Sumner, D.E., and H.G. Miller (2009). *Feature and magazine writing: Action, angle and anecdotes,* 2d ed. Malden, MA: Wiley Blackwell.

Warren, C. (1947). *Radio news writing and editing.* New York: Harper and Brothers.

Washkuch, F. (2009, April 6). "Plan for survival." *PRWeek*, 12, 11–16.

Wilkinson, J.S., A.E. Grant, and D.J. Fisher (2009). *Principles of convergent journalism.* New York: Oxford University Press.

• EXERCISE 1 •

Five news values that help editors to rank the importance of news stories have not changed much over more than a century. After reviewing these values, consider a local newspaper. Choose a story to evaluate based on the five news values.

- If the value is strongly present, give the story two points.
- If the value is moderately present, give the story one point.
- If the value is weakly present, give the story ½ point.

Add the points below to determine the likely placement an editor would give to this story. Consider below your evaluation. For example, most editors would give a nine- or ten-point story top treatment on the front page. Did this publication's editor?

A story earning three points or less would probably merit treatment as a brief, and buried on an inside page. Did this publication's editor play it more prominently?

Now take a look at that publication's website. Was the story handled in the same way? If not, why would it be handled differently on the website?

Point totals
Consequence=_____ pts.
Timeliness=_____pts.
Proximity=_____pts.
Human interest=_____pts.
Prominence=_____pts.
Total points=_____
Your evaluation:

• EXERCISE 2 •

One of an editor's functions is to think ahead to future story ideas. This means editors need to monitor current events to determine what might be of interest to their audiences.

a. Go to a mainstream news website. Based on today's front-page stories, develop three story budgets for tomorrow's top news: one each for local, regional and national audiences.
b. Go to a profit or not-for-profit organizational website. Based on current news and events related to that organization and its key publics, develop a story budget for next week's newsletter.
c. After listing your story ideas, discuss how you would present these stories across platforms. Consider the communication channels and images (still or motion) you would use as well as how you would engage your stakeholder groups (e.g., inviting them to share their images, opinions or ideas). Then compare your ideas with those of other class members.

Prepare and discuss your budgets in writing.

• EXERCISE 3 •

You have been asked to compose 10 perfect tweets about your chosen discipline (e.g., advertising, journalism, broadcasting, public relations). Assume you would post these on Twitter later. You must write in complete sentences with proper punctuation—no texting abbreviations. You must also use AP style. If you like, though, you can include links and hashtags in your tweets.

Now exchange your work with someone in your class so you can edit each other's work. Did your partner catch anything that you didn't? Did he or she understand what you wrote in the way that you intended? Why or why not?

TWO

Editing Begins with the Writer
Mavis Richardson

All media writers, whether beginners or seasoned reporters, instinctively know good writing starts with good fact gathering. But the best digital recorder full of facts doesn't necessarily lead to a good story if those facts get lost in a thicket of incorrect grammar, punctuation and spelling, and ignorance of Associated Press style. All of these areas require careful attention if the writer is to produce clear, concise copy that appeals to a consumer.

Writing is a process, and a key part of that process is editing. Editing begins with the reporter herself or himself. Students should learn that the first *draft* is not usually their best attempt, and they should expect to edit and change their work as a part of the writing process. More importantly, students may one day find themselves in the role of copy editor, editing newspaper or Web copy, public relations work such as news releases, annual reports, etc., or other media-related copy. The editing they do is a process. It begins with that first draft and continues until the reader sees the finished product.

What is an editor? That's a broad question. Consider the world of media from corporate websites to community newsletters. The products we call media vary so much that sometimes they don't even seem to speak the same English. But one thing is common: editors. Editors are defined by the scope of what they do. They usually edit copy: they correct grammar and word usage, check fact errors, judge style, both AP and in-house, and even second-guess the spill chucker now and then (such as in this sentence). That's a beginning. Editors also prepare material for the world of multiplatform media, considering design and visuals, while remaining close to the audience whose loyalty they can't afford to lose. They may edit blogs. They may create their own. They may tweet. They may promote and advertise, if they work in the public relations and advertising world. One thing is certain, however: good editors begin their work with the written word.

This chapter is organized into four sections: Section I will address common grammar errors. Section II will address common punctuation mistakes. Section III will address clarity and conciseness. Section IV will cover four common Associated Press style mistakes.

While those who master this material will establish a good basis for growth as a strong copy editor, this chapter makes no attempt to offer an exhaustive study of English grammar and style usage. Students whose grammar needs a relaunch from scratch are urged to consult one of the many print or online grammar guides.

I. Common grammar errors

Each semester, some instructors distribute a basic grammar/punctuation/spelling diagnostic exam to media writing students. The exam elicits common responses such as:

"Everything I learned about grammar I learned in elementary school." Or "I know this stuff so why do I have to take the exam?" In response to these questions, instructors ask a simple question: "Yes, you may have been taught proper grammar techniques in elementary school, but do you practice what you were taught in your writing?" Scores on these exams provide the answer: *No*.

Grammar makes communication possible to the large audience an editor aims to attract. You may text to your friend, "C U b4 cls, ur tat is gr8, imho, tty 18r, BBF!" Perfectly clear to you. But as an editor, you know some people may read, "Columbia University buffers its calls, urgent that his GR 8 optical disk imports home, teletype 18 reserved, be back in a few!" Professional copy editors consider an audience of more than BBF; therefore, writers need to be clear and concise. Students commonly make some errors over and over. Let's get into the five most common grammar mistakes:

1. incomplete sentences.
2. subjects and verbs that don't agree.
3. subjects and pronouns that don't agree.

QUIRKS O' THE TONGUE: THAT DASTARDLY LANGUAGE

To learn English grammar well takes years of school, and a keen interest in reading widely and writing often. As well, it has to be said that English is peculiarly difficult because it is based on a broad collection of all sorts of languages, with no accent marks as a guide, and rules with many exceptions. We suffer, for instance, from 16 different word combinations with the pronunciation "sh," and no grammatical guide as to that combination's pronunciation.

In fact, research has shown that dyslexia, a condition in which people find it difficult to read, is rare in countries such as Spain and Italy. Natives speaking these languages emphasize pronunciation of every letter and rely on nearly universal rules guiding that pronunciation. Dyslexia is, however, more common in France and England, whose languages have many letters unpronounced, or pronounced in a way not obvious by spelling. We're lucky that for most of us our first language is English.

4. confusing possessives and contractions.
5. poor word choices.

✳Error #1: The incomplete sentence.

Overwhelmingly, the most common mistake in student work is (drum roll, please): the incomplete sentence. A sentence is a group of words that expresses a complete thought or idea. At the bare minimum, it contains a subject (something or something that is the doer of the acton, or receiver) and a verb (which provides the action): Josh texts. Kristin reads. The professor pontificates. The canoe overturned.

For example: **John ate.** "John" is the subject; "ate" is the verb. Two words that make an impact because they tell the reader a person named John consumed something. Another example: **All of the candy** is not a sentence. It is a phrase. But, combine the two and you have a complete sentence: **John ate all of the candy.**

Exceptions are sometimes acceptable. Occasionally, a writer will choose to use a one-word sentence, usually just a verb, to provide impact to the story. These become imperative sentences with an understood "you." **Stop! Run! No!** Caution: use sparingly.

✳ Error #2: Subject/verb agreement.

A verb also must be consistent with the grammatical number of the subject of the sentence (singular or plural). If you have a singular subject, you need a singular verb. If you have a plural subject, you need a plural verb. Editors whose first language is English usually don't make a mistake editing for simple subject/verb agreement: **The professor has (not have) her students study grammar every day.** But look at the following sentences, all of which contain subject/verb agreement errors:

The cause for the three deadly fires have yet to be determined.
(The true subject is the singular noun *cause* so the singular verb **has** is needed.)

A team of writers agree on their list of changes to the screenplay.
(Team is singular so use the singular pronoun **its.**)

Deciding whether the subject of a sentence is singular or plural causes more problems and mistakes. Memorizing the following "always-singular subject" items will help make the decision automatic.

As the subject of a sentence, these pronouns always take singular verbs: **each, either, anyone, anybody, everyone, everybody, nobody, somebody, someone, much, one, no one, neither, and nothing.**

No one is ever alone.
Everyone goes to his cell phone nowadays for correct time.

Yes, we know many writers will use "their" in a sentence such as the one above, perhaps to avoid sounding sexist ("his") or awkward ("his or her"). This is, nevertheless,

QUIRKS O' THE TONGUE: WILY PASSIVE VOICE

Perhaps three-quarters of the time you need to emphasize active voice in media writing. It's livelier, more immediate, more like the way we actually talk. It emphasizes, well, action. A thief stole the Mona Lisa. Protesters demonstrated against banks. The president signed the bill.

Can we ever make an exception? The truth is that passive voice comes in handy for a variety of reasons, some of them rather sneaky. Passive voice is helpful when the recipient of an action is most important. Below are other common usages.

- You need to vary sentence structure. Writers look for sentence variety, and an occasional passive voice can offer that.
- You're not sure of the facts. For instance, if you're not sure of the precise amount of tax increase (was it 30 percent or 35 percent?), you can just say, A tax increase of about one-third was approved. Similarly, if you aren't sure who performed the action (Did Jones really hit Nern with his cane?), you can slip into passive voice: Nern was hit with a cane. Who did the hitting? We can't say.

Using passive voice to avoid assessing personal responsibility can be taken into a realm of policy, official or not. For instance, academic researchers in the sciences often rely on passive voice to avoid emphasizing the significance of a research team, but instead to emphasize the results of the research. An experiment was performed. Results were analyzed. Conclusions were made. Probably this is legitimate usage of the passive — readers in this case are more interested in research results than in performers. But in the business world such an approach can be used to hide responsibility behind critical decisions. A decision was made to lay off several hundred workers. Who did the firing? We're not telling.

An interesting case study of the power of passive voice to eliminate responsibility from a paper trail can be made by tracing the investigation following the Space Shuttle *Challenger* explosion of 1986. Investigators examining documents provided by the manufacturer of shuttle parts that failed tried to pin responsibility on those who made decisions that led to the disaster. It was difficult, because documents relied on passive voice: this decision was made, that action was taken, this was done. Who did it? By relying on passive voice, decision-makers can avoid taking blame.

---

incorrect. Editors who wish to avoid an awkward construction without a grammar error may be able to reconstruct the sentence slightly:

Everyone goes to a cell phone now for the correct time.

When **each, either, every,** or **neither** is used as an adjective, the noun it modifies always takes a singular verb:

Every day brings a new beginning.

When the phrase "number of" is the subject of a sentence, it always takes a singular verb, no matter what quantity is indicated by the noun in the prepositional phrase:

The number of bicycle thefts is dropping.

(The words "of bicycle thefts" is a prepositional phrase, not the subject of the sentence.)

Collective nouns denoting a unit made up of two or more members always take a singular verb. These include **team, choir, band, group, club, organization, university, company, senate, faculty, audience, board, herd, public** and **a country** such as the United States, Canada, Mexico. One of the most common problems writers face is forgetting they are talking about a collective noun and so incorrectly begin using a plural verb:

The team is (singular) playing this Saturday and they're (plural) expected to win. (You could also rewrite the sentence, breaking it into two separate sentences: **The team is playing this Saturday. Players expect to win.**)

The best way to avoid switching from singular to plural in midsentence is to keep a sharp eye on these pronouns: **they, them and their.** If you use one of these words, look for a plural noun. If no plural noun is in sight, then switch to a singular pronoun.

Pronouns such as **any, none,** and **some** and nouns such as **all** and **most** take singular verbs if they refer to a unit or a general quantity. They take plural verbs if they refer to an unspecified amount or individuals: **All of the forest was destroyed by fire.** (General quantity because we do not know how many trees are in the forest.) **All of the theater receipts (an amount that can be counted) are missing.**

Error #3: Pronoun usage.

Pronouns are substitutes for nouns and constitute the focus of the third most common grammar error. Pronouns are common because they bring a certain economy of words to a sentence. It sounds awkward to write: **John went to class. John sat at the back. John opened his laptop. John checked his Facebook account. John paid no attention to the professor.** Instead, you'd want to write, **John went class. He sat at the front. He opened his laptop, and began taking notes.**

Journalists and other mass media writers need to follow the same grammatical rules concerning pronouns that all writers follow. However, journalists not writing blogs or opinion pieces rarely write in the first person ("I have discovered…") when using personal pronouns. Instead, journalists try to remain apart from the story, neutral observers. Using the first person singular suggests a subjective judgment.

Here's a short refresher. First-person singular pronouns include **I, me, my, mine, myself,** and first-person plural pronouns include **we, us, our, ours, ourselves.** Second-person singular pronouns include **you, your, yourself,** and second-person plural pronouns include **you, your, yours, yourself.** (Note: singular and plural second-person pronouns are the same.) And, finally, third-person singular pronouns are **he, she, it, his, hers, him, her, its, himself, herself, itself.** Third-person plural pronouns are **they, them, their, theirs, themselves.** Journalists use the third-person singular and plural pronouns most often.

A pronoun requires an antecedent (a noun to which the pronoun refers), and its link to the antecedent (reference) is critical. When more than one person is involved in a sentence, writers have to be careful that the reader understands which person they are referring to.

For example, to whom do you think the pronoun *she* refers to in the following sentence?

Just seconds after the officer told the reporter and the photographer to get out of the line of fire, she dashed to her car.

Any guesses? Well, it could be the photographer (the closest noun). Or it could be the officer (the main character). But, don't forget about the reporter. Or even someone else. The point here is that you the editor must make it absolutely clear who *she* is referring to in your sentence. As an editor, you may have to ask the writer to clarify. Then, rewrite the sentence.

Just seconds after the officer told the reporter and the photographer to get out of the line of fire, the *reporter* dashed to *her* car.

Another common error in pronoun usage is number. If you use a singular noun, you must use a singular pronoun. **Bill turned in his assignment. The boys completed their work.** If you use a plural noun, you must use a plural pronoun. The problem occurs when the writer does not indicate the gender of the subject. For example: **The student did not turn in their work.** Correct usage: **his/her.** Another choice is to use **s/he,** or **his or her** work. As we noted, the use of **they** and **their** appears to be gaining popularity with writers in our politically correct atmosphere because neither pronoun indicates gender, and both are less clumsy. The plural form may be acceptable sometime in the future — but not yet.

Error #4: Contractions.

The fourth most common mistake involves contractions. These few simple tips on how to avoid this common mistake can make you a better, faster editor. Contractions are a combination of two words. The most common problem involves misspelling and incorrect usage of **they're/their, it's/its, who's/whose** and **you're/your.** Writers often mistake the pronoun for the contraction. To edit, simply say the contraction as two words. If it makes no sense, you have the wrong spelling.

Example: **The magazine replaced its** (possessive) **or it's** (it is) **reviewer. Its** is correct because the magazine did not replace "it is" reviewer. Do the same for they're/their, who's/whose and you're/your. One note of caution: Don't use "there" (an expletive) if you mean "they're" or "their."

Wrong: **They helped there brothers move.** Be forewarned: Spell Check does not recognize this usage as incorrect so read copy carefully. (However, Grammar Check does recognize the difference.) Correct: **They helped their brothers move.** And a final note: *its'* does *not* exist! Even though you see it often in real life, or perhaps in real low-life.

QUIRKS O' THE TONGUE: THE ENGLISH MISHMASH

In ye olde tyme of early medieval English grammar, commas, and indeed all punctuation, were thought to be unnecessary. Even spaces between words—who needs 'em?

thelanguagewasstillreadablebutitbecamesuchachoretoconcentratethatmuchall-thetime

The language hoarded words from all over — French, Latin, Norse, Celtic, Germanic. No one thought to throw much away, and so today English boasts the world's largest vocabulary, with no guide to pronouncing all those words borrowed from all over. Still, it has become the first language of 380 million people, and the second language of 300 million more (www.englishlanguageguide.com). It also is the official or unofficial language of tourism, aviation, science, the internet and diplomacy — much to the chagrin of France, which still remembers when diplomats spoke in French.

Error #5: Word-choice mistakes.

Finally, the fifth most common error concerns word-choice mistakes: **than/then, who/that, that/which** and **lay/lie.** Other troublesome errors are **affect/effect, principal/principle** and **who/whom.**

Than/then.

The word **than** is used to show comparison between two equal items: **I would rather stay home than dine out. Then** is used to indicate next in order or in time: **Drivers must first turn left on Pine Street and then turn right into the first driveway.**

Who/that.

Who is the pronoun used for references to human beings and to animals with a name. **A man who left no name called. Susie the cat, who was scared, ran to her basket.** Use that for inanimate objects. **I switched the chairs that had been broken.**

That/which.

That is also used to introduce material that restricts the meaning of the noun: **A campfire that got out of control in the Gifford Pinchot National Forest is now threatening two nearby towns. Which** is used to elaborate on meaning: **The Gifford Pinchot fire, which thus far has consumed 800 acres, may be brought under control this weekend.** These two words are *not* interchangeable. Tip (courtesy of the AP *Stylebook*): If you can drop the clause and not lose the meaning of the sentence, use **which**; otherwise, use **that.** In the examples above, you can remove the **which** clause, and the sentence still makes sense. But if you remove the **that** clause, you end up with a wee campfire threatening two whole towns. How could that happen? Note: A **which** clause is surrounded by commas; no commas are used with **that** clauses as shown in the above examples.

Lay/lie.

Lay is the action word. It is transitive; that is, it takes a direct object: **He lays the book on the table. Laid** is the past tense of lay: **The defense laid blame on the victim.** But **lie** indicates a state of reclining along a horizontal plane. It is intransitive; that is, it does not take a direct object: **She lies down every day at 3 P.M.** The past tense is **lay. Yesterday she lay on the sofa for an hour.** Notice the past tense of **lie** is the same as the present tense **lay.** This confusing usage leads to mistakes so common that it actually sounds clumsy to say **He lay [not laid] on the couch for two hours yesterday.** Additional forms and examples can be found in the *Stylebook* under "lay, lie."

Affect/effect.

Affect is generally used as a verb and means to influence. **The game will affect the standings. Effect** can be used as both a verb and a noun. **The effect was overwhelming. He will effect many changes in the country.** Always use **affect** as a verb and always use **effect** as a noun. Remembering this principle, if you edit copy containing the common phrase, "has an effect on," you know it must be **effect,** because **affect** can only be used as a verb. True, the rule is muddied by the phrase "effect change." But note this less common usage of **effect** as a verb is nearly always followed by "change."

Principal/principle.

Principal is a noun or adjective meaning someone or something of importance. **Principle** is a noun that means a fundamental truth, law, or basic doctrine. Try this to keep the correct spelling for the correct term: The **principal** (a person or thing of importance) is my "pal," and so needs to have a companion noun. The use of "pal" should indicate the correct spelling for a reference of "importance": **principal.** If there is no reference to a person or something of "importance," use the other spelling. Example: **A principal rule of this editor is to always tell the truth.** (Note reference to "rule.") But **She explained the seven principles guiding company policy.** (No reference, no "pal" accompanying the word.) Annoying exception: **principal** as a noun also may refer to a sum of money. But usually we can remember this less common usage as it applies to financial stories: **Interest is 2 percent, with a goal of preserving the principal.**

Who/whom.

Who is also used when it refers to the subject of a sentence, clause or phrase: **The woman who rented the room left the window open. Who is there? Whom** is used when someone is the object of a verb or preposition: **The woman to whom the room was rented left the window open. Whom do you wish to see? Whom** is becoming less common, particularly in spoken English. Perhaps someday we'll see it become as archaic as "thou" and "thy" are today. But not yet.

Section II: Common Punctuation Mistakes

Have you ever had trouble figuring out what a writer's story meant? The reason could be improper punctuation, such as the following sentence: **Punctuation, mistakes,**

Woman Without Her Man Is Nothing.

What Did You Say?

Woman: Without Her, Man Is Nothing.

Punctuation Saves Lives!

Punctuation adds meaning.

that mess up good, writing. Punctuation marks, such as periods and commas, help readers understand the story.

Take the title of a popular punctuation guide, *Eats, Shoots & Leaves: The Zero Tolerance Approach to Punctuation.* Much discussion followed on the meaning of the first words in that title. The book was about punctuation and the author used an animal, a panda, as the main character. One interpretation for the title could be that the panda eats (something), fires a gun (shoots) and leaves (for some place). Eliminate the comma and the title makes more sense. A panda eats shoots and leaves.

Periods

Periods ("full stops" in British usage) denote the end of a sentence. But periods are needed for more than that in writing. Periods are also used to end an abbreviation such as for a time (A.M./P.M.), month (Nov.), and a title (Sen.). Periods are also used in addresses (Ave.) (Minn.) (U.S.).

Commas

While the period presents some opportunities for error, the **comma** can change meaning in sometimes amusing and deadly ways. Note the difference a comma makes in the meaning of the two sentences:

Let's eat Grandpa. (Someone has decided to eat grandpa.)

Let's eat, Grandpa. (Grandpa is being addressed. He is being summoned to eat.)

Commas are the most used and most misused form of punctuation. Inserting a comma whenever you feel like taking a breath is a bad rule. Still, that's how lots of people

---

QUIRKS O' THE TONGUE: THOSE WEIRD ENGLISH POSSESSIVES

In addition to their use in contractions, apostrophes in English are used to indicate possessiveness. This peculiar linguistic construction is not part of Latin-based languages such as French and Spanish, and it causes confusing mistakes. On the good side, it does streamline word usage. The minister's book is a smoother read than the French or Spanish equivalent, The book of the minister. (*Le livre du curé; El libro del padre.*) In any case, we're editing in English, so we do not use an apostrophe to indicate plural.

While we don't see many college editing students making these mistakes, they are common in the larger English-speaking world. Apostrophes sometimes labor in a new and ungrammatical role to indicate noun plurals: Sale today on pre-owned computer's! Who would shop at a place liable to such egregious grammar errors? But this rule should be easy. Just remember: no apostrophes in plurals. Ever. One book. Two books. One car, three Toyotas. One egg. I have a dozen eggs. No apostrophes. No sweat. Except...

Indicating the *possessive* of a noun means adding apostrophes—somewhere. Where depends on if it's plural or singular. The apostrophe goes before the s for singular possessive, after the s for plural. I have a dozen eggs. *But* This egg's shell is cracked. (Singular possessive.) The car's battery needs to be replaced. (Singular possessive.) *But* The cars' batteries were ruined in the recent flood. (Plural possessive.) Folks seem to forget apostrophes more often than they add them where they don't belong. For instance, time and date expressions need apostrophes when used possessively. In one year's time I'll be done with school. The professor's assistant says two hours' time is long enough for the exam. *But* The professor says two hours is enough for the exam.

decide where commas should go, and the breathing concept works about three-fourths of the time. All you have to do is learn when to take a breath.

To help us with the "breath principle," we have rules for when and where to use commas. Some commas are essential for clarity, and others please the grammar gods. Commit the following rules to memory. Perhaps that seems like a daunting task, but most make logical sense. Memorization of these rules will eliminate most common comma mistakes. More items can be found in grammar style guides.

Introductory phrases and clauses

Set off long introductory phrases with a comma: **After a long spell of dry weather, farmers may have to replant crops.**

Short introductory phrases and clauses do not necessarily have to be set off with commas. If the meaning suffers from a lack of a comma, put it in. **With careful planning (,) we'll succeed.**

Set off introductory subordinate clauses with a comma: **Because she had decided early she wanted to be a doctor, she took a heavy concentration of biology courses.** If the subordinate clause appears elsewhere in the sentence, it may not need a comma. **She took a heavy concentration of biology courses because she had decided early she wanted to be a doctor.** Independent clauses joined by the short conjunctions— and, or, nor, but, yet, for, and so— are separated by a comma before the conjunction. **He thought he could make the trip faster by plane, so he bought two tickets for himself and his wife.**

When independent clauses are short, most agree the comma can be omitted. **James left home early but he returned soon.**

Don't confuse two independent clauses with a sentence that has a single subject and a compound predicate (two or more verbs that serve the same subject). Don't use a comma between two predicates: **He left early but returned before noon.** "Left" and "returned" are two verbs but there is only a single subject, "he."

Generally use commas between elements of a series. Journalists drop the comma before "and" and the last element. **Sarah bought bread, milk and butter at the store.**

If a sentence needs commas within the elements of a series, separate the elements with semicolons: **New officers are Jim Smith, president; Sarah Lang, vice president; and William Boyd, treasurer.**

Use pairs of commas to set off the year when it follows a complete date, and to set off the state when it follows a city (or countries that follow cities and similar constructions). **Amy Smith was born Jan. 12, 1989, in Jamestown, Va. Sarah Jones was born in Oslo, Norway, and immigrated to Minnesota in 1919.**

Do not use commas between a month and year when no date is used: **Amy Smith was born in January 1989.**

Essential/nonessential

Commas do not set off essential appositives. In the sentence: **This is my brother Bob,** Bob is an essential appositive, meaning that among several brothers, the only one being introduced is Bob. In the sentence: **The company CEO, Thomas Jones, spoke first,** the commas are needed because a company has only one CEO, so his name, while it adds information, is not essential.

The rule concerning essential and nonessential appositives extends to phrases and clauses as well: **Lake Washington, a popular resort area, is 15 miles east of Mankato.** ("A popular resort area" is a nonessential appositive.) **Lakes in northern Minnesota are less popular.** ("In northern Minnesota" is an essential prepositional phrase.)

Parenthetical expressions

Use pairs of commas to set off parenthetical expressions. Parenthetical expressions are nonessential, but they do add meaning or tone to the sentence. **It is possible, of course, to take the test in less than 20 minutes. She left no doubt, however, as to what she meant.**

Indirect/direct quotes

If an attribution is used within an indirect quote, use commas to set off the attribution: **Early spring weather, he said, is unpredictable.**

Use a comma to set off attributive phrases that precede, interrupt or follow a direct quote: **She took off her coat, turned to the audience and said, "Please be seated."**

Do not use commas when the attribution at the beginning of an indirect quote is essential to the sentence: **She said her vote could decide the issue.**

Do not use a comma when the direct quote is not a complete thought in itself but is a partial quote within an unquoted sentence: **The governor said he was pledging to support the issue "with as much effort as I'm able."**

Change of direction in sentence

Use a comma to indicate a change of direction in a sentence: **The commission voted to fund the first three groups, but not the last two.**

Colons and semicolons

Colons and semicolons sometimes also present problems. A **colon** introduces formal statements. **In his formal address Lincoln said: Four score and seven years ago....** A colon also may be used to introduce lists or series: **Officers were chosen to represent their classes: Jim Jones, freshman; Emily Nern, sophomore; Justin Time, junior.** Do not use a colon after verbs such as **are, includes** or **were** introduce a list (New class officers are Jim Jones, freshman, etc.).

Semicolons are used to punctuate lists of three or more names followed by identifications: **New officers are Jim Jones, president; Emily Nern, vice president; Justin**

QUIRKS O' THE TONGUE: JUST WHEN YOU THINK YOU KNOW IT ALL

I take it you already know
Of tough and bough and cough and dough?
Others may stumble but not you
On hiccough, thorough, slough and through.
Well done! And now you wish perhaps,
... To learn of less familiar traps?

Beware of heard, a dreadful word
That looks like beard and sounds like bird.
And dead, it's said like bed, not bead —
for goodness' sake don't call it "deed!"
Watch out for meat and great and threat
(they rhyme with suite and straight and debt).

A moth is not a moth in mother,
Nor both in bother, broth, or brother,
And here is not a match for there,
Nor dear and fear for bear and pear,
And then there's doze and rose and lose —
Just look them up — and goose and choose,
And cork and work and card and ward
And font and front and word and sword,
And do and go and thwart and cart —
Come, I've hardly made a start!
A dreadful language? Man alive!
I'd learned to speak it when I was five!
And yet to write it, the more I sigh,
I'll not learn how 'til the day I die.

— Origin uncertain.

Time, secretary. Semicolons are also used to separate independent clauses when the second clause begins with adverbs such as **however, furthermore, therefore, consequently, but,** etc. **John said he and his wife would accept the appointment; however, his wife had not been consulted.**

Hyphens

Hyphens tie a single idea from two or more words. Modern informal usage tends to avoid hyphens, unless ambiguous meaning needs clarification. This happens most of the time when writers use compound adjectives before a noun. For example, **A little known politician has decided to start a new caucus.** The politician may be little, and may be known. But with the hyphen, he becomes **a little-known politician.** Generally stick to hyphens in compound adjectives before a noun: **The team enjoyed a 15-point**

lead during most of the game. She found a full-time job in multimedia editing. **The bluish-green subtractive primary is called cyan.** On the other hand, many compound adjectives after a noun don't need a comma: **She is working full time as a multimedia editor. The team's lead reached 15 points by the third quarter.** Exceptions: Adverbs (they end in ly) do not need hyphenation for clarity: **A lightly traveled road took the reporter to an abandoned farm.** On the other hand, compound adjectives after a form of the verb "to be" often do need hyphens for clarity: **Cyan is a bluish-green subtractive primary.** Check the AP *Stylebook* for more.

III. Clarity and Conciseness

Media writing should be crisp, lively, factual and concise. (In fact, shouldn't all writing be?)

- Keep words simple.
- Keep sentences short.
- Keep paragraphs brief.

If a word lacks meaning or function, it can be deleted or perhaps the sentence can be rephrased in a more concise manner. In other words, rephrase concisely. Make every word count. The following observations may help you delete some of the more obvious verbal deadwood.

1. Passive and active voice construction. An effective way to change from passive to active voice is to rewrite the sentence using active voice. However, passive voice is necessary to avoid confusion and/or when the recipient of the action is the most important fact. For example: **The mayor was robbed Tuesday** is much clearer than **A robber robbed the mayor Tuesday.**

With active voice the subject does the acting. Take the two examples below:

A report was given by Tom Olson concerning the need for bylaw changes. (passive, 13 words)

Tom Olson reported on the need for bylaw changes. (active, nine words)

Indefinite pronoun phrases such as **it is, it was** or **it will be** are related to passive voice and allow a journalist to avoid telling who did it. Make an actor do the action:

It was proposed (The mayor proposed)

It is hoped (Committee members hope to)

It has been reported (Miller reported)

2. The article **the** can be deleted if its omission does not create awkward flow. This is most often possible before plural nouns. **(The) college presidents will meet in Mankato to talk to (the) legislators about (the) tuition problems.**

3. Relative pronoun phrases beginning with **that, which, who** and **whom** can often be tightened:

VOCABULARY AND JARGON FOR EDITORS

Appositive.

A noun or pronoun that adds information to another noun. **Irving Nern, a veteran at the desk, serves as a mentor to many.** "A veteran at the desk" is an appositive.

Desk.

Journalese for copy editors.

Direct object.

Noun or noun substitute that answers who? or what? Usually it is affected by a verb: **Josh threw a party.** Threw what? A party.

Predicate.

A complete predicate talks about the subject. **The bureau chief hired three new copy editors.** "Hired three new copy editors" is the complete predicate. A simple predicate is the verb without modifiers. "Hired" is the simple predicate.

Prepositional phrase.

A group of related words used together, and beginning with a preposition. **Ron worked at the taco shop. The soda is on the table.** "At the taco shop" and "on the table" are prepositional phrases.

Pronoun.

Replaces a noun. **You may see him now.** "You" and "him" are pronouns.

Styles: APA, Chicago, MLA, and AP.

Consistency connotes quality. Many English words and expressions can correctly be written several ways. Is it 9 P.M., 9:00 P.M., 9 PM, or 2100 hours? All are correct, but editors need to choose one for consistency. AP choice is somewhat arbitrary, even quirky, but that's what most editors for the mass media have agreed upon. On the other hand, editors in the social sciences usually use a style set up by the American Psychological Association, APA. Historians might use University of Chicago style. English scholars might use Modern Language Association (MLA) style. These are not intrinsically incorrect, but they are wrong if you're editing for most mass media.

Subordinate clause.

A group of words that can't stand on their own in a sentence. The professor gestured toward his PowerPoint slide, and the class laughed. The professor was angry because he had drawn the stick figures himself. In the first example, each clause can stand alone: "The professor gestured toward his PowerPoint Slide. The class laughed." In the second, the phrase "because he had drawn..." is dependent on the subject and can't stand alone as a complete statement.

We bought the house (that is) in the 2700 block of Madison Avenue. SPJ, (which was) organized in 1978, meets weekly.

4. The adverbial pronoun **that** can usually be deleted after the attributive phrase: **She said (that) she would run.**

5. Prepositional phrases beginning with **of** can often be changed to adjectives or possessives: **Minnesota Gov. Mark Dayton** (instead of **Mark Dayton, governor of Minnesota**); **PRSSA meets Tuesday** (instead of **the meeting of the PRSSA club**).

6. The preposition **on** can be omitted before a day or date. **The concert will be (on) Sunday.**

7. Weak modifiers such as **very, quite, rather, sort of, kind of, really** and **somewhat** can often be deleted.

8. Phrases beginning with **there,** such as **there will be, there are, there is** and **there was** have no specific meaning. **No more scholarships will be given this year** rather than **there will be no more scholarships given this year.**

9. Avoid the "will be doing syndrome." **She will sing** rather than **she will be singing.**

10. **Located** is commonly used deadwood: **The building is located on Tenth Avenue** can be shortened: **The building is on Tenth Avenue.**

11. **Nominalizations** make four words out of one. **Made an investigation of** is a nominalization of the simple verb **investigated. Made a study of** can be **studied.**

IV. Common AP style mistakes

The first Associated Press *Stylebook* came out in 1953. It was 60 stapled pages, and grandly called itself the "most definitive and inclusive work ever undertaken by a group of newspapers," according to the 2009 edition foreword. The *Stylebook* today is a collection of rules—part dictionary, part encyclopedia and part textbook. Though the book has undergone several revisions, it remains committed to its original mission: "to provide a uniform presentation of the printed word, to make a story written anywhere understandable everywhere" (*Stylebook* foreword).

Buy the book. Keep it next to you. Refer to it frequently. Or buy online access. (Go to www.apstylebook.com. Sadly, it's not a free download.) The book contains an abundance of material and may appear insurmountable to memorize. It is. To help get you started in learning the multitude of style rules, below are 10 style rules media editors use often. This is generally true throughout the world of media: public relations, advertising, online media, magazines and newspapers generally rely on AP style. (Note: *AP style* is not the same as *APA style,* the academic style most students learn in social science courses. That style is a product of the American Psychological Association.)

1. Never abbreviate the following words: days of the week; the months of March, April, May, June and July; the states of Alaska, Hawaii, Idaho, Iowa, Maine, Ohio, Texas and Utah; percent (and it is always one word, not two); company or corporation; department; assistant; associate; association; attorney, government; building; department and geographical locations of alley, road, drive, circle, terrace and highway.

2. Spell out single-digit numbers (zero to nine), and use numerals for numbers 10 and above. However, note the exceptions. Always use numerals for ages (3 years old); weights and heights (9 pounds, 7 ounces; 8 feet high); dimensions (2-by-4; 5 inches); dollars and cents ($6; 6 cents); speeds (5 mph); scores (6–10); votes (3 votes);

percentages and ratios (4 percent; 2–1 ratio) and temperatures (4 degrees). Commas should be used after every three digits of a long number, such as 29,875. But when you reach millions, billions, and trillions, rely on the easier-to-read word, with a decimal:

The new stadium is expected to cost $82.5 million.

3. Use figures for time and a colon to separate hours from minutes (3:30 P.M.). Delete zeros and the colon with no minutes (10 A.M.).

4. Do not put a 12 in front of noon and midnight, and do not capitalize either word.

5. Spell out fractions below one, using hyphens between the words (one-third).

6. Use more than and less than with numerals (more than $20).

7. Use the abbreviations Ave., Blvd. and St. only with a numbered address (1600 Pennsylvania Ave.). Spell them out and capitalize when part of a formal street name without a house or building number (Pennsylvania Avenue). No commas in addresses:

He lived at 29875 South Sugar Land Road.

8. Spell out the names of the 50 U.S. states when they stand alone in textual material. Use state abbreviations when used in conjunction with the name of a city, town, or village (Brainerd, Minn.) and with political party affiliations (D-Minn.). Note the AP has not adopted the United States Postal Service two-letter state abbreviations, unless zip codes are included in an address.

9. Use Web to indicate the World Wide Web. Also, use website, Web page, webcam, webcast, webmaster. Online is lower case, without a hyphen.

10. Use quotation marks only (no **bold**, *italics* or underlining) for all book titles, computer game titles, movie

The

Associated Press

Style

Book

The original AP Stylebook, 1953.

titles, play titles, album and song titles, television and radio program titles and titles of lectures, speeches and works of art. Do not use quotation marks, **bold**, *italics* or underlining for newspaper names (New York Times).

Subject/verb

In identifying the actual subject of the sentence, let's consider first what a subject is NOT:

It is *not* the object of a preposition.

It is *not* a phrase that is parenthetical to the true subject. (The **fitness center** [subject], **along with the cafe and wine bars** [parenthetical phrase], **was** [verb] destroyed in the fire.)

Additional "always-singular subject" items to memorize:

When used as a subject of a sentence, the personal pronoun *it* always takes a singular verb.

Subjects that stand for definable units of money, measurement, time, organization, food and medical problems always take singular verbs. (**Six hours of swimming has turned him into a giant prune.**)

A singular subject followed by such phrases as *together with* and *as well as* always takes a singular verb because those phrases merely modify their subjects. (**The new Internet company, as well as two off-shoot businesses, has attracted the attention of venture capitalists.**)

When all parts of a compound subject are singular and refer to the same person or thing, the verb is always singular. (**The president and board chair is Jane Smith.**)

Additional "always-plural" categories to memorize:

When the compound subject is joined by the conjunction *and*, it always takes a plural verb if the subjects refer to different persons or things and if the subject cannot be considered a unit. (**Ten men and one woman have been arrested on burglary charges.**)

As the subject of a sentence, indefinite pronouns such as *both, few, many* and *several* always take a plural verb. (**Many are cold, but few are frozen.**)

Well-recognized plurals require plural verbs if they do not represent a singular unit. (**Your criteria for grading my paper are unfair. The news media are under attack for their coverage of the election.**)

Know more

The Associated Press Stylebook (2011). New York: Basic.

Brooks, B., J. Pinson, and J. Wilson (2013). *Working with Words. A Handbook for Media Writers and Editors*, 8th ed. Boston: Bedford/St. Martin's.

English Grammar, http://www.englishgrammar.org.

Kessler, L., and D. McDonald (2008). *When Words Collide: A Media Writer's Guide to Grammar and Style*, 7th ed. Boston: Wadsworth.

Truss, Lynne. (2006). *Eats, Shoots and Leaves: Why, Commas Really Do Make a Difference*. New York: Gotham.

Webster's New World College Dictionary. Merriam-Webster.com

• EXERCISE 1 •

Incomplete sentences

Correct the sentences below as necessary.

1. Police are investigating a stabbing. That left a 20-year-old man injured Monday night.
2. Although what John Reina was saying has a lot of truth in it. The memo did make FOX biased in many ways.
3. Levine doesn't follow all five principles of ethical journalism. Although he believes that what he is doing is correct.
4. Film critics have proclaimed Steven Spielberg's new film a critical success. But a commercial failure.
5. One woman killed and three injured Tuesday. When their sports car skidded on icy roads and collided with a truck.

• EXERCISE 2 •

Subject/verb disagreements

Correct the sentences below as necessary.

1. The media is to blame for the economic problems of this country.
2. Politics are a topic to avoid at parties.
3. The film's producer believes each of these movie scripts have great box office potential.
4. Creating new investments opportunities are the CEO's biggest concern.
5. Neither she nor her partners has reported for work.

• EXERCISE 3 •

Subject/pronoun disagreements

Correct the sentences below as necessary.

1. The network is very biased because they use their own frames to choose their side in many situations.
2. The company explained that they had conversed with Jeb Bush's office and they apparently denied all allegations of voter fraud.
3. The CEO claims the company makes all their products with natural ingredients.
4. A team of writers agreed on their list of changes to the screenplay.
5. The Minnesota Vikings will end its lease with the Metrodome at season's end.

• EXERCISE 4 •

Confusing possessives and contractions

Correct the sentences below as necessary.

1. Sheriff Townsend said the suspect had gone to his parent's home asking for money.
2. Smarts salary will be $95,000.
3. The plot has two aspiring producer's trying to make it big on Broadway.
4. Temperatures remained near the freezing mark, leading many to believe that its going to snow tonight.
5. Police Chief Anderson continues to speculate on whose responsible for the rash of car breakins.

• E X E R C I S E 5 •

Poor word choices

Correct the sentences below as necessary.

1. The main age group the store sees is the 30- to 60-year-olds who are still in love with the vintage albums from their youth.
2. A local couple is dead after a family argument turned to disaster.
3. The team has participated in the national tournament for four years, reached the semifinals twice and took home the title in 2010–2011.
4. Sigler volunteers her time by providing pro bono work to various top rated civic organizations.
5. Georgetown University announces Lucinda Smart as its next head women's basketball coach.

• E X E R C I S E 6 •

Punctuation mistakes

Correct the sentences below as necessary.

1. The Wayland, Mass. native came to the conclusion that history was the answer for his future career.
2. Japan declared war on the United States with its Dec. 7, 1941 attack at Pearl Harbor.
3. "Here we are, moreover, here we go again," declared the protestors.
4. Unfortunately the story aired only overseas, through the BBC.
5. Smart was offered the position—which pays $95,000 annually.

• E X E R C I S E 7 •

Clarity and conciseness

Correct the sentences below as necessary.

1. For example, the author talks about how FOX was talking about an environmental special and how it should show both sides but to not lean towards the pro-environmental side.

2. The letter basically exposed the network by explaining the inside scoop of what goes on inside the newsroom.

3. Network executives hint at then which way they want the story to go which makes the stories come off as biased because they are leaning towards a side and it makes us as viewers perceive the message as they please.

4. The resolution was approved after a unanimous vote in favor by all council members.

5. A man was shot to death by his son after the man shot his wife to death during a family dispute in Johnstown Tuesday night.

• EXERCISE 8 •

AP Style quiz

The following examples touch a few of the most common mistakes beginning journalists make regarding AP style. The quiz also will help students become familiar with the *AP Stylebook*.

4:00 P.M. in the afternoon
March ninth
X-Mas day
Fri., Apr. 20, 2009
sheriff Sam Smith
who's book
He visited Cal., Tex. and Ohio.
eight percent; two per cent; 3%
$.15
fifteen thousand dollars
Sun Valley, Ida.
has a masters degree; has a bachelors degree
in the 1990's
2500 Americans
7 year old boy
Mass Communications department
degree in Mass Communications
24 yard touchdown
won 19 to 16
scored three power play goals post season
50 pound box
2,700 block of Madison Ave.
second and third degree burns
Senator James Madison, Republican of Georgia
Dallas, TX and Minneapolis, MN
son, eight, and daughter, six
vice-president
Doctor Samuel Smith
19-years-old
the NBC TV Today program

Gone With The Wind
web site, internet, emale
Brigadier General Tom Brady
12 midnight

• EXERCISE 9 •

The following story has several grammar, punctuation, spelling and AP style mistakes and contains words and phrases that should be eliminated (25 to be exact). Your assignment: Read through the story and cross out unnecessary words and phrases and correct the AP style mistakes without altering the meaning of the sentences or changing indirect quotes to direct quotes.

A woman named Shirley Anne Hall has up until December 8 to clear up her Garden Grove house of rotten oranges that have gone bad, cobwebs, vehicle parts, musty newspapers and a year's worth of dirty dishes that have not been washed.

Hall who is age 54 must remove overgrown weeds in her yard and other debris from her yard which is located in the 12,000 block of Barlett Street, Orange County, superior court judge Randell Wilkinson said on Wednesday. If she fails to comply with the order which judge Randell Wilkinson made on Wednesday, the city will bring in work crews and send Hall the bill for the work the crews have done.

The city has been trying to persuade Hall to sort through her mess since the year of 2001 city attorney Stuart Scudder said.

Hall, a woman who is diagnosed with chronic depression, said the city is harassing her and that the stress that the city has caused her by harassing her has prevented her from making any progress.

The Dayle McIntosh Center for the Disabled in Anaheim is looking for volunteers who of their own volition will offer to help Hall to clean up.

• EXERCISE 10 •

The following story has several grammar, punctuation, spelling and AP style mistakes and contains words and phrases that should be eliminated (25 to be exact). Your assignment: Read through the story and cross out unnecessary words and phrases and correct the AP style mistakes without altering the meaning of the sentences or changing indirect quotes to direct quotes. Check your answers with the key provided at the end of this chapter.

Power was cut off to nearly a 3rd of the residents of Mankato last night after a violent storm ripped thrugh the city around six o'clock.

Police chief Robert Dye said that power was restored to most homes within about two hours, but a "substantial number of people," had to go without power for most of the night.

Chief Dye said that many of the city's traffic lights were knocked out by the storm, and traffic problems developed on several of the more busy streets.

Chief dye says that everything should be back to normal today.

A power company official said that over 1500 homes were without electricity for some part of the night. He said, that crews worked throughout the entire night to get people's power tuned on.

The storm dumped over 2 inches of rain on the city in about 30 minutes. The power failure was due to lighting hitting one of the power companys substation in the Western part of the city.

KEYS

Exercise 1

1. Police are investigating a stabbing that injured a 20-year-old man Monday night. **BETTER:** Police are investigation the stabbing of a 20-year-old man which happened Monday night.

2. Although what John Reina was saying has a lot of truth in it, the memo did make FOX biased in many ways. **BETTER:** The memo did make FOX appear biased in many ways, according to John Reina.

3. Levine doesn't follow all five principles of ethical journalism but believes that what he is doing is correct.

4. Film critics have proclaimed Steven Spielberg's new film a critical success. However, low box office receipts indicate it is a commercial failure.

5. One woman was killed and three injured when their sports car skidded on icy roads and collided with a truck Tuesday.

Exercise 2

1. The media **are** to blame for the economic problems of this country.

2. Politics **is** a topic to avoid at parties.

3. The **film** producer believes each of these movie scripts **has** great box office potential.

4. Creating new investment opportunities are the **CEO** biggest concern. **BETTER:** Creating new investment opportunities are the biggest concerns for a CEO.

5. Neither she nor her partners **have** reported for work.

Exercise 3

1. The FOX network is very biased because **it** uses **its** own frames to choose **its** side in many situations.

2. The company explained that **it** had conversed with Jeb Bush's office and **it had** apparently denied all allegations of voter fraud. **BETTER:** Make two sentences. The company explained that it had conversed with Jeb Bush's office. Bush's office denied all allegations of voter fraud.

3. The CEO claims the company makes all **its** products from natural ingredients.

4. A team of writers agreed on **its** list of changes to the screenplay.

5. The Minnesota Vikings will end **their** lease with the Metrodome at season's end.

Exercise 4

1. Sheriff Townsend said the suspect had gone to his **parents'** home asking for money.

2. **Smart's** salary will be $95,000.

3. The plot has two aspiring **producers** trying to make it big on Broadway.

4. Temperatures remained near the freezing mark, leading many to believe that **it is** going to snow tonight.

5. Police Chief Anderson continues to speculate on **who is or who's** responsible for the rash of car breakings.

Exercise 5

1. The store **caters to** 30- to 60-year-olds who are still in love with the vintage albums from their youth. (Leave out "The main age group" because an age group is listed.)

2. A local couple is dead **as a result** (or) **following** a family argument. (Leave out the word "disaster" as it indicates an opinion expressed by the writer.)

3. **Rewrite:** The team (take out "has") participated in four national tournaments, reaching the semifinals twice and taking home the title in 2010–2011.

4. Take out volunteers her time by **OR** pro bono work as both indicate the same action.

5. **Rewrite:** Linda Smart has been named as the next head women's basketball coach at Georgetown University.

Exercise 6

1. Add a comma after the state abbreviation.
2. Add a comma after the year.
3. Make the quote into two sentences.
4. Add a comma after "unfortunately" and remove the comma after "overseas."
5. Remove the dash between the words "position" and "which.

Exercise 7

1. Use two sentences. For example, the author used an environmental special to demonstrate how FOX slants perception to one side. The network should have included sources from all sides of the issue.

2. The letter exposed the behind the scenes working of the network.

3. Network executives hint at which way the story should be written. Hence, viewers will perceive a biased message.

4. The council unanimously approved the resolution.

5. The problem: too many unidentified pronouns (his). One possible solution is to write a shorter lead: "A son shot his father during a family dispute in Johnstown Tuesday night." The second graph should provide more details, including proper names.

THREE

Think Like an Editor

Deneen Gilmour

Yes, a copy editor must exhibit an excellent command of grammar, punctuation and Associated Press style. Yes, a copy editor must be capable of editing under extreme deadline pressure. Yes, a copy editor must display design skills equal to his or her editing skills.

However, a truly effective copy editor is more than a grammar geek or an AP style whiz. In the course of developing as a professional, an effective copy editor intuitively learns to think like an editor. That notion of "thinking like an editor," equates for the most part to developing the skill set needed to make judgments about the use and presentation of words and images.

Successful copy editors possess intellectual curiosity that propels them to seek information beyond personal interest areas. Intense intellectual curiosity drives a good copy editor to read widely—far beyond the reading required in the workplace. Copy editors who satisfy their intellectual curiosity develop the ability to conduct on-the-job audience analysis, and that, in turn, feeds the ability to make sound judgments while the deadline clock ticks.

Students who aspire to become copy editors show intellectual curiosity and strong grammar and AP style knowledge. These provide the building blocks needed to pass the demanding editing tests often administered as the gateway to internships or job openings. If you wonder what questions might be on an editing test for an internship or full-time career position, conduct an online search for the Dow Jones test. No matter what type of mass media career you're planning—public relations, online journalism, photojournalism, print journalism, broadcast media or advertising—the editing test handed to you likely will include some or many aspects of the Dow Jones News Fund Editing Test. Of course, the firm or media outlet testing you may change the test to fit the firm's needs or niche. However, looking at the Dow Jones test is likely to drive home one point: "Wow! That's a tough test." Wise students then busy themselves with becoming the type of broadly educated and well-read individual who can pass such a challenging test. The five-page, one-hour test includes 11 sections on grammar, current events, editing and headline writing.

The fact is that preparing yourself to be an editor means you must go far beyond what's taught to you in a textbook and by teachers. We can give you a start. But only you can take the initiative to prepare yourself to think like an editor.

Essentially, a copy editor is a person who edits words, photos and graphics produced by others and prepares that mix of words and images for presentation to an audience. Ultimately, that translates to this nugget: A copy editor is a decision maker, an astute decision maker who uses keen judgment skills to make the best decisions for a given audience and for the colleagues whose work is edited. Judgment skills grow and develop with time and practice, but novice copy editors can do several things to jump start their prowess as astute decision-makers.

1. Read, read, read

Editing is a skill that can be improved three ways. Amazingly, two of the three ways do not involve practicing the skill of editing itself. (1) Yes, the first and most obvious way to become a better editor is to edit, edit and edit some more.

(2) The second way is to revise your own writing. The process of revising your work — amping up the acceptable to the memorable — demands that your mind install the revisions in the "hard drive" between your ears; and in the process, you begin your next editing project at a higher level of effectiveness.

(3) Finally, a copy editor must read widely. The very process of reading puts new words, phrases and syntax construction patterns in your mind, and those new patterns will naturally flow out in your editing work. It seems reading books and magazines has declined in popularity as other forms of media vie for our attention. If you want to be an effective editor, you absolutely must read for pleasure and read for professional improvement and enrichment.

Here are a few suggestions for developing a reading habit:

Carve out quiet, private reading time in your daily schedule and guard that time zealously. Begin by reading for pleasure — whatever genre brings you enjoyment, whether it is the sports section of the newspaper, historical fiction novels or fashion magazines.

Next, include professional improvement magazines, journals and books. Reading the magazines electronically or on paper makes no difference. What matters is you are taking in information that inspires you to improve your editing skills and you are putting high-quality writing and editing patterns into the "hard drive" in your mind.

Finally — and this suggestion is the most important on the pyramid of transforming yourself into a well-read editor — make it a daily ritual to read newspapers (on paper or online) and a weekly ritual to read news and cultural magazines (again, paper or online doesn't matter). If you are unsure what to read consider these titles:

- Your local daily newspaper and perhaps the newspaper of the next largest city plus a highly reputable major national daily newspaper such as *The New York Times* or *Washington Post*.

- Weekly news magazines such as *Time* and *The Economist*. Cultural/policy analysis magazines such as *The New Yorker, The New Republic, Atlantic Monthly, National Geographic, Smithsonian* or more entertainment-oriented magazines such as *Vanity Fair, Rolling Stone* or *Sports Illustrated*.
- "Best of" books such as *Best Newspaper Writing: American Society of Newspaper Editors Award Winners and Finalists*, a book series published each year; *The Best American Magazine Writing*, compiled by The American Society of Magazine Editors; or *The Best Newspaper Design*, a compilation of prize-winning entries from the annual Society for News Design contest.
- Made-for-the-Web e-zines such as "Salon.com," Slate.com" or "TheDailyBeast.com" also offer excellent, ever-changing content along with ideas for online design.

2. Seek mentors

Try your best to put your work and ideas out for others to critique. After all, the work of a copy editor eventually goes before a public audience. So there's no sense to be secretive or defensive about your work or work process. The first challenge is finding mentors who are a good fit for you. Ask your instructor, or call someone whose writing you admire. The second challenge is to listen to your mentors. Rather than reflexively defending your ideas, editing or designs, try to quietly contemplate your mentor's suggestions and at least try applying their wisdom. People who enjoy input from a nurturing mentor discover that taking the advice of a mentor actually helps decrease the burden copy editors often feel. That is, after developing the habit of incorporating a mentor's ideas into one's work process people report feeling less like they are walking a tightrope alone. Copy editing is, after all, often a fast-moving, deadline-driven type of work. Accept all the help you can get. As a novice copy editor you can connect with strong, nurturing mentors and listen to your mentors' suggestions before and during the editorial decision-making process.

3. Discover the benefits of criticism

Seek critiques of your work. Having your work critiqued can range from asking instructors or co-workers for input to entering contests and applying for scholarships sponsored by professional associations such as the American Copy Editors Society (http://www.copydesk.org).

Most copy editors entered the profession with an appreciation for words but the truly good ones develop a love and respect for the power of words, and they live a life of intellectual curiosity that channels knowledge into their work life and helps build sound judgment.

People in media professions often joke that copy editors make great trivia team members because copy editors see a parade of news and information go past their eyes each day, read widely and explore the world of ideas. A copy editor's brain is an organic repository of information that by mid-career is often chock full of a rich array of facts and information equal to the computer databases that support computerized trivia games.

The view from the copy desk

Roger Whittle, Omaha, Neb., has worked as a copy editor for more than 20 years. Rather than decrying the state of "kids these days"—as some veterans in any profession do—Whittle says each year's crop of college graduates who enter the copy-editing profession are brighter than the ones the year before.

A question-and-answer session with Whittle provides a glimpse into the realities of copy editing today.

Whittle's resume at a glance:

Education: Bachelor's degree in journalism, South Dakota State University.

First job: Began career in 1986 as sports editor in Glenwood Springs, Colo. Since then he's climbed his way up, working for nine daily newspapers as he navigated the career ladder to larger newspapers.

The call of copy editing: "I became a copy editor at my second newspaper when I realized the copy desk enjoyed higher pay and better hours and worked fewer weekends than sports editors.

"I've stayed because I actually enjoy the work."

Current job: Copy editor at the Omaha, Neb., *World-Herald*.

Q: Although novice copy editors arrive with academic training in AP style, grammar, headline writing and ethics, what "big picture" things does a copy editor need to know or possess in order to succeed?

A: Schools teach the basics of accuracy, fairness, readability, etc. But that doesn't seem to be enough today. With more competition and declining readership, newspaper managers want copy [editors] to produce stories that also are "engaging," "forward-looking," "interactive" and other hard-to-define qualities.

Q: What are the daily tasks of a copy editor today at a metro newspaper?

A: In my experience, copy editors are doing a lot more than they did 10 or 20 years ago. As newspapers have reduced staffs to balance budgets, copy desks seem to take [the] brunt of the cuts. Nobody wants to reduce the size of their reporting staffs given the emphasis on websites, but everything else is fair game. Copy desks, therefore, are [editing] more stories with fewer people. New technology also gives copy editors the ability to pick up the work of paginators and, to a certain extent, graphics people as well.

Copy editors have also taken on extra work for online editions, posting breaking news and photos to websites. This wasn't the case even three or four years ago before budget woes forced staffs to shrink.

Q: Has technology made copy editing easier or more difficult?

A: Technology has both helped and hindered copy editors. It has made some parts of the job much easier: electronic libraries and Internet search engines make fact-checking much simpler than it was 20 or 30 years ago. Computers have also made obsolete such skills as headline-fitting and copy fitting. On the other hand, such technologies have enabled newspapers to eliminate jobs such as paste-up people and paginators, putting even more work on the plates of copy editors.

Q: Have you noticed a pattern of certain aspects of the job that tend to cause copy editors to leave the profession?

A: Fear of losing their jobs is about the only thing I've noticed that drives copy editors out of the business. It's a matter of getting out before getting laid off. Other than doing more work, most copy editors I know still like their jobs. But the fear of layoffs, furloughs and pay cuts often overpowers any job satisfaction.

4. Editing style correlates with interaction style

In mass media settings where words and images are edited to produce a publication, press release or website, the copy editor often functions as the tie that binds the otherwise disparate parts of the creative team together. That's because a copy editor brings together text, photos and graphics and thus interacts with all the professionals who create or produce the text, photos and graphics.

The manner in which you, as a copy editor, deal with people during the editing/design process goes beyond simply asking a photographer, "When will the photo be ready?" or telling a reporter you need to discuss a confusing quote with him. The manner in which copy editors deal with other media professionals sets an overall tone for interactions in the workplace. Interestingly, the three general styles that copy editors employ when dealing with others in the editing/design process also are the three general operating styles of managers in mass media. Perhaps that's because managers tend to rise from the ranks of copy editors in print newsrooms and the ranks of producers in television newsrooms, a job that correlates to that of a print editor. The interaction styles are more than the way you treat people when editing their writing, photos or graphics. It's also a style of relating to other professionals in the media workplace. The three general interaction styles are the following:

The authoritarian style.

Anybody who's had a job will recognize the authoritarian style as the "I-will-decide" or "I-know-best" management style. The boss decides with little input from staff. When it comes to editing, the authoritarian editor often unilaterally edits others' words and images without consulting the person who wrote the words or created the images.

The team-building style.

The team-building style often is characterized by a desire on the part of managers to build consensus and to lead by example. When it comes to editing, a team-building copy editor is likely to meet with writers and other creative professionals, or even sit beside them while making decisions about wording, headlines, photos and design. In the team-building style, copy editors try to build good will by explaining how editing can best be done, thus leading by example and from experience, and sometimes teaching in the process.

The coaching style.

In a practical sense, the coaching style functions via one-on-one collaboration and decision-making in the workplace. Coaching, of course, is a term borrowed from sports. According to Roy Peter Clark and Don Fry in *Coaching Writers*, the term "coach" entered mass media lexicon at the *Boston Globe* in 1978 when Don Murray became perhaps the first in-the-newsroom writing teacher at an American newspaper. Since Murray's groundbreaking work as a writing coach who collaborated and strategized with writers to make the story in front of them better and build skills for the next story, "coaching" has become a concept used in newsrooms and classrooms worldwide. Editors who use a coaching style often suggest two or three strategies for improving copy or design and the writer or designer makes the choice, leaving the writer or designer with a feeling of autonomy and creative empowerment.

A textbook can't tell you the most appropriate editing style. Maybe no one can; we develop a style that fits our personalities. But a book can tell you what editors of any style look for in copy that is compelling — something that will make an audience want to pause, want to begin, want to continue and want to read all the way to the end.

So approach the desk. Grab that digital blue pencil. Think.

5. Getting started behind the desk

Just how does one go about effectively editing a story? Many editors approach copy in the methodical manner by reading each story three times"

1. Read the story.
2. Edit it thoroughly.
3. Re-read the edited story.

It's easy to skip the first and third step of this process, especially if you're under deadline pressure. However, it's important to read the story through once so that you know what it's all about. If you don't understand the purpose of a story, and manner in which it is written, you can hardly edit it effectively. Also important is to re-read the story to make sure you caught everything — and to make sure you didn't introduce any new errors. It's embarrassing for an editor to add errors that weren't there originally, but it happens more than you might think. Editors can get pretty smug about their ability to make things better.

Similarly, avoid changing a writer's way of putting words together just because it's not the way you would have written it. Consider: Is it really necessary to change, and why? Good editors don't discourage reporters by working over their copy with a blue

THINK LIKE AN EDITOR: AVOIDING CLICHÉS

Clichés are those cute, once original phrases or expressions that have become tired from overuse. It's sort of like hearing the same joke for the third or fourth time. Good writing ought to be fresh and original, and while clichés are often part of our everyday speech, they are less part of written work. We can divide clichés into three categories of offensiveness.

Common phrases.

Category one is the old common phrase, often a metaphor, sayings that have been around for perhaps centuries: Beehive of activity. Thorn in his side. Chicken with its head cut off. Easy as pie. Sometimes they evoke barnyards or other experiences long gone from our day-to-day lives. How many of us have seen a chicken with its head cut off? But your great-grandmother might have. Writers can occasionally find a fresh and amusing version based on an old cliché. He opened Pandora's Box is an old cliché, but in a story about lawyer advertising regulations being made more flexible, a writer tried He opened Pandora's briefcase. You're groaning. Right. This kind of witticism draws a fine line between clever and corny.

A variety of old cliché is journalese, trite expressions particularly common in the journalism or business world: acid test; long-smoldering; the bottom line; finalize; impact (as a verb); firestorm of criticism; cautious optimism. A dictionary of clichés for reference: http://www.clichesite.com/.

Pop culture clichés.

A second cliché category is material not so old, but quickly made popular from television programs or movies. Usually they are fad phrases that come and go. From the 1960s, '70s and '80s, for example, we had Sock it to me! (*Laugh In*); Sorry about that, chief! (*Get Smart*); Isn't that special. (*Saturday Night Live*); Well, excuuuse me! (*Saturday Night Live*); I can't believe I ate the whole thing. (Alka-Seltzer commercial).

All of these phrases are way out of style, but more recent clichés include: You are the weakest link; Been there, done that; Yada, yada; Same old, same old; The mother of all…; I hate it when that happens; What's wrong with this picture? No-brainer. No doubt you can think of more. And no doubt they'll soon be as moldy as Sock it to me!, which once sounded groovy, man.

A Society for Professional Journalists *Quill* magazine columnist writing about stereotypes noted someone probably could write a dissertation examining writers who copy dialogue from television. Why would people rather copy fake dialogue of fake characters living false lives instead of making real-life conversation? Of course, it's easier to let someone else be clever. But not in our media editing. People hear enough stale clichés at school and work — why should they have to read them in the media as well?

Stereotypes.

A third level of clichés is perhaps more insidious, and more dangerous. These clichés are the things you write based on assumptions, without ever having been to a location or experienced a culture. That is, stereotypes. They may be based on our prejudice or ignorance of a society, or a country, or a part of the world. A few years ago, a report of an airplane crash said the plane went down in Florida, in a "snake-infested swamp." Actually, however, this is not true of all the Everglades, particularly the area in which the plane crashed. And one could argue that animals don't really "infest" anything—they just live there. It's a stereotypical cliché someone wrote without thinking. Similarly, writers from elsewhere often cover a story based on stereotypes. "Those crazy Californians." "Those knee-jerk liberals from Massachusetts." "Those backward hillbillies from Arkansas."

In North Dakota visiting media writers feel compelled to include weather clichés that have nothing to do with the topic. During the 2004 presidential campaign a Democratic candidate visited that state. AP writers from California squeezed in the usual clichés of the "remote state," "frozen north," "braving frigid temperatures." Would Dakotans do the same thing writing about those nutty Californians? Or perhaps "the state that's always going broke?" What clichés do you recognize about your state?

Most dangerous is the tendency for us to compartmentalize minority groups, professions, hobbies or physical characteristics. Most of us would edit material that branded African-Americans as "ghetto-blasting drug dealers" or Native Americans as "lazy boozers." Most of us would change a description of a "homeless cripple." But sometimes we let go stereotypes such as the "attractive blonde coed," "wild-eyed feminist," "farmer looking for another government handout," "lazy know-it-all college student," or even those "rumpled, absent-minded college professors." Stereotypical labeling actually drives the thinking of many radio commentators, bloggers and politicians—but likely they don't enjoy the benefit of good editors.

pencil (or its digital equivalent, a cursor) without good reason. If you're concerned about the way something is written, it's best to talk to the reporter, to give the writer the opportunity to make the changes.

That having been said as fair warning to over-zealous copy editors, the principle remains: You can't let poorly written content into public view. Yes, an editor has a responsibility to writers, but also a responsibility to readers. If writing really does need more work, and you don't have time to get back to the writer, don't let it go to spare the person's feelings.

Editors usually keep in mind a hierarchy of goals in considering a story. At the basic level are the technical things: spelling, grammar, typos, AP style. Many editors try to consider these first. Second, they take on the lead, because if time is limited, the most important part of a story is that first "nut graf." Then they consider the rest of the story, tightening awkward construction and considering clichés, wordiness, bias, missing information (What would the reader want to know?) and potential libel.

After the first read-through, it's not a bad idea to ask yourself the following questions:

1. Does the story make sense?
2. Is it complete?
3. Is it fair?

4. Should more sources be contacted? Note that a single-source story is usually inadequate, unless it's a meeting account.

5. Do all quotes have complete attributions? Every story needs actual quotes from sources to give it authority and realism. Each person quoted must be identified by first and last name, plus position, such as, "Tex T. Book, superintendent of schools, said...."

Many editors will check spelling of every name, unless they are certain. Misspelled names tend to creep into stories written on deadlines. They are serious errors: People really can't forgive a publication that misspells their name in public. It is, after all, a pretty important part of who they are. Many undergraduate journalism students have experienced the old-fashioned editor turned instructor who gives "automatic F" to any exercise turned in with a name misspelled.

When an editor must change wording, it's worth trying to be sensitive to the writer's style. Instead of just inserting words you'd use yourself, look back into the story to find words the author uses and work with that vocabulary. You might write, "April Bloom brings a plethora of orchids to brighten her office," but if he writer doesn't use the unusual word "plethora," it will look like someone else's writing. As an editor you still have to remember it's not, after all, your story.

Often not considered by beginning editors is the need to read skeptically. Non-staff written stories sometimes contain far-fetched claims off the Internet, perhaps even lies the author tries to squeak past a tired editor. Every once in a while you hear of a journalist duped by a prankster who stages a bogus wedding, or even a bogus funeral. Urban legends come and go, whether about the cat in the microwave oven, the hoax computer virus or a more recent favorite, a supposed think-tank listing presidential IQs starting with Franklin Roosevelt. As the old-time copy editor warned: "If your mother says she loves you, check it out."

Related to skepticism is the oft-heard admonition to new editors joining news-rooms: "To be a good editor, you have to have a dirty mind." It's easy to catch obscenities, the usual four-letter words. Some media operations okay them in direct quotes or blogs. A very few even let them go generally, but you have to consider your reader's response. It's not that most readers are prudes. It's just that seeing "those words" in print is so startling it disrupts the reader's understanding of the story.

Less obvious are the double-entendres, expressions that have a naughty meaning to readers with "dirty minds." Any version of the verb "to come" has potential: "She said she had a wonderful time on the date, and hopes to come again soon." Sometimes double-entendres end up on the funny page of *Columbia Journalism Review*, or advertising mistakes on the back page of *Consumer Reports*. That's worth a hearty guffaw for everyone. Except for the embarrassed editor who missed the mistake.

6. Boring leads: The top five

As an editor you will rarely write leads on news stories, feature stories or press releases. However, you certainly will edit leads. Some leads should be avoided because they are overdone, trite, annoying to the audience or simply the hallmark of a lazy or lackadaisical writer.

Here are five leads that a copy editor should edit or send back to the original writer for a revision:

1. The question lead.

Do you have any idea how many sex offenders live in your city?
Or, *Had it with freezing cold temperatures?*

The first lead asks the reader — someone who's paid money for the publication or at least paid time for the online version — to do the intellectual work. The role of a publication is to tell a reader something, not to ask the reader something.

The second lead is trite and cliché. Copy editors usually purge clichés from any placement in writing, most certainly the lead, and triteness is not endearing to audiences.

2. The quote lead.

A quote generally is used to provide voice, flavor and context to a piece of writing. Voice, flavor and context usually cannot find a comfortable home in the first sentence of a piece of media writing. A quote in a lead usually confuses readers and makes them wonder, "Who's talking and what are they talking about?" Confused readers click to something more understandable or turn the page. For example:

"There are 25 sex offenders threatening this city's children." This is how mayor candidate Irving Nern began his press conference Friday.

This clumsy lead beginning with a quote could be strengthened as a paraphrase:

More than two dozen sex offenders threaten the city's children, said mayor candidate Irving Nern Friday.

3. The long lead.

These days long leads are definitely no-nos. The length of leads has been shrinking along with people's attention spans. If a lead is longer than 20 to 25 words it probably needs trimming. If a lead is longer than 40 words it needs to be rewritten or split into two sentences. Example:

Freezing temperatures are uncommon in August, but meteorologist Rainer Snow said data from the past 100 years show at least five cold summers, sending residents scurrying to cover their plants and their children from an unexpected cold snap, "like swimmers from an alligator," joked Mayor Irving Nern.

That weighs in at 47 words. A copy editor would shorten (and probably change to active voice):

Think like an editor: The bigger picture

People who work in the media business often don't stop to realize — or perhaps just downplay — the power their words have to influence readers. Words published have a power beyond words spoken, in that their appearance in print or even on the Web gives them the credibility of permanency. We believe it because "it was published in a book," or in a magazine, or sometimes we don't even remember where. This book's editor has had discussions over the years with people who declare their statements to be absolute fact, because they "read it in a magazine somewhere." We as students or scholars often do research and mistakingly think adding a reference to statements indicating it was published somewhere automatically gives it unquestionable credibility:

According to recent research, the earth is flat (Johnson, 1971).

Looking up (Johnson, 1971) on a reference page might bring you to a publication such as *Journal of the Flat Earth Society*. Credible? You can decide that, but the point is, publication gives statements more authority — no matter where they're published.

Accepting that we as (nearly) media professionals have some ethical responsibility to consider carefully what we are publishing, we can begin by identifying three kinds of statements:

Facts.

Interpretations.

Judgments.

1. Facts are verifiably true statements made by the writer or by someone quoted, that is, a source.

By the writer: The weather yesterday was bright and sunny in Fargo.

Fact, easily verifiable.

By someone else quoted: It was bright and sunny yesterday on Wisconsin's Big Placid Lake, according to Placid Mayor Sandy Beach.

You weren't there, but still it's pretty easily verifiable by consulting weather reports, or asking other people who were at the beach.

By someone else quoted: It will be sunny tomorrow, according to chief meteorologist Sunny Phorcas.

This one is a bit more tricky. It's verifiable in that the writer could probably prove Phorcas said it, perhaps by digital recorder. It's not verifiable in that tomorrow hasn't arrived. But it soon will be verifiable. Meanwhile, we rely on the fact of this sentence by examining the credibility of the person who said it. In this case, it is presumed that a meteorologist would make this prediction based on scientific methods of analysis proven to be generally accurate.

By someone else quoted: It will be sunny tomorrow, according to Ross Collins, professor of communication.

Fact? Here we have to question the credibility of the source. But one thing is certain: it will soon be easy to verify.

The point is that a *fact* presented using a *source*, the usual way information comes into published media, may depend not only on an objective ability to verify, but also on the credibility of the source. If an editor presumes something published is a "fact" because "the source was quoted accurately," she or he is missing an important point: readers presume the quote is accurate but still need to know if the fact that as asserted by the source is accurate.

But most often, no matter who said it, a fact is reasonably easy to verify independently.

It is interesting to note that "fact checkers" who go through stories on large publications will sometimes verify facts by making sure the source exists and was correctly quoted. They will not necessarily verify that the material in the quote is correct.

2. Interpretations are comments based on facts, often made by the writer following a quote from a source:

"It was bright and sunny yesterday," said Placid Mayor Sandy Beach, giving boaters and anglers the opportunity to enjoy a relaxing day on the lake.

Sounds like a safe bet. But do we know this interpretation to be true? Not necessarily — maybe it was too hot to go boating and the fish weren't biting. Maybe water skiers bothered the anglers and aggressive turtles ruined the day for everyone. Far-fetched, perhaps. But interpretation is conjecture. We can't say verifiably that everybody on the lake enjoyed themselves.

Interpretations can get tricky, particularly in more complex stories about important issues. For instance, if you read: Crime on campus has increased 20 percent in one year, making the university a less safe place for students.

The first clause is a fact. The second is an interpretation based on that fact. But is it a reasonable interpretation? Maybe not. If crime on campus consisted of three thefts and two attempted rapes one year and went up to four thefts and two rapes the next, would you feel less safe? On a campus of 4,000 students? On a campus of 40,000? Maybe yes, maybe no.

Interpretations can also suggest judgments.

3. Judgments are statements which indicate something is good or bad. Supposedly in "straight news" writing, editors are taught to avoid judgments. That is, we only write "opinions," declaring something good or bad, in columns, blogs, editorials or tweets.

It was a really nice day on the lake yesterday, according to Placid Mayor Sandy Beach.

Did Beach say this in her statement quoted above? No. She said it was bright and sunny. The writer presumed that was a good thing, and made a value judgment, calling it "nice." A safe judgment? Probably. But not everyone likes sun.

Interpretation gets sticky when it's part of more complicated stories. Researchers call it the "fully/only" conundrum. For example, you read:

Crime at the university has increased fully 20 percent in just one year.

The word "fully" suggests an interpretation, as does the word "just." Or I could write

Crime at the university has increased only 20 percent during the entire year.

Just two little words changed, but a pretty different statement. Reporters can't ethically include judgments in an "objective" news story. But they can disguise judgments as interpretations based on interviews. How? Let's say a reporter interviews four people on campus apparently qualified to speak about crime: the campus police chief, vice president for student affairs, student senate president and chief of the city's police force downtown. Three out of four say this 20 percent increase in crime is not a significant amount. "While we would like to see zero crime on campus, this represents very few crimes, after all, and it might be just a coincidence," says the campus chief. But the student senate president is not convinced. "I really think crime on campus should be zero. Not only do we have some worrisome crimes—two near-rapes is two too many—but crime seems to be increasing, not going down."

How do you portray this difference of opinion? If you as the writer believe crime trends are worrisome, you have a handy way to report it without saying it yourself. You can write:

> The up-tick in crime on campus is a real concern, according to Student Senate President Irvin Nern. Concerning a 20 percent increase in just one year, Nern said, "Not only do we have some worrisome crimes—two near-rapes is two too many—but crime seems to be increasing, not going down."
> University administrators and law enforcement officials were not as convinced that the increase is meaningful. Campus police chief Iva Badge did note, "We would like to see zero crime on campus." But clearly campus crime is a concern among university leaders.

As an editor, do you feel this story represents the facts as the reporter collected them? Is it fair? Objective? Two things are certain: no one was misquoted, and every word presented was a fact. The interpretation is what's more important here, as well as the suggested judgment. Obviously, you could easily turn this story around to reflect the "only" interpretation.

Judgments declare something good or bad. So according to accepted media writing values, a writer can't say in a news story:

It will be a nice sunny day tomorrow on Big Placid Lake.

The word "nice" is a good/bad judgment. But the writer can quote someone else using a judgment he'd like to use:

"It will be a darned fine day at the lake tomorrow," said letter carrier Stan P. Cancel. "I wish I didn't have to work."

The ethics of how writers use facts, interpretations, and judgments, disguised or not, often becomes one of the great challenges for editors. Gatekeepers hold viewpoints sometimes dramatically different from one another. Some editors tell reporters what kind of story they want to see even before the reporter goes out on assignment. That is, the reporter's interpretation is dictated before the event or interviews actually take place. Is this ethical? Other editors let the reporters decide how to cover the story. Reporters would like to claim this approach is more ethical, because you can't know what the story is about until you cover it. We can't tell you as an editor how to proceed on all such questions, but we can make you aware of some complications in the simple principle, "be objective."

City residents seldom see freezing temperatures in August. But meteorologist Rainer Snow said century-old data show it's happened at least five times.

4. The buried lead.

Buried leads have become more common in recent years as reporters try to make their stories more "interesting"—to rev up the story to capture reader attention. Or writers will make sweeping, general statements. A good copy editor will tell you it's often better to state the news specifically instead of trying to come at it from an angle. Related to the buried lead is the "flowery feature lead" on a news story. Cut the flowers and get to the point. Examples:

The Cass County Commission met Tuesday at its regular meeting. The agenda was approved. Several matters were discussed. Commissioner Polly Tique made a motion to raise property taxes 10 percent. The motion was approved unanimously.

No one would learn about the tax increase. It's buried so far into boring generalities that the only readers likely to reach that point would be the commissioners themselves, and the writer's spouse. Be direct:

Cass County residents will see a 10-percent boost in property taxes, the Cass County Commission decided Tuesday.

This reporter perhaps felt inspired by the good earth:

The American Midwest is a windswept rolling prairie extending for hundreds of miles. Students of East Shoe State University plan to travel those windy grasslands next month in an effort to restore historical farmlands threatened by time and neglect.

Most editors would lop off the flowery first sentence:

Students of East Shoe State University next month plan to travel to eastern Montana in an effort to restore historical farmlands threatened by time and neglect.

5. A lead with the word "program" in it.

When you see the word "program" in a lead you know the audience is likely in for a snooze and you, the copy editor, are in for, at best, a test of your editing mettle, and, at worst, a discussion with managers about whether the story merits getting ink or space on a website. Programs are static, dull and generally boring to read about but programs are, oh, so easy for reporters—possibly struggling to find a story in a news slump—to write about:

A program has been launched to provide more decorative trash bins on Front Street.

In public relations, writers sometimes erroneously write about a program when they should instead write about people with problems or needs. After all, most programs are developed to solve human problems and needs. Focus on people, not programs:

Front Street joggers will no longer have to zig-zag around dozens of empty fast-food containers, as the city plans to install a decorative trash bin at every corner.

7. Quotes are sacred, but use them sparingly.

Quotes are sacred in the world of writing for mass media. A writer should never ever change a quote. A quote is to be presented exactly as the speaker said it. A copy editor should never ever change a quote without speaking to the writer who put the

---

THINK LIKE AN EDITOR: USING OBSCENITIES

Are editors who change obscenities just being prudish and old-fashioned? A number of years ago as an intern the editor of this textbook wrote a story for a small-town newspaper about a 5-year-old who had open heart surgery. This was quite unusual back then, and worth a feature. He interviewed the father, a crusty but lovable sort, who cast a glance at his son romping around, and said, "He's supposed to be taking it easy, the little shit." Thinking this quote captured the spirit of the story, he repeated it in print. Small newspapers have limited resources, and sometimes articles get published without editing. Such was this intern's luck, or fate. What happened? Shocked calls from readers: "I can't believe you published THAT word in MY paper." (Small-town readers often feel a real sense of ownership over their town's newspaper.)

Afterward he wished he hadn't done it. Not because he thought it was particularly obscene or inappropriate, but because it ruined the impact of the story. A reader moves along without roadblock until he reaches that word, and then — thunk! Communication ends, because while the reader can continue, he can't get out of his mind, "they actually used THAT word in the newspaper." So avoiding this kind of material is more than just bowing to the priggish.

---

quote in a piece of writing. A copy editor may think he or she has found an error in the quote or want to shorten a long quote. However, the copy editor was not at the interview at which the dialog took place between the reporter and interviewee. The copy editor didn't *hear* the way the words were spoken or see the expression on the speaker's face. Thus, a copy editor must speak with the interviewer to ascertain the meaning and context of the speaker's words before making any changes, even if a well-meaning copy editor believes the editing will improve the overall piece of writing.

Further, writers and copy editors must never rob a sentence of context so as to alter the meaning of a quote or, conversely, edit context into a sentence so as to alter the meaning of a quote. Many a well-meaning copy editor has accidentally edited an error into a quote.

If you change words in a quote, you must take the quote marks off, turning it into a paraphrase. Warning: Never add quote marks to an existing paraphrase. Consider this sentence:

Free Internet-based content threatens legacy news operations, said Frank O'Pinion, editor of the West Shoe Gazette.

Can you add quotes around O'Pinion's comment? *"Free internet-based content threatens legacy news operations," said Frank O'Pinion.*

You'd better not! This is a *paraphrase,* and the source may not have used these actual words. In fact, what O'Pinion might have said was, *"This free Internet stuff is really hurting our newspaper business model."* The same idea, perhaps. But not the same words.

VOCABULARY AND JARGON FOR EDITORS

Blue pencil.

Pre-computer editors of the last century often used blue pencil to work through hard copy. Today to "blue pencil" someone's work means to change and delete, often unfavorably. Blue pencil or felt tip also was used to indicate instructions or make changes in "camera-ready" material, that is, copy ready for production. Large process camera film was not sensitive to blue.

Dow Jones News Fund.

Charles H. Dow founded the *Wall Street Journal* in 1889. The company grew to one of the strongest newspaper chains in the country, with world-wide holdings. The Dow Jones internship program has placed university students in prestigious summer journalism internships since 1960. In 2010 84 interns were lucky enough to be chosen for the program.

E-Zine, zine.

A magazine-style website, usually independently produced or self-published. Webzines may be online versions of print magazines or based totally in cyberspace.

Gatekeeper.

The person in a news operation who decides what will and will not get published or posted. Usually that's an editor. Communication scholars have done extensive research on the gatekeeping roles of the press.

Legacy news media.

Slightly pejorative term for news media that predate the Internet: newspapers, magazines, radio and television.

News magazine.

A legacy medium, printed magazine distributed weekly as a digest of world news for the busy reader. Henry Luce established the genre with *Time*, launched in 1923.

Graf.

Journalese for paragraph.

The use of quotes is changing in most forms of modern media writing. A decade or two ago, writers were instructed to quote as much as possible. In today's style of writing the rule of thumb is to quote only when a quote will transmit information more effectively than a professionally trained writer can transmit the information. For example, if someone who was interviewed for a story says something in a unique way, then quote it. Or if a speaker says something in a way that reveals motive, personality or emotion, then quote it. Often, however, a professional writer can more succinctly convey information to an audience than can a series of quotes or quote set-up paragraphs.

Follow these guidelines for editing quotes:

• Check to make sure the writer has been consistent with the style of attribution.

That is, the writer should use either "said" or "says" but not both interchangeably in the same piece of writing. Often the past tense is used in hard news stories, and the present tense in features, but the rule is to be consistent.

Other forms of attribution like "admit" or "claim" tend to cast doubt on the speaker's veracity, and so should be carefully edited.

Verbs of attribution such as "chuckled" or "chortled" tend to disrupt the story flow and thus distract the reader. It's best to avoid them.

• Check to make sure the writer fully identifies the speaker the first time the speaker is mentioned. A good identification includes a person's first and last name, middle initial if the person has a common first and last name, his or her city of residence, and age or occupation if age or occupation is pertinent to the rest of the story. Thereafter the speaker should be referred to by last name unless the person is less than 16 years old, in which case the person should be referred to by first name.

• On first reference: *"A storm tore up our house," said Dr. Jessica Johnson, a neurosurgeon at St. Mary's Hospital in St. Paul, Minn.*

On second reference: *"The storm came without warning," Johnson said.*

• In general, you should put the person's name before "said." The name is more important to readers than the verb of attribution.
"The tornado sounded like a roaring jet engine," Johnson said.

However, it is preferable to put the person's name after "said" when a long title precedes the person's name. For example:
"The tornado sounded like a roaring jet engine," said Johnson, a St. Paul, Minn., mother of triplets and chief of neurosurgery at St. Mary's Hospital, also in St. Paul.

• Put attribution (said or says) at the end of the first sentence if a quote is more than one sentence long.
"The children and I stayed in the basement until the storm passed," Johnson said. "When we came up from the basement we saw trees uprooted and roofs torn off houses."

• Only one person can speak in a quote. Avoid the temptation to have two or more people saying something together: *"I hung onto my mom during the storm," said the Johnson triplets.* In reality, one person says something and others repeat it or add to it.

• When writing a section in which multiple people are quoted, begin a new paragraph each time a new speaker starts speaking: *"I hung onto my mom during the storm,"* *said 8-year-old Jill Johnson.*

"And I hung onto the railing," added her mother.

• Punctuate quotes and attributions with punctuation inside the quote mark (United States usage). Use commas, not periods, unless the quote ends the sentence.

Incorrect: *"City crews will clear tree limbs from the streets." the mayor said.*

Correct: *"City crews will clear tree limbs from the streets," the mayor said.*

Also correct: *"City crews will clear tree limbs from the streets," the mayor said, "but crews won't move out until the flood danger has passed."*

Know more

For those who want to learn more about the coaching method for editors and writers:

Clark, R. P. and D. Fry. (2003). *Coaching Writers: Editors and Reporters Working Together Across Mediums.* Boston and New York: Bedford/St. Martin's.

For those who wonder where the soul of a media practitioner ends and the professional mind begins:

Willis, J. (2003). *The Human Journalist.* Westport, CT: Praeger Publishers.

Tune up your revision and self-editing skills by taking an interactive online course from The Poynter Institute's NewsUniversity at http://www.newsu.org/courses/course_detail.aspx?id=newsu_getmerewrite05. "Get Me Rewrite: The Craft of Revision" is fully interactive and free. The course is taught by Chip Scanlan, senior faculty member at The Poynter Institute for Media Studies in St. Petersburg, Fla. Expect the course to take about 30 minutes.

• EXERCISE 1 •

Editors: How smart do you need to be?

One way to find out is to take the Dow Jones editing text. Tests from past years can be downloaded with answer keys at http://www.editteach.org/specialprojects?id=8.

• EXERCISE 2 •

Avoiding clichés.

Rewrite clichés you encounter in the story below. Note if no quote marks surround a comment, it is a paraphrase, and can be rewritten.

A dozen East Gulch State University sororities and fraternities created a beehive of activity at the student union Tuesday, as members worked to recruit new students. Irving Nern, the university's Greek life coordinator, said membership was a no-brainer. "It's a way to get involved, but more," he said, noting membership in a campus Greek organization can impact positively a student's career.

Erma Smith, an attractive blonde co-ed who chairs the membership drive, emphasized the life-long friendships and camaraderie of sororities and fraternities. Many hands make light work, the Sorority Girl emphasized, as teams from the Greek houses often volunteer to improve life both on campus and off. Volunteer work may be the ace in the hole for students hoping to enhance employment prospects.

Applying is as easy as pie: men can visit the fraternity house of their choice, and girls the sorority, during an informal series of newcomer events. More information: www.westgulchgreeks.com.

• EXERCISE 3 •

What is a fact?

The sentences below contains facts, interpretations and judgments. Based on the textbook reading, identify the nature of each statement from published news sources.

1. This year's city-wide walking festival will raise fitness awareness and offer a fun weekend activity for community residents.

(Circle one.)
Fact.
Interpretation.
Judgment.
A combination of the above.
Why?

2. Last weekend's Comic-Con Convention featured the greatest series of DC Comics characters ever to attend a local convention.

Fact.
Interpretation.
Judgment.
A combination of the above.
Why?

3. On the announcement that DC Comics was reinventing its 80-year-old cast stable of characters, however, the old-time fans freaked out.
Fact.
Interpretation.
Judgment.

A combination of the above.
Why?

4. The wellness center offers group exercise from 2 to 6 p.m., featuring Cardio Mix, Cardio Kickboxing and High Intensity Interval Training.

Fact.
Interpretation.
Judgment.
A combination of the above.
Why?

5. Your professors are getting rich on your tuition: according to new research, 350,000 educators in the United States are millionaires.

Fact.
Interpretation.
Judgment.
A combination of the above.
Why?

• EXERCISE 4 •

Boring leads.

Rewrite the leads below based on principles as outlined in the text.

1. The East Gulch State University Student Senate met Wednesday. Several agenda items were discussed. A motion was made to approve the minutes of the last meeting, and unanimously approved. Student Senator Erma Smith made a motion to increase student fees by 10 percent to support staff travel. The motion was approved unanimously.

2. Do you know how much it will cost to replace the East Gulch City Park gazebo? That's the question considered Monday by the East Gulch City Commission. Based on contractor estimates, $250,000 will be required to replace the aging concrete structure.

3. "My goal is to spend my money now. I'm not planning to leave an inheritance to my daughters." That's how 60-year-old Clarice Smith explains her decision to spend every last dime on herself after retiring. Smith's approach reflects that of today's Baby Boomer generation, according to a survey of millionaires between the ages of 50 and 70: fewer than half believe it is important to leave an inheritance.

4. A program to improve first-year student success has been launched at East Gulch State University. Erv Nern, vice president for student affairs, emphasized that the voluntary series of workshops have the goal of increasing student retention as well as performance in general-studies classes.

5. Clara Smith has been named the new director of the East Gulch Neighborhood Revitalization Project, besting more than 50 candidates, and replacing Erv N. Nern, who resigned in July to take on a new job as principal of a private high school in Appleton, Wis.

• EXERCISE 5 •

Using quotes.

The story below includes mistakes made using quotes, as described in the text. Edit to improve.

North Gulch State University's women's volleyball team defeated Snowshoe State Saturday in front of a crowd of 4,000 spectators. "We were excited to see one of the largest crowds ever," said coach Amy Nern, who added the win puts the team at an early 6–3 record. Laurie Smith agreed, saying, "We played some great volleyball last night, and our fans made the difference."

The hardest part for the women was finding a way to stop SSU's well-balanced attack, says Nern. The team put up one heck of a fight during the final minutes, she said. "but our players came through with enough kills to reach a team record." The record had stood since 1998.

"I wasn't sure if we could pull it out, but we did," said Nern and Smith. Nern was pleased with her team's performance. "Laura had a record 10 kills. Marla Digg had a record 23 assists. That made the difference," said Nern.

KEYS

Exercise 2

Clichés in **boldface**.

A dozen East Gulch State University sororities and fraternities created a **beehive of activity** at the student union Tuesday, as members worked to recruit new students. Irving Nern, the university's Greek life coordinator, said membership was a **no-brainer**. "It's a way to get involved, but more," he said, noting membership in a campus Greek organization can **impact positively** a student's career.

Erma Smith, an attractive **blonde co-ed** who chairs the membership drive, emphasized the life-long friendships and camaraderie of sororities and fraternities. **Many hands make light work**, the **Sorority Girl** emphasized, as teams from the Greek houses often volunteer to improve life both on campus and off. Volunteer work may be the **ace in the hole** for students hoping to enhance employment prospects.

Applying is **as easy as pie**: men can visit the fraternity house of their choice, and girls the sorority, during an informal series of newcomer events. More information: www.westgulchgreeks.com.

Exercise 3

1. Fact and interpretation. That the walk is scheduled is a fact. That it will raise awareness and offer a fun activity is an interpretation.

2. Fact and judgment. That the event took place is a fact. That it featured the greatest characters is an opinion (good or bad), so a judgment.

3. Fact and interpretation. That the announcement was made is a fact. That some fans became agitated is an interpretation based on their behavior.

4. This is a fact, easily verifiable.

5. This is an interpretation based on a fact as reported in a research study. Journalists commonly make interpretations based on such data.

Exercise 4

Problems with leads above.

1. Buried lead.
2. Question lead.
3. Quote lead.
4. Program lead.
5. Long lead.

Exercise 5

1. Comma inside quote mark, third line.

2. Incomplete identification for Laurie Smith. Presume it's a player, but may be better to remove the quote.

3. Period inside quote mark at end of paragraph.

4. Second paragraph, second line includes an inconsistent attribution ("says" and "added.") Choose past tense, "said."

5. Do not add quote marks to the phrase "The team put up one heckuva fight during the final minutes." As the original does not include quote marks, it must be treated as a paraphrase, and should be changed to more formal wording.

6. Change "says" to "said" in the second line.

7. Delete period after "said" in the third, line, insert comma.

8. Fourth paragraph: One person speaks in a quote. In this case, you are not sure if it was Nern or Smith. You may delete the quote, or change to paraphrase with a less specific attribution such as "Coach and team late in the game worried they could not hold onto their lead, but rivals never caught up. "

9. Move attribution in the last quote to appear after the first sentence: "Laura had a record 10 kills," Nern said. "Marla Digg had a record 23 assists. That made the difference."

Four

Editors, Ethics and the Law

Paulette D. Kilmer

In ethical media operations, editors understand that their job involves maintaining consistency, credibility and integrity as well as assigning stories, marking up copy and serving as a gatekeeper. That moral obligation may mean catching a typo, but it also might mean something a lot bigger: catching theft and lies. When writers make these dishonest choices, they risk shattering public trust in the news operation or other publication and may destroy the company itself under the weight of a lawsuit. It is often up to one person to avoid such dire outcomes. That individual is an editor, who remains invisible like an automobile mechanic, until a crisis threatens to stall or stop the delicate engine of information exchange between readers or viewers and media outlets.

Communication majors learn in college that everybody expects writers to practice accuracy (stick to the facts); unfortunately, knowing this rule does not always result in compliance. Indeed, if people followed experts' advice, some hospitals and cemeteries would certainly accommodate fewer clients. For example, Notre Dame psychology professor Anita Kelly pointed out in August 2012 that, like eating vegetables and sleeping long enough, telling the truth actually improves people's health. While this finding no doubt will fascinate ethics and philosophy professors, it probably will not convince human beings to give up telling white lies to spare feelings or cut corners. Moreover, some journalists will continue to tell lies because learning the truth is time consuming. Under pressures to make a deadline, to avoid having to track down a phone number, or for personal gain, journalists will occasionally offer unverified assumptions (if not falsehoods) in place of facts. Therefore, editors understand that they must constantly check copy to protect the public, whom all journalists serve, from convenient, malicious or profitable lies.

Although deliberate lying permeates our culture, ABC journalist John Stossel pointed out that untrue reports often arise from illogical conclusions, like announcing that diet soda causes obesity just because overweight people drink that beverage. In 2006, he expanded his *20/20* segments on popular misperceptions into a book, *Myths, Lies and Downright Stupidity: Get Out the Shovel — Why Everything You Know Is Wrong*, noting that journalists often lack the background to effectively report on medical or scientific research. This example reflects how the complexity of modern life challenges writers who try to reveal the truth to serve the public as well as compels editors to crack down on misinformation presented for many reasons, including ignorance, carelessness or greed.

Therefore, editors must catch these five big lies:

1. Plagiarism.
2. Fabrication and falsification.
3. Invasion of privacy.
4. Misappropriation.
5. Libel.

What is plagiarism as opposed to ethical usage?

Plagiarism is claiming someone else's words, ideas, graphs, or other visual materials, including video and online creations, as one's own original work. It is derived from the Latin word for kidnapper, "plagiarius." *Black's Law Dictionary* notes that in civil law, "plagiarium" refers to "enticing away and stealing men (which here includes women) and slaves" as well as encouraging or helping slaves escape from their masters. The theft of words and ideas constitutes a form of kidnapping that robs victims of the fruits of their imagination. It is perhaps the most common threat an editor must face in a digital world.

The plagiarist's habit in America often begins in college. Getting away with it once makes it easier to try again. Soon plagiarism becomes a habit. Perhaps it's a matter of ignorance. Some people assume because they can easily download stuff that whatever appears on the Internet must belong to everyone. However, copyright laws protect all authors and artists regardless of where their work appears. The consequences for students of committing plagiarism usually involve receiving at least a zero on the assignment and more likely an "F" for the course, even expulsion. At the University of Toledo, Ohio, any "F" given for academic dishonesty remains on the transcript even if the student earns a higher grade. Anyone looking at the transcript knows how often an individual was caught cheating. Sadly, some people do not realize they are plagiarizing. But as editors, they need to know, to protect both their writers and their media organization's business reputation. Here are some ways to avoid deception.

Don't improperly attribute direct quotations or paraphrased passages

Perhaps writers get in trouble most often for not adequately attributing words, ideas, images, or other material from the Internet. Students sometimes cite a search engine (Google, Yahoo) but not the precise publication information: the author, article title, journal, publication date, page, and if found online the Web address and date of access. This habit transfers to working journalists who use the Internet for research, but prefer not to admit that, and so claim borrowed material as their own.

Even high-profile writers make this mistake, and editors sometimes fail to catch it. In August 2012, CNN commentator Fareed Zakaria, who regularly published articles in the *Washington Post* and major magazines, apologized for failing to attribute passages in a *Time* article on gun control. The work had originated in historian Jill Lepore's feature that the *New Yorker* had published in April. The consequences: CNN and *Time* suspended Zakaria.

Don't purloin passages by changing just a word here and there

The point of doing journalism is to recast ideas into the writer's own words to offer fresh facts and interpretation. When writers change passages slightly but still regurgitate another writer's text, they steal that author's views and words. Instead they can paraphrase key sentences to capture the spirit as well as the original writer's meaning. Paraphrasing requires rewriting a passage using different words. Writers analyze each source and then synthesize or pull together the key ideas. Ideally, this process involves making an independent inference, a judgment call based on facts, and recognizing the original authors to highlight a fresh interpretation.

Don't forget to attribute paraphrased sentences

Sometimes beginning writers get so caught up in the process of relating one idea to another that they forget to attribute passages they have paraphrased. Paraphrases need attribution.

Don't borrow your buddies' work

While it's true we often learn a lot from the people we meet along the way, if we rehash their old work into versions we attach our bylines to, we have committed plagiarism. This deceit begins often when a journalist is still a student. However, it's becoming more dangerous. Electronic submissions and bottomless online storage have empowered professors to keep copies of past assignments. For example, on Feb. 2, 2006, Greg Grisolano explored "'Cut and Paste' Plagiarism: Copying Assignments from the Internet, a Growing Trend," on Pittsburg, Kansas, State University's *CollegiOnline* news site. He interviewed John Rodrique, a graduate-student teacher of English composition, about his *déjà vu* while grading an essay. He told Grisolano, "It just so happened that I ran across phrases that I just knew I had read somewhere before. I went through my files and found this certain one, and sure enough it was a dead-on match." The cheater, who consequently received a zero, had submitted an essay that a former student had written. Sophisticated software makes it possible to identify work procured from other writers or the Web. Editors do know about these tools, but according to Craig Silverman, writing in the *Columbia Journalism Review* in March 2010, most journalists don't use them because the services are expensive, time-consuming and not always accurate.

Don't kidnap published works

Occasionally, procrastinating writers wait too long to do an assignment or maybe succumb to the temptation to get the story fast and first without taking time to actually do the legwork. Then again, some liars live by deception and plan from the beginning to doctor someone else's published article and turn it in as a work of their own genius. In a bizarre twist on this form of plagiarism, brazen souls tweak published, sometimes famous, memoirs or other first-person accounts to claim as their own personal experiences. One of the silliest examples of this breach occurred on the chapter author's campus a few years ago when a student from a suburb of Cleveland recycled a section of Ernest Hemingway's short story, "The Snows of Mount Kilimanjaro," into an essay on "my most memorable experience."

Don't juggle pixels or steal visual material

Computer programs make it possible to rearrange photos or reconstruct the image. Especially in the mass media world, shuffling the pixels in somebody else's picture to claim the outcome as personal creativity is unethical. All visual material must be properly cited to give creators credit for their endeavors.

How do editors recognize and respond to plagiarism?

The most common way you as an editor can catch writers who commit word larceny is simply by scrutinizing their style and nuances. The best way for novice editors to learn how to do that is to listen to the pros. In the last chapter you were encouraged to find mentors to guide your copy editing knowledge. In this chapter, we present some of those guides; we consult with editors and writers who have investigated plagiarism and fabrication, two of the most dangerously common practices in journalism. "Every copy editor now knows of the 'danger signs' of plagiarized copy—abrupt shifts in vocabulary or syntax, aspects to a story that don't seem like the writer's usual work, single-sourced stories," Jill Rosen, the assistant editor of the *American Journalism Review,* said in the June/July 2004 issue. In "We Mean Business," she asked editors of many newspapers what lessons they had learned from recent instances of star reporters lying at the *New York Times* and *USA Today.*

Editors fact-check published stories

At the Fort Worth, Texas, *Star-Telegram,* editors conducted a reverse lottery every week. Ombudsman David House numbered each article and then transferred that digit to the back of a ticket. The editor drew one ticket from a shoebox. House and the editors verified every fact in that story. The stakes, loss of respect among readers, are too high to ignore. Therefore, across the country, journalists are tackling the problem of dishonesty head on. "Editors [have started] tightening ethics policies, having heart-to-hearts with their staffs, monitoring corrections, tracking expense reports and learning about software that detects plagiarism," Rosen explained.

Sometimes new writers inadvertently commit plagiarism through inexperience. Bob Rosenbaum, a media consultant who has worked for many years as a publisher, editor, reporter, and everything in between, graduated from the Medill School of Journalism at Northwestern. He has personally confronted both writers who unintentionally erred and those who blatantly cheated. Copy and assignment editors rely upon two skills outsiders often overlook: listening and asking questions. Martin Baron, an editor at the *Boston Globe*, told Rosen that editors question reporters and are leery of anonymous quotations that just sound too good to be true. Moreover, complaints from readers and tips from staff members often expose wrongdoing. Loud whistle-blowing from staff members as well as the community maintains ethics in the newsroom. The *Boston Globe* "welcomes" readers to comment via fax, e-mail, or phone and runs corrections prominently.

Ironically, sometimes editors unmask unscrupulous conduct through compliments. For example, John E. McIntyre, assistant managing editor of the *Baltimore Sun* copy desk, recalled an incident involving an obituary featuring a phony mourner. The editor uncovered the ruse when a family member asked for help in contacting the wonderful stranger who had expressed beautiful memories of her loved one. Another reporter was caught copying quotations from a competitor and then claiming to have called the official, who said no one had spoken to him. The layers of lying between plagiarism and fabrication often blend so that a nabbed quotation is attached to a false attribution.

When readers complain about stories lifted from a competitor, the newspaper loses face. It does not matter whether the plagiarism occurs in print or online. In either case, the dishonesty erodes the readers' trust.

Editors read widely and therein detect stolen items when they see an article the second time. As a board member for FutureHeights, the publisher of the *Heights Observer*, a neighborhood newspaper for Cleveland and University Heights, Ohio, Rosenbaum usually works with untrained reporters. Nearly everybody contributes without compensation to the Cleveland news enterprise, hoping the paper and website by and for the citizens will inspire them to be engaged in the community and, thus, help shape the destiny of their neighborhood. But the Web has not only made it easier to plagiarize, it has made it easier to detect plagiarism. The Web presence at www.heightsobserver.org increases the likelihood of someone exposing purloined passages. Although factual errors are embarrassing and can be deadly to credibility, as long as people perceive these missteps as honest errors, the public may forgive the lapses. However, actually hijacking another reporter's article requires choosing to lie, and that assault on truth offends people's sense of decency and fairness. The damage is far harder to repair than slips in spelling or other reporting problems.

Most folks know that neophyte reporters unwittingly blunder. On good days, the editors remove the bloopers before publication. For instance, while finishing her account of a meeting, a *Heights Observer* news correspondent committed plagiarism inadvertently. Because she had not covered a meeting before, she missed details. Unfortunately, the rookie did not understand that she could not fill in her account with liberal amounts of information from the Cleveland, Ohio, *Plain Dealer*.

"The volunteer editor, who reads the *Plain Dealer*, recognized a passage that had appeared in its coverage of a meeting," Rosenbaum said. "He caught the error before the story went to press. That was a miracle."

The reporter apologized and acquired her own facts via phone interviews before rewriting the article.

The rise of aggregation

News folk have borrowed from fellow journalists as long as journalism has existed. This borrowing is OK only when it is sanctioned by a contract. For example, Associated Press members freely share each other's work. Although some publishers tolerate local broadcasters giving a recitation from that morning's newspaper instead of a real newscast, *Toledo Blade* editors won a lawsuit against local radio stations that had used its news items without attribution.

Moreover, a policy of basing entire articles solely on unattributed material drawn from rivals can easily slide into plagiarism. The advent of "aggregators" who make mash-ups from others' work has sullied the reputations of some of the nation's most respected news sources.

Aggregators at the oldest continuing newspaper in the nation, the Hartford, Conn., *Courant*, composed articles based solely on other journalists' reporting. As part of their job description, aggregators cherry picked the competition's scoops for material. An economic crisis had triggered a major layoff that left the paper short-handed. In the summer of 2009, the once highly regarded newspaper lost prestige when its competitor proved reporters had committed plagiarism.

In "Plagiarism Follies at the Courant: TribCo Unit Fumbles a Scandal," a *Columbia Journalism Review* feature published Sept. 8, 2009, author Dean Starkman concluded that the *Courant* continued to "chew off its own legs" with its tepid response to the allegations. The newspaper admitted taking items from competitors, including its "arch rival, the *Journal Inquirer* of Manchester, N.H., and from other Connecticut newspapers without their permission," Starkman said. When management replaced all the dismissed reporters with one person assigned to covering numerous beats simultaneously, they chose expedience over public service.

By November 2009, the *Journal Inquirer* had filed a lawsuit for copyright infringement against the *Courant*, arguing that recycling facts even with attribution gave the *Courant* an unfair economic advantage and irreparably harmed advertisers, competitors, and the public. "But the *JI*'s main point, as expressed in lawsuits and columns, is that

WHAT IS PLAGIARISM? A PRACTICAL GUIDE

Some writers know very well they are plagiarizing. And they think they'll get by with it. They sometimes become the Jayson Blairs and Jack Kelleys of journalism. As time goes on, and editors too enthusiastic about a good story to check for sources let it go, the plagiarists take the next step. Why borrow from someone else when you can just borrow from your imagination?

But let's not make hasty judgments, not yet. We realize some people are honestly a bit confused about how to use material others have written. Is it wrong to copy names and dates from other writers? Is it all right to copy and paste paragraphs from other writers? The rule should be clear cut. Usually it is: if you copy and paste another person's work without giving that person credit, you are plagiarizing, that is, stealing another person's work. Okay, but here are some nuances. If you copy and give credit, but don't put quote marks around the copied text, is it plagiarism? For instance, from an online history lecture you read:

"Hitler's interest in media control and propaganda was so strong that he created a ministry for it, headed by Dr. Josef Goebbels (1933–45). Goebbels set up a control so sweeping that nothing in Germany escaped; effectively content of all the media was dictated by the government. The ministry relied on Hitler's belief that propaganda must appeal to 'the masses,' and not 'the intellectuals,' and that it must be based on emotional themes, simple slogans and themes, repetition, common enemy, a hero figure, cult of violence, and lies or half-truths. Propaganda was extremely successful in Germany. Censorship was complete."

You copy this paragraph in your own work, adding (Collins, Reading Six) after. Is that wrong? What if you copy and paste a number of paragraphs? Well, here we're in a gray area, but the general standard is this: do your own writing. That means do not copy a large quantity of text, even if you cite a reference, unless it's absolutely necessary. And if it's absolutely necessary, indent the paragraph as a separate text block:

> Hitler's interest in media control and propaganda was so strong that he created a ministry for it, headed by Dr. Josef Goebbels (1933–45). Goebbels set up a control so sweeping that nothing in Germany escaped; effectively content of all the media was dictated by the government. The ministry relied on Hitler's belief that propaganda must appeal to "the masses," and not "the intellectuals," and that it must be based on emotional themes, simple slogans and themes, repetition, common enemy, a hero figure, cult of violence, and lies or half-truths. Propaganda was extremely successful in Germany. Censorship was complete. (Collins, Reading Six.)

This makes it perfectly clear that the text is a direct quote, and not your own words. But it's much better to copy smaller pieces and put them in quote marks. This means that basically you develop the text yourself, based on knowledge you've gained from probably several sources.

Let's take an example. On a class website a professor writes about newspaper development in the paragraph below.

> Technology has often driven changes in mass media, and the new technology of the 1880s was the telephone and typewriter. The telephone allowed true reporting as we know it today, as reporters could now put together a story in hours instead of days or

weeks. The typewriter, along with a machine called the Mergenthaler (inventor's name) Linotype, which set lead type automatically, also made it easier for newspapers to reach more people faster. The great economic growth of the United States during this time coincided with great interest in culture and the importance of education. By 1900 there were 6,000 high schools in the country, compared with 100 in 1860. While it's true that at the turn of the century the average American still only had a fifth-grade education, this was enough to read. Literacy reached 90 percent.

Let's say you want to use some of this information for your own writing. How might you do it? Well, based on all the information you gathered and read for your report, you might begin in this way:

> Two of the most important inventions that made modern mass media possible were the telephone and typewriter, common by the 1880s. Both made possible the kind of fast production of news we expect today. "Reporters could now put together a story in hours instead of days or weeks." (Collins, Reading 11.) Now that people could get their news faster, they also demanded faster production of news. And beyond that, more people could read, and the more they could read, the more they wanted to read. High school education became more and more common, as high schools were built — 6,000 by 1900, compared with 100 only 40 years earlier. (Collins, Reading 11.) Even without a high school education, most people could read by 1900.

As you can see, the information in the second paragraph is basically the same, but you put it together in a new way, with insights from your other research. Actual figures (or historical names) are credited with a reference, but are not necessarily copied word for word. Direct quotes also are referenced, but are short, and in quote marks.

It's sometimes hard to write longer stories or essays using your own words if you base your information on one or two meager sources. That's because you really don't know enough about the topic. You haven't learned enough from several sources. After you've interviewed or consulted several sources, though, you've gathered information from a variety of approaches. The key is this: if you rewrite using your own words, it's your own work, and not plagiarism, even if you don't write as well as the original author. And you never will, if you just copy and paste.

Changing a few words.

If you are supposed to write using your own words, what about changing a few words, such as those below in bold face?

> Hitler's interest in media control and propaganda was so strong that he **set up** a ministry for it, headed by Dr. Josef Goebbels (1933–45). Goebbels set up a control so **vast** that nothing in Germany escaped; effectively content of all the media was dictated by the **authorities**. The ministry relied on Hitler's belief that propaganda must appeal to "the masses," and not "the intellectuals," and that it must be based on emotional themes, simple slogans and themes, **repeating the slogans**, common enemy, a hero figure, cult of violence, and lies or half-truths.

The answer is that changing a few words is not enough. It's still considered plagiarism.

Borrowing ideas.

Generally, you can't plagiarize general concepts and ideas, although if you present an idea as if it's original to you, someone who reads your work is going to say, "what a jerk, he stole that idea from someone else." How to tell? It depends on the idea. For instance, if you write, "World War I can be blamed on many global currents at the beginning of the twentieth century, but Germany probably is most directly responsible." Did you borrow someone else's idea? Well, yeah, but not really one person — this is a generally accepted version of many historians. But if you write, "World War I can be blamed on war-mongering politics and treachery based on expansionist ambitions of Luxemburg," well, that's a unique interpretation. If it's not your own development, it needs to be credited to its author.

it's not fair for one paper to have to pay to send reporters to gather news for meat-and-potatoes stories only to have the salient facts lifted by another, even *with* attribution," Starkman concluded. "As a result the *Courant* suffered criticism and condemnation in journalism circles throughout the country," the *JI* reported on November 19, 2011. In that same article, the *JI* announced a settlement had been reached in the federal lawsuit. Shortly after the *JI* had sued the *Courant*, its editors apologized and stopped aggregating copy.

Repeating the facts gathered by someone else saves time but erodes democracy by eliminating the opportunity for a second look at the situation that frequently results in slightly and sometimes greatly different accounts. The nuances empower the public to consider multiple factors rather than just one view. If the concept of the aggregation editor spreads during financially bleak years, when the good times return, news will no longer constitute a public forum of a diverse multitude of voices.

"It's pure economics," said Cleveland-area media consultant Rosenbaum. "When a lot less manpower gathers the information, the risk of plagiarism increases dramatically."

Social media networks focus a spotlight of disapproval on frauds

About 90 percent of the time, especially with minor incidents, no one detects plagiarism, Rosenbaum estimated. But that is probably changing; the Internet and social networking channels increase chances someone will notice lifted passages. He pointed out that if the *Heights Observer* editor had missed the rookie's misstep, the *Plain Dealer* certainly would have objected to the stolen paragraphs but dropped the complaint upon receiving an apology.

Yet Rosenbaum was more generous than some college professors who give automatic Fs to plagiarists. "Everybody makes mistakes," Rosenbaum said. "The first one is free usually if the offender sincerely apologizes. Then everybody can move on. The second scenario involves the people who matter the most: the readers. While competitors' demands of accountability remain invisible, when a reader catches the error, everybody knows about it."

Of course, via Twitter, Facebook, and multiple quick messaging networks, word spreads fast. Mike Sallah, the coach and member of an investigative reporting team at the Miami, Fla., *Herald*, also noted in an e-mail interview that although in the past offenses frequently stayed off the public radar, today's instant messaging makes detection likely.

"In the age of the Internet, a reporter who's busted for such practices is usually exposed online, especially in the blogs," Sallah said. "Then it becomes extremely embarrassing for the publishing entity. The reporter should be summarily fired for such offenses."

The convergence of print, broadcast and the Internet has simplified the process of inserting stolen words into articles, but the convenience of "cutting and pasting" has not justified the theft. Editors know that overworked and underpaid reporters may cut corners. Many have begun restricting anonymous sources as well as calling individuals mentioned in accounts after publication to verify information. A quick check of city directories and online "people finders" also enables editors to discover "phantoms" who exist only in the reporter's mind. Combining made-up identities with passages grafted from already printed articles is a chilling practice that has compelled more editors to be skeptical and to ask questions.

Print and Web journalists share the same ethical concerns. Many Internet sites consider fighting plagiarism a professional duty. The *Online Journalism Review* hosts *Plagiarism Today*, which Jonathan Bailey founded to combat cyber thieves. The Annenberg School of Communication at the University of Southern California maintains the *OJR* site as part of the Knight Digital Media Center, a venture that also includes the University of California Berkeley Graduate School of Journalism. Besides covering the future of journalism in the digital age, the *Review* also provides a forum for denouncing copyright infringement, aggregation and deception.

A sin similar to stealing another writer's facts without attribution has arisen with the cut and paste ubiquity of the Web. The Baltimore *Sun* has spiked stories that in Frankenstein fashion were cobbled together with parts harvested from several published articles. For example, in "We Mean Business," Rosen quoted McIntyre of the Baltimore *Sun*, who remembered skullduggery from the fall of 2003. A routine Google spelling check of a place name unearthed two stories that contained passages repeated in a *Sun* article without attribution.

Letting the staff know the editors' expectations is crucial to cracking down on plagiarism and its cousins, fabricating, lying, and deceiving through omission. The assistant managing editor of the copy desk at the Boston *Globe*, Baron, pointed out to his staff that he relies on them to alert him to suspicious behavior. Both Baron and Deputy Managing Editor of the Charlotte, N.C., *Observer* Cheryl Carpenter emphasized to Rosen the need for dialogue. "The pain at the *New York Times* and *USA Today* have given us all reasons to talk about [this problem] more and think about it more," Carpenter said. "It's a constant conversation that has gotten louder." Pamela Luecke, editor of the Lexington, KY., *Herald-Leader*, pointed out that ethics must permeate the culture within the newsroom. "What is our expectation? What is our standard? These are not simple conversations. But it creates a sense of shared values in a newsroom. And it sends a message that newsroom leaders are committed to a high standard."

What happens if editors look the other way?

To borrow from the adage of Edmund Burke, all it takes for evil to triumph is for good editors to do nothing. Indeed, a review of the hit parade of worst stinkers in the ranks of journalists who have committed plagiarism shows that the perpetrators got away with their crimes against integrity partly because no editor paid attention to early signs of skullduggery. However, Rosen noted editors of United States publications are training their staffs to promptly detect and report dishonesty. Portland, Ore., *Oregonian* Executive Editor Peter Bhatia, former president of the American Society of Newspaper Editors, said he had not faced any recent problems involving plagiarism or fabrication, but he underscored the need for industry-wide concern. "This [the Jayson Blair and other cases of unethical conduct] is a real crisis," Bhatia said. "We're kidding ourselves if don't think it's had an impact on our credibility."

Bhatia was referring to one of the most famous recent cases of plagiarism and its logical companion, fabrication. Fabrication might start with plagiarism, borrowing without credit. But why borrow from others if you can just make things up? Writers tempted to make a quote just a little stronger, by adding just one or two words, soon slide away on a slippery slope, first making up whole quotes, then entire interviews and finally complete stories. In the 2003 movie, *Shattered Glass*, a drama featuring the disastrous career of *New Republic* writer Stephen Glass, a rival checking one of his stories declared that only one fact definitely could be verified: a state Glass referred to did indeed exist.

Two notorious recent cases of fabrication embroiled two of the largest news operations in the country, *USA Today* and the *New York Times.* Jack Kelley and Jayson Blair fooled nearly everyone for a while. Charm, good looks and popularity masked furtive, dirty tricks. Commenting in "Plagiarism Antecedents and Situational Influences," Norman P. Lewis noted in the summer 2008 *Journalism and Mass Communication Quarterly* that too much emphasis on originality has encouraged reporters to avoid attribution rather than appreciate it as an integral component of stories. Neither Kelley nor Blair acknowledged the origin of pilfered material and probably embroidered stolen words with fabrication.

When *USA Today* editors hired Kelley, a graduate of the University of Maryland journalism school, his work ethic impressed them. Within four years he had risen to becoming a national star whose scoops revealed his ability to get people to tell their most damning secrets. Over the next 21 years, Kelley became a living legend known to "dodge bullets and sidestep landmines," Rosen observed in "Who Knows Jack?" an *American Journalism Review* feature in April/May 2004. Kelley outran Chetchen Mafia thugs in Russia, witnessed suicide bombings in Jerusalem, and trekked through snow-packed mountain passes with rebels in Afghanistan. He sent back gripping accounts of danger and mayhem, always witnessing thrilling scenes and routinely barely escaping death.

"For a decade, he had a hand in nearly every major international news event, hitting A1 [the front page] constantly with his trademark vivid accounts of violence and strife," Rosen said.

While most of his colleagues and editors believed him and respected his ability to unearth seemingly impossible interviews and gain access to folks and places denied to everybody else, skeptics had raised doubts— at least among themselves, for many years. Kelley's editor maintained the intrepid foreign correspondent worked like a dog and always got the story. Nevertheless, he fell from grace swiftly when a single lie triggered an investigation. Kelley had convinced a translator to pretend to be a witness to a contested interview.

When *USA Today* editors showed Kelley proof of his treachery, Rosen said he claimed "the lie was a one-time deal, a mistake made under pressure, that has nothing to do with his stories, all of which he [stood] firmly behind." The inquiry proved otherwise. He was found guilty of making up things and stealing words from others 24 times. Rosen reported that *USA Today* called Kelley's journalistic sins sweeping and substantial. Kelley, who was then 43, resigned.

Another whiz kid graduated from the University of Maryland and also parlayed charisma into trust and flair in talking his way out of corners. Jayson Blair, like Jack Kelley, impressed folks with his can-do attitude and hustle. "You felt like you knew him," UM professor Carl Sessions Stepp explained to Rosen. ("All About the Retrospective," *American Journalism Review*, June 2003.) "Some people have the magic touch when it comes to ingratiating themselves, making friends, making sources— Jayson was one of those guys," Sessions added. "He always wanted to play — he came to play every day."

Blair, like Kelley, aspired to greatness. Blair spun through the UM *Diamondback* student newspaper office like a whirlwind, leaving an avalanche of stories in his wake. But errors and sloppy reporting prompted editors to warn him that he needed to reform. Against their wishes, the editorial board appointed Blair to serve as editor despite his shaky record. As editor, Blair's lying, fabricating, and just goofy behavior increased. Still, Blair served internships at the Boston *Globe* and the *New York Times*.

But in the end, like Kelley, Blair's deceptions destroyed his career. The energetic national reporter had copied a story from a San Antonio, Texas, newspaper that the *Times* subsequently ran on its front page. Investigators eventually found 36 errors in 73 national stories and fabrications in more than 600 other articles, Rosen said. On May 11, 2003, the *Times* devoted the front and four inside pages to Blair's crimes against accuracy and honesty. He resigned, explaining that personal problems had caused his unethical behavior.

Cheating often costs reporters their honor and career. The longer they lie without detection, the greater their fall when, inevitably, they are exposed. Thefts have occurred even in the mass media world of comic books. Nick Simmons, son of Gene Simmons of "Kiss" rock group fame, salvaged his career as an artist but lost respect in the anime world of graphic illustrations when in 2009 he copied the designs and dialogue of *Bleach,* a series in the genre popular during the early 2000s. According to Michele Reed, reporter with the University of Houston *Cougar*, on May 3, 2010, Simmons apologized and warned on his own website that anybody who stole his images would pay in cash.

Plagiarism in public relations and advertising

Since both public relations and advertising deal with marketing, they often are considered together. Unlike journalists, PR writers do not usually expect a byline for their work. In advertising, slogans are not protected under copyright laws. Maintaining an image through improving the company or client's reputation depends upon media exposure, and so PR agencies are delighted when print or Web publications replicate press releases. They do not care if a news staff member's name appears at the top. However, the public expects honesty from all news venues. "Looting press releases" deceives the public, according to Roy Clark, a senior Poynter Institute scholar, who advised editors to insist the story contain additional reporting, verification, and rewording.

Public relations consultants who work for politicians and celebrities may not need to claim objectivity, but they still need to avoid plagiarism and fabrication. Most public relations professionals do not employ professional editors and so must act as their own editors. Many politicians and celebrities hire ghostwriters to help them tell their story. Routinely, PR agents ghostwrite speeches, articles, and books; but although they may eschew recognition, they are expected to reflect the ideas of their clients and to acknowledge material they do not generate. "Practitioners must not misrepresent themselves by using the intellectual properties of others," Kathy Fitzpatrick and Carolyn Bronstein warned in the 2006 edition of *Ethics in Public Relations: Responsible Advocacy.* Advertisers, like public relations agents, get in trouble if they are caught claiming someone else's work as their own. The vocabulary changes a bit, but the principle remains the same. Advertising textbooks, such as the 2007 edition of Gerald J. Tellis and Tim Ambler's *The SAGE Handbook of Advertising,* frequently do not consider "plagiarism" per se. Nevertheless, they warn against misappropriation (using someone's name or likeliness without permission) and trademark infringement as well as emphasize uniqueness and creativity as crucial to selling goods. To advance in marketing, practitioners must heed the call for originality and produce new twists albeit very often on old ideas.

Falsification, misappropriation and privacy

Falsification refers to deliberate acts of deceiving others to gain prestige or make a profit. Think of a sandwich. The simplest form is two pieces of bread smacked together — not very tasty! However, adding toppings increases the heft and the appeal of the subway. Likewise, the most basic form of falsification, "lying," may amount to a white lie that is told to spare someone's feelings or embroider a tall tale. In falsification,

VOCABULARY AND JARGON FOR EDITORS

Daily

The task of printing and distributing many thousands of newspaper copies every day, or even every several hours, requires careful organization and enormous expense. Advertising traditionally has paid for most of this cost in the United States. But the Web as an alternative removes the financial weight of multi-million dollar presses, fleets of trucks and small armies of delivery personnel. Some publishers suspect that as soon as many newspapers amortize their current presses, they will abandon the paper product.

Edward R. Murrow

One of the pantheon of great American journalists, Murrow gained fame for his radio coverage of World War II London bombings. He successfully jumped to television in the early 1950s with "See It Now," a program that brought respectability to television news.

Freedom of Information Act

Journalists have fought for greater openness in government through most of the twentieth century. Open records campaigns beginning in the 1940s succeeded at the state level in all but a few states. In 1966 President Lyndon Johnson signed the federal Freedom of Information Act to give citizens the right to request access to most government records. In 1977 the Sunshine Law required many federal agencies to hold their meetings in public.

Pulitzer Prize

Joseph Pulitzer, a Hungarian immigrant, became one of the most famous publishers in American history. In 1904 he made an endowment to fund an award for high achievement in journalism, the Pulitzer Prize. Prizes have been awarded since 1917; beginning in 1999 nominations for online journalism were accepted.

Society of Professional Journalists

The largest broad-based society of working journalists and journalism students began in 1909 as Sigma Delta Chi, at DePauw University, Greencastle, Ind. It offers awards for high-quality journalism, works to defend journalists' freedom and publishes *Quill* magazine.

---

the more layers of deception, the more potential for harm. While finger foods normally benefit from embellishment, many other arenas of life do not. The degree and act of stealing someone else's creativity legally may be deemed plagiarism, false light, misappropriation or trademark violation.

Like plagiarism, "false light" bends the truth for self-gain. False light law cases focus on privacy, the right to control the spread information about oneself. The courts have defined these variants of false light: intruding into someone's solitude or private circle, publicly announcing embarrassing facts of no legitimate concern to the community, releasing information that gives others an untrue impression, and using commercially an individual's photo or name without permission.

For public relations and advertising people, misappropriation typically focuses on the false light tort of borrowing someone else's name or physical likeness for spurious financial reasons. For example, putting Lady Gaga's picture on pickle bottles without her permission would entitle the popular singer to sue all involved in the heist of her identity. Trademark violations also involve misuse of legally protected material: a symbol, word or design. Companies, organizations and individuals register original emblems to protect their business' unique names. For instance, nearly everyone recognizes McDonald's golden arches, NBC's rainbow peacock and Nike's swash. Cartoon characters too are registered. Editors must obtain permission to use them. Public relations and advertising practitioners in particular may face hefty lawsuits if they nab images protected by trademark agreements.

Falsification erodes the credibility of PR and advertising

Naturally, advertisers craft puns, cultural adages and jokes into new messages designed to sell products. Steffan Postaer, a veteran ad copywriter with a shelf full of awards, lectures around the world, serves as a consultant and writes a blog, "Gods of Advertising." In his Jan. 5, 2010, post, "No Longer Smiling: It Appears My Favorite Commercial of the Year Was Plagiarized," he pointed out that sometimes the line between cliché and plagiarism is not distinct. Ads draw upon consumer recognition to tie products to embedded community values and human aspirations. Nevertheless, even the most respected companies occasionally cross the line between originality and deception, thus damaging their credibility and ultimately sales.

Focusing on marketing drives advertisers and public relations representatives to operate under a different relationship to truth than print or online journalists who serve the public. PR agents write speeches, direct quotations, letters, and even chapters or books for others as normal practice as long as the ghostwriters get permission for every statement from the people they name as the authors, Patricia J. Parsons explained in the 2005 edition of *Ethics in Public Relations: A Guide to Best Practice*. They serve clients. In advertising, pitches inherently build from vestiges of popular culture. Dancing trees, philosophical shredded wheat and wiseacre magpies snap to life in commercials that blend fantasy with product information. In fact, exaggeration amuses consumers, unless the ad contains harmful claims or misleads folks.

In addition to weight-loss products, tobacco goods have generated frequent litigation based on allegations that the ads have presented products in a false light. For instance, in March 2010, the Vermont attorney general's office won a case against R.J. Reynolds, a tobacco company. WCAX.com. in "Vt. wins cig lawsuit" noted, "The judge sided with the state, saying the company's advertising of their Eclipse brand of reduced-risk cigarettes was deceptive and misleading." Lies in ads or PR copy, as well as in the news, whittle away public trust and foster a climate of fear and cynicism that erodes the hope and optimism essential for building strong, altruistic, moral communities.

Libel and invasion of privacy also shatter trust

The Associated Press *Stylebook*'s "Briefing on Media Law" analyzes statutes that editors, PR practitioners and advertising agents need to know. Of course, libel tops the list. Libel, which is normally written defamation of character, involves damaging someone's reputation or exposing that person to hatred, contempt or ridicule.

Slander, the spoken form of defamation, is usually reserved for private contexts. Public communicators, like broadcasters, reach a wide audience and are charged with libel instead of slander.

Consider the popular animated TV show on the Comedy Central network, *South Park. South Park* always begins with this disclaimer: "All characters and events in this show — even those based on real people — are entirely fictional. All celebrity voices are impersonated ... poorly. The following program contains coarse language, and due to its content, should not be viewed by anyone." In a November 2005 episode, Tom Cruise and John Travolta refused to come out of Stan's closet. On Nov. 16, the *Chicago Tribune* pointed out sending both action-movie heroes into Stan's closet implied they had hidden their homosexuality from the public. When tabloid websites spread similar allegations, Cruise protested that questioning his manhood threatened his income and harmed his reputation among his fans.

Since Cruise welcomes the spotlight of fame, he is considered a public figure. To win a libel case, he must prove actual malice, which means that journalists either knowingly or recklessly published false information. Since *South Park* parodies contemporary society, the First Amendment protects the writers. Truth, which is the major defense against libel suits, does not pertain here because people recognize satire as not literally true, and therein it is not actionable legally. Editors know the legal bar is high for public figures and so are more likely to permit strong and unfair criticism. But editors also are guided by a sense of ethics. Can a writer call the president of the United States "an idiot" in print? Legally, yes. Ethically? It depends on the writer, the context, the media and, finally, the editor.

Consider an example that spotlights the gray area where people enjoy some celebrity simply because of their work but really are not public figures in the same sense as politicians or movie stars. Chris Healy on the website *Reporters Committee for Freedom of the Press* related a case in which privacy and political humor clashed. After the Colorado legislature slashed the operating budget of the University of Northern Colorado's student newspaper, senior English major Thomas Mink and some friends created *The Howling Pig*, a satirical online publication. Students doctored photos of professor Junius Peake to resemble Gene Simmons, the lead singer of Kiss, and declared "Junius Puke" their editor-in-chief.

Assistant District Attorney Susan Knox filed felony charges against Mink in behalf of the state but lost. However, the American Civil Liberties Union and Mink countersued and after an eight-year battle settled in December 2011 for $425,000. Healy concluded with this quotation from an ACLU press release: "This case reaffirms that satire, parody, and expressions of opinion are fully protected by the First Amendment." Peake's involvement on campus and in the community had given him name recognition.

On the other hand, private figures (an ordinary person, like a neighbor or colleague, who does not seek publicity) only must prove negligence, undue carelessness and falsity of the depiction. Unknown individuals may qualify as limited public figures due to circumstances, but all details must pertain to the news event. High-profile crime, war, natural and man-made disasters as well as a willing or persistent effort to occupy the spotlight of public attention may qualify. State definitions of public figures vary, but courts consider basic factors including fame, political power and level of public interest. Most elected officials are automatically public figures as long as the coverage involves their work. Status as "household names," like Bill Gates, Oprah or Lady Gaga also makes someone a public figure.

Truth, the unassailable defense in libel, does not apply to privacy cases

Privacy is the right to be left alone and to control the distribution of information about oneself. Privacy lawsuits arise when someone intrudes into personal affairs or space, reveals embarrassing personal facts without permission and lies or makes exaggerated claims about an ordinary soul. Media may run afoul of trespassing laws not only by actually entering private property, but also by pointing a telephoto lens at a window. Yet an editor may find invasion of privacy to be a concept difficult to apply on deadline. Images often are particularly challenging. A photographer may take a picture of folks on public property. What if they are on private property, but in plain view of sidewalk passers-by? What if they are in a house, but in plain view of a camera from above, say, from a satellite?

In fact, Google faced charges of privacy invasion with just such a camera. A family was upset that the search engine's street views on its map service showed their home without their permission. The 3rd U.S. Circuit Court of Appeals in Philadelphia dismissed the privacy charges because Aaron and Christine Boring had not indicated that the camera had revealed activity inside the home; moreover, the photo of their home and pool that is accessible online via a "street search" would not offend anyone. However, the court allowed the trespass charges. "Here the Borings have alleged that Google entered upon their property without permission. If proven, that is a trespass, pure and simple," Debra Classens Weiss wrote in "Privacy-Loving Couple Allowed to Pursue Only Trespass Count Against Google Maps," posted Jan. 29, 2010, on the American Bar Association's *ABA Journal Law News Now* site. On Dec. 2, 2010, PCMag.com writer

Chloe Albanesius reported that the Pennsylvania district court had ordered Google to pay the couple $1.

Over the centuries, views of "private" and "damning" facts have changed. While editors have to consider privacy laws today, such a right was not part of the original U.S. Constitution. Samuel Warren and future U.S. Supreme Court justice Louis D. Brandeis were offended that newspapers carried a list of guest names at a dinner party. They responded by issuing the country's first calls for privacy protection in the *Harvard Law Review* of 1890 and 1891.

United States privacy laws today limit an editor's reach, despite the country's comparatively liberal free speech laws. Photographers and reporters are not allowed to take pictures of victims in ambulances or hospitals. They may take distance shots as long as they shoot them from public spaces, like a sidewalk or the edge of a road. Usually, empathy and a sense of decency keep photographers from zooming in to frame closeups of the injured or dying. Journalists must stay behind the yellow tape at crisis or crime scenes.

Editors are likely to face situations involving private cell phone photos, accident photos or embarrassing personal information. The only defense for including highly private facts in a news article is if these details are vital to the public interest in terms of governing, not gossip, and also are integral to the story. For example, facts about alcoholism would be inappropriate in a feature profiling an all-star gardener but might be highly relevant in a news account describing an automobile accident. The Society of Professional Journalists Code of Ethics' command, "Do no harm," does not direct reporters to cover up wrongdoing. Doing harm means adding gratuitous information to satisfy unhealthy curiosity or providing only one perspective. When people break the law, they have already hurt themselves. The most editors can do, which is a lot, is to treat all sources fairly and report the details of offenses accurately.

Conclusion: Why does Andrew Vachss say his personal hero is a flawed journalist?

Blogs and other social media remind editors that decency requires actions beyond what the law says *must* be done. Acknowledging each other's original creations provides incentives to strive for public recognition. Moreover, attributing the ideas, photos, paintings, stories, and other productivity stretches the intellect, forces the mind to explore new possibilities, and, therein, motivates personal growth that translates into professional skills.

Traditionally, journalists have answered the call to serve the public by opening windows on the world that reveal the truth. Shady behavior diminishes people's trust in the press, which ultimately prompts them to stop monitoring the news. Without fair, balanced, in-depth accounts of current events, citizens cannot participate rationally in democracy; elections become beauty contests focused on "character" rather than issues.

"Journalism is the protection between people and any sort of totalitarian rule. That's why my hero, admittedly a flawed one, is a journalist," Andrew Vachss, New York attorney, novelist, and essayist, concluded (www.vachss.com). "Journalism is what maintains democracy. It's the force for progressive social change."

But if editors allow reporters to plagiarize online, on TV, or in print; to make up sources and quotations; to libel; to invade privacy; to steal and misappropriate — the lies magnify the loss of independent thought and perspectives from multiple sources vital to a marketplace of ideas. Eventually, the world shrinks until choice evaporates, and not only are all restaurants Taco Bell, but all minds close to new possibilities. The cost, ultimately, is erosion of liberty and freedom of expression essential to democracy.

Know more

Notes

Garber, M. (2009). "The public editor and the Internet: The Match Game! Clark Hoyt builds up the case of The Times v. The Blogger. Behind the news." *Columbia Journalism Review,* May 26, 2009.

Lewis, N. P. (2008). "Plagiarism antecedents and situational influences." *Journalism and Mass Communication Quarterly,* 85(2).

Linkins, J. (2009). "Online poll: Jon Stewart is America's most trusted newsman." *Huffington Post,* July 22, 2009 at 2:10 P.M. Retrieved 25 November 25, 2009, from http://www.huffing tonpost.com/2009/07/22/time-magazine-poll-jon-st_n_242933.html.

Rosen, J. (2003). "All about the retrospect." *American Journalism Review,* June 2003.

_____ (2004). "Who knows Jack?" *American Journalism Review,* April/May 2004.

Slack, M. (2009). "Young Americans see Colbert, Stewart replacing traditional news outlets: Poll; what's your reaction?" *Huffington Post,* March 25, 2009, updated April 25, 2009. Retrieved November 24, 2009, from http://www.huffingtonpost.com/2009/03/25/young-americans-see-colbe_n_178884.html

More recommended reading

Barton Carter, T., J. L. Dee, and H. L. Zuckman (1994). *Mass Communication Law in a Nutshell.* St. Paul, MN: West.

Bugeja, M. (2007). *Living Ethics: Across Media Platforms.* New York: Oxford University Press.

Grant, S. (2007). *We're All Journalists Now. The Transformation of the Press and Reshaping of the Law in the Internet Age.* New York: Simon and Schuster.

• EXERCISE 1 •

Media ethics discussion topics for editors

1. Contrast a recent case on www.plagiarismtoday.com with one mentioned in this chapter.

2. Compare and contrast a case involving plagiarism with one involving fabrication. How are they different? Why do writers often comment on plagiarism and fabrication together?

3. Visual messaging is rapidly seizing the public imagination. Therein, plagiarism involving digital manipulation and theft will occur. What can editors, public relations executives, and others who rely upon graphic elements do to prevent plagiarism? What can they do to detect it?

4. How do advertisers' attitudes about plagiarism differ from journalists? Why?

5. Make a list of consequences of plagiarism. Find an example online that supports one ramification.

6. Is "sampling," taking parts of songs and reconfiguring them into a new composition plagiarism? Find two sources that support your view and two that refute it.

7. Manipulation of pixels to generate a new picture raises new issues about plagiarism. What do you think? Find evidence to support your ideas and also review the opposition view.

8. What is wrong with the argument that everyone does something? Do you think plagiarism arises from social or peer pressures?

9. Why do think some once famous journalists committed plagiarism? What happened to their credibility? Their news venue's reputation?

10. Find a newspaper article, blog, or magazine item that exposes an instance plagiarism in the field you intend to build your career. What can we learn from the mistakes people made in this instance?

FIVE

Headlines and Headings

Chris Roberts

One of the hardest parts of the copy reader's task is to write head-lines over the sto-ries he edits. Usually a reporter does not write the head-lines over his own stories. One reason for this is that his article often is completely changed when it comes out of the copy reader's hands. Another is that it is wise to make every statement undergo the scrutiny of a second pair of eyes before it can get into the composing-room. But the chief reason is that head-line writing is an art in itself, and the copy reader must be an expert in this work. It is as difficult to write good "display hands" as to write good verse.

—*Practical Journalism: A Complete Manual of the Best Newspaper Methods* (*Shuman*, 1903, p. 91)

There is nothing new under the sun, as the Old Testament book of Ecclesiastes says. This quote is as accurate today as it was a century ago, especially after you change "copy reader" to "copy editor," know that the "composing room" died with the rise of electronic page-design software, and remember that women are at least as likely as men to write stories and headlines. Regardless of whether the headline is for a print publi-cation or online, written to meet exact page specifications or written with the purpose of being found by search engines, the task of headline writing remains as much an art as it was when all the work was done on paper.

Writing a hed (the industry's shorthand term for "headline") is an act of contra-diction: A hed has only a few words to summarize a long story. Heds must draw readers into the story without giving too much away or promising something the story does not deliver. They must reflect the story without stealing from it. Headline writers follow rules yet must be nimble with words and know when it's OK to break the rules. Heds can often be clever, but never should they be cloying or crude. They are usually written in minutes, long after the writer took hours (or weeks) to hone the story. Heds are written as part of an assembly-line process, but each product is unique.

No wonder, then, that many students shy from the task. At the very least, they stop grousing at the hed atop their published stories, and they gain respect for the unsung heroes who write heds. Even if they never compose a hed outside of an editing class, smart writers put suggested heds atop their stories because they realize that if they can't summarize their own stories in just a few words, why should they expect anyone else to be able to? More likely, however, students understand that nearly all word-focused journalists will be writing heds as the industry sheds jobs and workers are forced to multitask. This skill is becoming especially necessary for online content, as some reporters post blog and Twitter entries that do not pass through conventional copy desks (Russial, 2009). Simply put, every writer should learn to be a headline writer.

This chapter focuses on the art and science of hed writing. It discusses:

- the jobs that heds perform
- the basics of writing heds: Print and online
- how to write a print hed
- tips when you're stuck
- how to write online heds, how hed writing is different for websites, and what makes for a good Web-focused hed

The jobs of the headline

Find a copy of a centuries-old newspaper and you'll find that journalism historian Wm. David Sloan was right in writing that "[b]y today's standards, these early newspapers were not impressive," that "[g]rayness pervaded each page," and that even the most important stories of the day were published under tiny one-column headlines at random places on the page (2011, p. 72). It was not until the late 1800s, when newspaper magnates William Randolph Hearst and Joseph Pulitzer were locked in the New York circulation battle that started sensationalistic "yellow journalism," that large heds stretched across multiple columns to draw attention to the stories underneath. Its purveyors noted that many of the stories they covered were no different from what other papers covered. The difference was the flashier design and bigger headlines. Indeed, "yellow journalism was distinctive mainly in its typography" (Sloan, 2011, p. 238). Before 1890, because metal type sizes were rarely larger than a half-inch, smaller heds stretched across multiple columns. Creating a taller headline meant carving it from wood. (Even today, some journalists refer to screaming headlines as "woodies.") Those big headlines drew readers into the stories and paper, and newsworthiness of stories began to be a deciding factor in where stories were placed on pages (Morano, 2002).

While "yellow journalism" is a derisive term today, the journalists of 120 years ago quickly learned the following truths about headlines that remain true today:

- Headlines attract attention, which translates to sales. How could you not stop to buy the *New York Post* on April 15, 1982, when "**HEADLESS BODY IN TOP-LESS BAR**" screamed across the front page? It broke the rules (because it has no verb), but it took on a life of its own and sold plenty of extra copies for a tabloid that has long depended upon single-copy sales. Traditional papers may not want heds quite so loud, but they crave powerful heds that can hike news-stand sales as home deliveries decline. In a time when readers can find news from multiple sources, a better hed can separate your news from the others. Not all stories scream like a brutal killing, but even a strong hed on a less-thrilling story will make a difference. Consider this hed atop a story about a same-sex marriage ceremony on a college campus: **They do, even if the law says they can't.** Audrey Kuo wrote it for the UCLA *Daily Bruin*, and it helped her win the American Copy Editors Society's 2009 hed contest for student copy editors (American Copy Editors Society, 2009). The deadline story was typical fare from a college newspaper, but there's no doubt that the hed enticed a few more people to stop and read the story.

- Headlines save time for readers. A typical reader doesn't take time to read every story on every page, or click on every website link. Headlines ("headings" on websites) at a minimum should give those readers a quick glance at the news, and a good hed entices them to wade further into the copy.
- Headlines reflect a story's tone. Tone can be a function of visual design and word choice. Some designers use color and different font styles and sizes to make the hed become part of the design on feature or centerpiece packages. These choices tell readers the story has a softer focus, while a more conventional hed tells readers the story is more serious. A flippant or sardonic hed atop a serious story can send a mixed message or offend readers, just as a too-serious hed can smother a bright story.
- Headlines tell readers what editors think is important. Journalists are gatekeepers and agenda-setters as they decide which stories to publish. The choice of the hed size, as part of the placement of the story on the page or website index, is another clue to readers about the relative importance of a story.
- Headlines play a vital role as part of a publication's or website's visual identity. The choice of typeface and the style of heds tell readers a great deal about a publication's purpose and goals. The *New York Times*' design reminds readers of that paper's tradition; *USA Today's* headline-heavy design is among its techniques aimed at capturing readers in a hurry.
- Headlines help stories be found online. Editors of even 20 years ago knew nothing of the Internet, but today's hed writers must consider the online implications of the heds they write. Today's hed writers learn "search engine optimization" techniques that will help readers find a story when they use Google, Bing or another search engine. As will be discussed, a perfectly good print hed may be the exact opposite of what's needed for the story to be found online.

The basics of writing heds: Print and online

Just as you cannot return to a place you've never been, you cannot write a useful and accurate headline for a story you do not understand. The understanding begins by reading the entire story. If you read the story and still don't understand it, then you may need to go back to the writer or the writer's editor to suggest that the story needs more work. When you do understand the story, only then you can write an accurate hed.

As you read the story, you'll pick up its tone — hard news or soft, serious or silly — and the type of hed you need to match the tone. It is a fundamental mistake to write a dull hed for a feature story, and maybe even worse to write a clever hed for a tragic story.

If your task is to write a straightforward hed, start by summarizing the key words and phrases as you read the story. Your goal is to boil down the story to its basic elements — those key nouns, verbs and quotes inside the story. Also, you might jot down key ideas — or puns, well-known sayings that you could use as a starting point — that pop into your brain as you read the story. All of that material will become raw material for the hed.

As an example, here's a six-paragraph story that would be late-breaking news for a news organization in a college town. To think about the headline, a smart copy editor would focus on the words in bold.

> FREEDONIA — A **fire** at a **Freedonia State** University residence hall **injured two** students and **destroyed a room** late **Saturday** night, authorities said.
>
> The two students suffered smoke inhalation and second-degree burns caused by **flaming popcorn**, said Fire Chief Ashton Smith. Neither injury was life-threatening, and residents of Harpo Hall were allowed back into their rooms shortly before midnight, he said.
>
> The fire on the second floor began at 10:30 P.M., when a student dropped a lighted **firecracker** into **bag** of just-microwaved popcorn. The explosion sent the flaming bag and its contents in all directions, Smith said, and several kernels caught nearby **drapes** on fire.
>
> "We were fortunate, because this could have been devastating," he said.
>
> Smith would not name the injured students, who he said were still being treated at Memorial Hospital.
>
> Efforts to reach a hospital spokeswoman were unsuccessful, and campus officials would not comment.
>
> A student in the room said he and his friends dropped the firecracker into the popcorn bag while **celebrating** Freedonia State's **victory** over arch rival Sylvania Tech.
>
> "It was the smelliest, scariest thing I've ever seen," said Louis Calhern, a sophomore. "We're all grateful that we beat Sylvania and that the fire wasn't worse."

The headline may well come from the key words: fire, Freedonia State, injured two, destroyed a room, Saturday, flaming popcorn, firecracker, bag, drapes, celebrating, victory. There's also the possibility of a hed built around phrases from two direct quotes: "could have been devastating" and "smelliest, scariest."

The next step is to write a declarative sentence that prunes those keywords to the essence of what happened. Start following a key rule of heds by using strong verbs: "A firecracker exploded in a bag of popcorn Saturday night, hurting two Freedonia State students and destroying a room in a residence hall." (The verb "exploded," for example, is better than the noun "explosion." It's always good to turn interesting nouns into verbs.) At this point, some of the secondary aspects of the story — such as it happened in celebration of the football win — fade away. You might come back to that secondary angle if there's space, but what happened is more important.

The sentence that summarizes the story isn't much more than a recast of the lede, but that's OK because the story was written in an inverted pyramid style. Most importantly, the sentence is accurate, and accuracy is the most important task of a hed. But the sentence is a problem because it fails to follow some rules that say it's best to write a headline in present tense and active voice.

- Present tense. Writing in past tense makes the news seem old. So heds tend to match the present-tense writing style of television news, where even "dies" is preferable to "dead." The exception is to use past tense for historical events.
- Active voice. As in any writing, try to place the true subject of the sentence as the first words in a hed (**Dog catches ball**) instead of as the object (**Ball caught by dog**), but there are times when the most important noun is the object. All these rules may go out the window in some cases, such as the story about the capture of a murderer who escaped from prison: "**Killer arrested**" is stronger than "**Police capture killer**" because the focus should be on the killer, not the police.

The next step may be to consider the tone of the story and how the hed should match. On one hand, a fire that hurts someone in your town may be too serious for a hed that plays off the obvious popping of corn and firecracker, or highlighting the quote in which the student mentions being thankful for the football victory before being thankful for the lack of injuries in the fire. On the other hand, a paper published far from Freedonia might run the story only because the bizarre nature of the explosion can let the hed writer have some fun with the fireworks and popcorn angle. In this instance, the news value is bizarreness, not the proximity or impact news values important to the Freedonia paper.

Regardless of whether the hed is for print or online, a few other considerations remain in place. Among the most important is the ability to think along "parallel tracks" — that is, to be able to write a hed that doesn't have a double meaning that you didn't want to include. Consider the hed **Man found dead in Pasco lake was lonely drifter**, published by the *St. Petersburg* (Fla.) *Times* (Sullivan, 2009). It unfortunately conjures the notion of driftwood and floating, which likely wasn't in the mind of the headline writer. Writing quality heds will require you to develop a nimble mind, have lots of practice, and find examples of bad heds. You can read examples of bad headlines on *Columbia Journalism Review's* monthly back page of flubbed heds.

Other useful guidelines when writing heds for online or print include the following:

Avoid libel

The need for shortcuts in a hed can lead to a trip to the courthouse. The previous hed **Killer arrested** implies that the person who was arrested is, indeed, a killer. That's true if the person is a convicted murderer, but not if the person has merely been charged with murder. Courts have ruled that a publication is guilty of libel if the hed is wrong, even if the story is accurate. The solution is **Murder suspect caught** or **Man arrested in killing** (not "for" killing, which implies guilt.)

Don't push a story beyond the facts

If the Freedonia State fire story had said the exploding popcorn might have been the fire's cause, then the heds you'll see later in this chapter need to be rewritten to steer clear of that unconfirmed fact or use modifiers such as "may have" to acknowledge that the information is unconfirmed.

Steer clear of alphabet soup

The hed **FSU blaze at HH hurts 2** might fit the available space on a page, but it doesn't make sense unless you know that Freedonia State is known as "FSU" and "HH" is Harpo Hall. Such little-known abbreviations especially weaken online heds, since people who search for FSU will find Florida State University and Fayetteville (N.C.) State University, too. Stay away from acronyms that aren't readily known.

Don't hide the news

A hed such as **Speaker discusses issues at meeting** tells readers absolutely nothing. Find the news in the story and put it in the hed.

Use quotations from the story effectively

A great direct quote from the story, or the most powerful words from that quote, might work well. The key is making sure that the hed as a whole makes sense, which is why quotes work best when teamed with a more direct main deck or subhed.

Be careful where you put quotation marks

While using a single quoted word from the story might be useful in the hed, the quotations around that word might convey to the reader that you think the person being quoted isn't really telling the truth. Example: Does the hed **President "eager" to mend fences with political foes** mean (1) the president is really eager, or (2) he's being sarcastic or lying? The quote doesn't make it clear; changing to "hopes" or "plans" (without the quotation marks) makes it clearer.

Include appropriate attribution

The hed **Freedonia fire injures two students** needs no attribution, because the story takes care of that factual information. But when the story focuses on a controversial topic, or on information not widely known, some level of attribution is needed. The hed to a follow-up story about the Freedonia fire, such as

> **Stupid student**
> **starts blaze**
> **in dorm room**

requires attribution to the speaker, such as **Stupid student/ started blaze, / fire chief says.** It might also be useful to put quotation marks around "Stupid."

Avoid labels

The hed **Fire at dorm** is a weakling because it has no verb — or does it? It could be a verbless label hed that means a dorm (or something in it) caught on fire? Or it could be read as a command aimed at someone holding a shotgun. Label heds are common on feature packages or magazine stories and work best when there's another element (such as a subhed or illustration) to explain the label hed.

Avoid redundancy

Try not to repeat the same words in the hed and subhed, and certainly do not repeat words in the hed. The hed **Firecracker sparks dorm fire** is redundant.

Ask questions appropriately

If you ask a question that a reader can answer with a "no," then you've lost that reader. (Example: **Do you love cats?** If you aren't a cat lover, then you'll answer the question and move on.) Moreover, the point of journalism is more closely tied to answering readers' questions than asking questions of them. Still, sometimes a well-crafted question with no clear-cut answer might pull readers into the story. Example: the hed

**What do president,
crates of oranges
have in common?**

would entice many readers to dig into the story to find an answer.

Keeping these principles in mind, the next steps depend upon whether the hed is written for print for the Web. In the following sections, we'll focus on specific needs for print and online heads, and then return for other considerations after the hed has been written.

How to write a print hed

It's hard to turn a long, complicated story into a six-word summary. It's even harder in a print headline, because the page design often puts the hed in a tight space with multiple lines spread across one or more columns. A good hed must fit the available space, because a hed that is too long cannot be printed and a hed that comes up short will look strange on a page. For example, the width of the hed **Dorm blast hurts 2** in 72 pt. times requires 48 picas of space. As editor you must write a hed to fit two columns in width. Two columns in your publication measures 21 picas. Will the head above fit? Hardly. You must either rewrite to shorten, write a new hed from scratch or reduce the point size to 30; 30 pts. requires only 20 picas.

A tip for publications whose hed writers are beginners: Use a centered hed style instead of a flush left style, because heds don't look as short when centered than when flush left.

Writing a hed for a print story requires the writer to know the following:

- The type of hed requested. (See Figure 1 for details about various types of headlines, each written with the Freedonia State University story in mind.)

• The hed order (or spec). The spec indicates the number of columns (width, measured in picas), the height of the hed (measured in points, a system in which 72 pts. equals one inch,) and the number of lines. For example, a 4-36-1 would require an editor to craft a hed that stretches across all four of the six columns of a newspaper page in half-inch type, and in just one line.

A 2-36-2 hed is tougher, since you've got just two columns written in half-inch type, but you must fill both lines. The key to a multiple-column hed is to make sure that "thought units" don't break from one column to the next. Consider the following hed:

Poe blows
away field

This hed wouldn't work because the first line ("Poe blows") leads to a secondary meaning you didn't intend. Also, avoid ending a line with a preposition or a conjunction because those parts of speech often begin a new thought unit. In the hed examples with the Freedonia story, look at the subhed (1-18-3 italic.)

Dorm blast hurts 2,
wrecks dorm room
at Freedonia State

Each is a complete thought. Now consider this hed:

Dorm blast injures
2, wrecks dorm
room at Freedonia

The break between "dorm" and "room" is a bad one because it might cause some readers to think "room" is "an availability of space," not a dorm room. The rules about breaks are not as strictly enforced with a one-column hed, but it's still good to read each line as its own thought unit to look for howlers.

Writing heds was even more difficult before pagination software, when editors had to consider the "count" of the hed based upon the width of the typeface, its height size and the number of columns set aside for the hed. Most publication fonts are proportional, in which the letters vary in width; the opposite is a non-proportional font such as Courier, in which all the letters are the same width. The "count" is the number of characters that can fit in the space. A typical lower-case letter is a single count in a proportional font, but the letters "f-l-i-t-j" (pronounced "flit-jay") and punctuation are a half count, and "m" and "w" are 1.5 counts. Most uppercase letters (and numerals) have 1.5 counts, while upper-case "f-l-i-t-j" have a count of 1, and "m" and "w" have a count of two. That's why "Killer," with a count of 5, is more likely to appear in a hed than the 9-count word "Murderer." While you may never have to deal with counts, knowing the "flit-jay" rules can help you find "smaller" words that fit the available space better than "bigger" words.

Banner hed: 4-36-1

Flaming popcorn injures 2 at Freedonia State

Banner hed: 4-36-1, with deck 1-18-3 italic

Students learn popcorn, firecracker don't mix

Dorm blast hurts two,
wrecks dorm room
at Freedonia State

Kicker: 24 point italic, with 2-48-2 main hed

Corn, 'crackers, kaboom

Freedonia State blast hurts two

Hammer: 42 point italic, with 3-24-1 italic deck

Pop! Goes the dorm room
Firecracker, corn blast hurts 2 Freedonia students

Sidesaddle: 1-24-4 rag left

Snack-sparked fire injures 2, damages dorm late Saturday

Lorem ipsum dolor sit amet, consectetur adipiscing elit. Suspendisse malesuada nisl quis nisi posuere auctor. Cras id erat ut felis vehicula rutrum.

Cumsociis natoque penatibus et magnis dis parturient montes, nascetur ridiculus mus. Cras a enim porta lacus scelerisque elementum eu at diam.

Praesent ac dui libero, sed feugiat magna. Quisque vel nulla id dui congue consectetur vel eu orci. In vel ligula sed do-

Figure 1: Banner hed, banner with deck, kicker, hammer and sidesaddle.

<u>*Subheds with justified text.*</u>

Labius, omni doluptate poris eum rectur, cumquid estrum eos experuptia veles evellan iscipsus siment est, in prori quae. Nam, toressi volorup tatemque et, quam dolores millit aspeditem ut quo con consed quatios et ellorae. Nam id que nullit ex ea plaut aut vendiati cum eaquias alitiatur?

Lorem Ipsum.

Sa comnimendem quas quidusant quatur sitatibus, voluptas accae porisitasi dus et, volorec ullores dolores seculluptas aut quam, quid quatia nam sapernam si volum aut is aut.

Tum que volorum ab inus volore numquiduntio es ium hariatur? Quiate nobit evendanis accum niendio volecepudae santis ullabo. Onsecum, net, sametusaped etum as esequis eius dolore comnisciet exped maione pro tecti untibea vellestecto doluptisim eaquid que voloriat.

Dolor Sit Amet.

Dit, quia debis exceatus sumquiate peritatum quossunt magnihilique nam qui cus.
Pa verunt. La quamentibusa con possitas erum ad molupta tiorecto est eiur, quas eos sim remporem. Apicipsunt minvel in rae culparchit.

<u>*Jump hed.*</u>

Flaming popcorn from page 1

<u>*Readin.*</u>

A dorm prank with a firecracker nearly ended in tragedy late Saturday, according to police. Reporter Irving Nern filed this report.

Dollorepe vent officip ictibus.
Et modigene pelit doluptate repudis quasperem quo cullibus iusant magniet voluptatet volore, omnimod ionsend itessim lam dit, inullam ipsunt.

Ignat porrumquae net doloreium re eumqui quiament.
Itatur aut maio. Et a si te niminctate nestorit reicipsam etust lit maios sequi deliquis nis dolupit volupta spiendae resserspit unt offic

Figure 2: Subheds, jump hed, readin.

How many counts fit in a column of type depends upon the typeface's height, which is measured in points. Type sizes in a typical newspaper headline range from 18 points to 72 points, depending upon the news value and the design requirement. Magazine heds vary much more widely in size because they are much more likely to be incorporated as an art element in the design.

Some newspaper copy desks develop "headline schedules" that explain how many units of space a hed writer has, based on the typeface, point size and columns needed

---

Hed chats: Points and picas

The arcane way of measuring type in points traces back to late 1700s France and to "hot type" days when letters were cast from a lead-tin alloy. (The industry mostly moved to offset printing in the 1970s.) The United States did not adopt the system until the late 1800s, and the size of a point or pica remained non-standard. Digital type foundries today have established, finally, one standard: a point is $1/72^{nd}$ of an inch. A pica (p) contains 12 points (pts). Six picas equal (about) one inch. So how many points in an inch? Of course it's 72. Editors used to actually measure type using a pica pole or pica rule — a metal ruler with a mushroom-shaped end to hook over pages.

Type sizes are standardized. Anything smaller than about 12 pt. is considered "body text," and is not used for heds. Bigger than that is "display type" for heds. Standard display sizes: 14, 18, 24, 30, 36, 48, 60, 72, 84, etc. So how big is, say, a 48-pt. head? You can figure out that one. Type of about 5.5 pt. is sometimes called "agate," used for fine print. Smaller than that you can't read without a magnifying glass. You see it in microprinting on some postage stamps.

We still use points and picas because the measurement it is easier than inches or millimeters. You want to use standard-size body type for your newsletter. You could choose type measuring .1314 inches. You could chose type measuring 3.528 millimeters. Or you could choose 10-pt type.

It's a little different online, as you also have the option of choosing type in pixels. Then the size depends on screen resolution, normally 72 pixels per inch (ppi).

---

to be filled. An example: A 30-point Bodoni bold hed has 10.5 units for a single column and 23 for two columns. The count for the two-column hed is more than double because of the gutter, the space between columns. Because page widths in different newspapers and magazines may vary, and because different publications use different type faces for their heds, there's no one-size-fits-all schedule.

Note that heds are never hyphenated, unless the hyphen is part of the word.

**City council
boosts li-
quor fees**

The headline above may fit the space better, but it must be rewritten to avoid the hyphen.

**City council
boosts taxes
on alcohol**

Types of print headlines

Newspapers and other publications generally publish the following eight types of headlines. Figures 1 and 2 above illustrates them.

Banners

The headlines that stream (and sometimes scream) across a page.

Decks

Heds that go under a banner or similar hed. They are often written in half the point size of the main hed. Writers use the deck heds to elaborate or expand upon the main hed, or to focus on a secondary news element in the story, not to repeat information in the main hed.

Kickers

A smaller hed published above the main hed, usually designed to tease or to provide additional information. These are sometimes known as "eyebrow" heds. Some papers use the kicker to identify the city or organization that is in the news, giving the hed writer the ability to focus on the news without having to waste hed space on identification.

Hammers

The opposite of a kicker, in which the larger hed is above the smaller hed.

Subheds

Short headlines inside stories that are typically designed to give readers a break from the columns of text in a long story.

HED CHATS: THAT PECULIARLY FAMILIAR LABEL HED

The label hed should be familiar to us: we see it in our book titles, in many magazine articles, in online essays, and even in our own term papers. For example, if you're writing at term paper about well-known newsman Anderson Cooper, would you write a standard hed for it? Anderson Cooper becomes celebrity announcer for CNN. Probably not. Instead, you'd write on the title page something like Anderson Cooper and CNN. This is a label hed.

Given their familiarity, then, we shouldn't have any problem writing them for media. But many students do. What seems hard to remember is that label heds normally have no verb. Cooper reports for CNN is not a label hed, because "reports" is a verb. Cooper announcer for CNN is not a label head either, because the verb "is" is understood. The Anderson Cooper era on CNN is a label hed, because it contains no verb. Note: it does contain an article, "the," normally not acceptable in standard heds.

Why would you want to use label heds in mass media content? Magazines and newsletters sometimes use them because they sound more literary, less like breathless breaking news. News media, too, sometimes use them, particularly on editorial pages or opinion pieces. That's because the label hed contains no verb. So the editor does not venture to suggest an angle the writer may or may not agree with. A label hed is more neutral. Governor's veto shows ignorance, arrogance can be neutralized with a label: The governor's veto.

Jump heds

Some newspapers write full heds that stretch across where a story is jumped. The best jump heds focus on information in the jumped section of the story and do not merely repeat the information from the previous headline or what's on the previous page. Other publications, however, use only key words that match the key words used just before the jump.

Sidesaddles

Heds placed alongside a story, not atop the copy.

Readins (and readouts)

A sentence or paragraph that summarizes a story. Sometimes, the first words or the last words are in a larger font and can stand alone as a thought.

Some space-saving rules for print heds

Because print space is at a premium, many traditional hed-writing guidelines are designed to save space. The general rules include using the following:

- Downstyle, in which only the first words and proper nouns are capitalized
- No period at the end of a hed. Use a semicolon if your hed would otherwise be two sentences.
- 'Single quotes,' not "double quotes"
- A % symbol of spelling out "percent," an exception to AP style
- Arabic numerals instead of spelling out numbers less than 10, as required by AP style (**Dorm fire injures 2**)
- The word "says" for attribution. Some publications use a colon for attribution (**Chief: Dorm fire 'could have been devastating'**) while others use a dash at the end (**Dorm fire 'could have been devastating' — Chief**). But don't write heds that can have double meanings (**'Smelliest, scariest thing I've ever seen' — Freedonia State student**).
- A comma to replace the word "and" (**Blaze injures 2, destroys room**)

Other considerations

Saving space is vital, but a headline's shortcuts should never be taken at the expense of accuracy and clarity. While some rules are more hard and fast than others, writing a good print hed sometimes requires the following:

- Use articles such as "a" and "the." Use articles with words that can be both verbs and nouns, such as "floors" or "hits." But avoid "a" and "the" at other times.
- Avoid proper names when the subject of the hed is not well known. In our Freedonia example, it's not likely that a typical reader would know the names of the two people quoted.

HED CHATS: COURIER AND TYPEWRITERS

Textbooks often indicate computer input instructions by writing code in Courier typeface. Courier is a monospaced font, meaning each letter takes up the same amount of space. To make that possible, narrow letters have large serifs, such as i, while wide letters are squeezed, such as m. The font goes back to typewriter days. A mechanical typewriter, using a metal arm with a metal piece of type at the end of it, couldn't type proportional letters.

But calculating proportions is exactly what computers are good at. So we shouldn't need monospaced fonts anymore. Why is Courier still ubiquitous? It is standard because it was the standard for so many years. U.S. State Department documents appeared for decades on Courier, until the government in 2004 dropped it for Times New Roman. Ironically, Courier was designed for IBM in 1955. Times New Roman was decidedly less American, designed by Stanley Morison for the *London Times* in 1931.

- Don't use abbreviations for days of the week, a person's name, or months (unless you follow AP rules that allow you to abbreviate a month that has a date following it.)
- Try not to pad. It's important to fill the space to make the hed fit the specs, but it's generally bad form to keep adding prepositional phrases or other needless words to make it fit: **Fire injures 2 people in dorm room at Freedonia State on Saturday** includes three consecutive prepositional phrases, a tipoff that the hed writer was padding. Another padding word is "people," because it wouldn't be news if it weren't people; make every word count.
- Focus on the latest development. This practice is important in stories that unfold over several days, so that old news isn't repeated.
- Steer clear of words you'd only find in a headline. The effort to make heds fit leads writers to use short words—"rips" instead of "opposes," or "thinclads" instead of cross-country running team, or "Jacko" instead of "Michael Jackson"—turns English into a foreign language for some readers. Read aloud, these heds sound like Tarzan is the speaker (**Prez eyes pay czar**, or **Solons nix fete, rap Reds at confab**). Use those shortcuts only when absolutely necessary. On the other hand, the word "dorm" will suffice in a hed regardless of the university's desire to use the more highfalutin' term "residence hall."
- Find the balance between clever and cloying.

David St. Hubbins in the 1984 movie *Spinal Tap* explains it well: "It's such a fine line between clever and stupid." The true headline writing artist can walk that line when writing clever heds that use a pun, a rhyme, a comparison or contrast with other words (**Freedonia players hot / on cold evening in 7-0 / victory over Sylvania**), alliteration (the **Crackers, 'corn', kaboom** kicker) or a twist on an well-known expression.

Heds might start with "how" or "why" when the story revolves around explaining a topic (the **Pop! Goes the dorm room** hammer).

But it's easy to go over the top and end up with something that is distasteful (**Shooter has it his way / in Burger King massacre**) or just plain goofy—although that's often in the eye of the beholder. Bottom line: Stay away from silliness in serious or sad stories, and ask the opinion of other people when trying to be clever.

Stuck? Think about this.

The frenzy of deadline, the assembly-line process, dealing with a deadly-dull story or simply having a bad night can make it tough to write consistently solid heds. While there's no perfect solution, John Schlander, executive news editor of the *St. Petersburg Times*, has a list of ways to think through a block (Schlander, n.d.). His suggestions include working to find the "perfect verb," using wordplay (that goes beyond puns and alliteration and instead uses contrasts or twists of phrases), looking for specifics inside the story to move past a vague hed and changing the perspective and writing about what the news means for the reader or the people affected, not the government agency that made the news.

And if all else fails, ask for help. Two heads can be better than one on a single hed. Or it just may be that the hed spec is too small to fit the news, which may require the designer to change the hed spec, add more space, or move the story.

How to write an online hed (heading)

The pain of writing a print hed involves finding the words to fit each line while balancing the need to be clever (but not too clever) and not give away the story. Fortunately, these are not the problems for a writer of online heds, sometimes called headings. The online hed serves two masters—delivering the news to readers and delivering the readers to the news.

The task of delivering the news to the readers is the central point of this chapter, and that task is slightly different for a Web editor. Editors signal a story's importance by where a story is placed on the printed page, the size of the hed and the typography of the hed. Online, however, this job is difficult because different browsers render pages differently, because Web browsers offer little variety in hed sizes, and because Web pages are often filled with ads (that sometimes resemble news content) and other links that compete for attention.

Typical online users read only a few words on the screen (usually starting with words on the left side), and readers can be easily overwhelmed as they look to see what's important and what links might be on the page. A useful Web hed delivers the news without adding to the clutter. It also assumes readers are in a hurry. So a just-the-facts hed works best. This approach is especially important as more readers use mobile devices to read the news. Readers quickly become frustrated if a hed fails to explain the point of the story, especially if readers only see a cute hed (which might work well on a print page) and must click to learn what the story is really about. For this reason, it's best to stick to simple heds.

VOCABULARY AND JARGON FOR EDITORS

Algorithm.

A series of steps to be followed in solving a problem. Mostly this term relates to computer programming; algorithms that tell computers how to search and sort can be used in Web search engines. Search Engine Optimization (SEO) headlines consider algorithms for best search engine placement.

Column.

A width of type on a page, usually measured in picas. Many magazines and newsletters have two or three columns on a page. Most broadsheet newspapers have six. Old-style broadsheets often had eight.

Hed Sked (Headline Schedule).

Editors use this style sheet to help choose sizes and styles. The hed sked lists possible headline choices based on the typeface chosen for a particular publication. Headlines that look unattractive or are hard to write are not included. For example, a Helvetica 6-14-2, that is, a six-column-wide, 14-point-high, two-line-long hed in Helvetica typeface in a broadsheet newspaper would be too small, and so difficult to write. On the other hand, a 1-72-1 would be impossibly large. (See page 107 for a discussion of type measurements.)

HTML.

Hyper Text Markup Language. This is a scripting language used by a computer to display a website. HTML was invented by Tim Berners-Lee in 1991, and today remains the basic skeleton of Web development. Editors working across media may be asked to understand HTML basics.

Pagination software.

Programs devoted to putting publications together, often called "desktop publishing software." The catchy name comes from Aldus Corp., the software company that gave the world its original computerized pagination software, PageMaker, in 1985. Programmer Paul Brainerd's company honored early Venetian typographer Aldus Manutius in the software that revolutionized graphic design.

Yellow Journalism.

Nickname for sensationalist journalism. It is based on the two famous New York rivals at the turn of the last century, Joseph Pulitzer's New York *World* and William Randolph Hearst's New York *Journal*. The name seems to be related to an early newspaper cartoon character, the "Yellow Kid," Its typically large heds helped to establish sensationalist traditions of newspaper design.

The second task—delivering readers to the news—is the crucial part of the Web-focused headline, because the goal of on online hed is to help the story be found on Google or other search engines. This task is known as "Search Engine Optimization," better known as SEO. As more readers are tossing paper and using the Web as their primary source of news and other information, and as search engines drive an ever-increasing number of people to sites on the Web, headline writers must master the rules of the SEO hed.

The SEO hed is one leg on the stool that makes a news organization's stories able to be found on the Web. The other legs include "meta-tags," the keywords that are unseen on the screen but embedded in the HTML of a Web page found by the search-engine "spiders" that crawl Web pages, and making sure the words in the hed match the words high in the text of the story. A good SEO hed includes the words that a typical reader would be most likely to use when searching for news about the topic in the story.

A good hed writer can find a way to meet both needs with a single hed. As an Illinois news editor explained, what's the same about print and Web heds is that editors "want people to understand what the story is about and read it" (Schmedding, 2009). While humans ultimately make those decisions about what to read, a SEO hed writer must take into account the fact that computer algorithms ultimately determine where a news story ends up on a search engine page. SEO heds must do the following:

• Use the specific words people are most likely to type when looking for news. In our example, a Google user might enter the terms "Freedonia State" and "fire" to find the story. But the words "popcorn" and "firecracker" and "dorm" might be useful, too, especially for readers who heard something about a popcorn-related fire but don't know where it happened. The SEO headline puts the references together: **Firecracker in popcorn causes fire at Freedonia State dorm room**. It's not the most exciting hed in the world, but it includes the key words.

Some of the clever words, synonyms and idioms that are perfect in print heds will work against you online. For a story about the declining value of the penny, the hed **Pennies aren't worth a dime a dozen** works well in print but may be lost online because the readers likely would not use the phrase "a dime a dozen" when they mean "decline in value." A simpler hed—**Pennies decline in value; worth less as coin money**—might be more effective. To summarize: When writing a SEO hed, ask yourself: What words would people type into a search engine site to find this story online?

• Break some of the rules of print heds. Use and spell out full names, dates and places. Don't abbreviate. If you're writing about Clinton, include more information so we'll know whether it's the former president, Obama's secretary of state, the county (nine states have a "Clinton County") or place (29 states have a "Clinton" city, town or Census-designated place) (U.S. Census Bureau, n.d.).

• Consider the juxtaposition of the words in the hed and the words in the text of the story. Web scammers try to fool Google by taking heds from news stories, hoping Google will place their links high on the results page. To stop the scamming, Google looks to see that the words in the hed match the words on the page, especially high in the story.

• Know that it's OK to be redundant—within reason. Repeating the same word in the metadata, hed and text can boost credibility with the Google search engine. But play fair, because Google will reject sites that it suspects use "keyword spamming" techniques to boost themselves.

Know more

Notes

American Copy Editors Society. (2009). Retrieved October 21, 2009, from http://www.copydesk. org/conference/2009/minne/headlines/D6.

Defense Information School. (n.d.). "DINFOS 'flitj' headline counter." Retrieved October 29, 2009, from http://www.dinfos.osd.mil/DinfosWeb/Students/headlines.asp

Morano, S. I. (2002). "Newspaper Design." In W. D. Sloan and L. M. Parcell, *American Journalism: History, Principles, Practices.* Northport, AL.: Vision.

Russial, J. (2009). "Copy editing not great priority for online stories." *Newspaper Research Journal,* 30 (2), 6-15.

Schlander, J. (n.d.). "Stuck for a headline? Try these tips." Retrieved November 15, 2009, from http://www.copydesk.org/words/headtips.htm.

Schmedding, T. (2009, May 2). "The SEO headline game." Retrieved October 29, 2009, from http://www.copydesk.org/conference/2009/minne/schedule/session/the-seo-headline-game/.

Shuman, E. L. (1903). *Practical Journalism: A Complete Manual of the Best Newspaper Methods.* New York: D. Appleton.

Sloan, W. D. (2008). *The Media in America: A History,* 7th ed. Northport, AL: Vision.

Sullivan, E. (2009, September 20). "Man found dead in Pasco lake was lonely drifter." Retrieved October 15, 2009, from www.tampabay.com/news/publicsafety/man-found-dead-in-pasco-lake-was-lonely-drifter/1037616.

Vanderbilt, T. (2004). "Courier, Dispatched." Retrieved June 7, 2010, from http://www.slate.com.

U.S. Census Bureau. (n.d.). "American Factfinder." Retrieved November 11, 2009, from http://fact finder.census.gov.

Recommended reading

A solid book on hed writing: Former copy editor Paul LaRocque's 96-page *Heads You Win: An Easy Guide to Better Headline and Caption Writing* (2003, Marion Street Press, Oak Park, IL) does an admirable job with dozens of good and bad heds, plus useful tips.

Keeping count: The U.S. Army's Defense Information School offers an calculator that does the hed counting for you. It's online at www.dinfos.osd.mil/DinfosWeb/Students/headlines.asp.

More about SEO: The Knight Digital Media Center offers a great deal of information about search engine optimization and journalism:http://multimedia.journalism.berkeley.edu/tutorials/seo-search-engine-optimization-basics.

For HTML tutorials and other Web-building resources, consult the World Wide Web Consortium (W3C), an international standards organization for Web development: http://www.w3.org.

• EXERCISE 1 •

A version of this story ran in *The State* newspaper of Columbia, S.C. Your task is to read the story and write a series of heds for it.

For Sarah Sheely and the dwindling thousands like her, the never-ending quest for Tab just turned closer to impossible.

Tab, once the nation's best-selling low-calorie soda, has vanished from the Columbia metro area.

Coca-Cola Consolidated of Charlotte quietly stopped selling Tab last month in its 12-state selling territory.

"It's a quality issue," spokeswoman Alison Patint said. "We have such low demand, it's hard to keep fresh product on the shelves."

Supplies won't be replaced as they dry up, she said.

Many of the few remaining Tab drinkers may not even know it's gone, since they've long lived with the here-today, gone-tomorrow nature of Tab on store shelves.

"It's really upsetting," Sheely said as she sipped a Tab during lunch Monday at Nursery Road Elementary School. "Tab is almost an addiction for the people who drink it."

Sheely became hooked as a teen-ager in the 1960s, a few years after Tab's 1963 debut and its groovy "Keep Tabs on your calories with Tab" slogan.

Coke began to ignore Tab after the 1982 arrival of Diet Coke. Coke franchisers decide what to sell in their territories, and many dropped Tab.

"It gets expensive and inefficient to manufacture and market and distribute a product that few people are buying," said *Beverage Digest* editor John Sicher, who collects "Tab-is-gone" stories nationwide.

In 1999, Coke shipped 4.6 million cases of Tab and 843 million cases of Diet Coke. While Diet Coke sales jumped 24 percent in the 1990s, Tab sales slid almost 75 percent.

"Diet Coke is the mega-brand," Sicher said. "Tab is out there on the fringe."

But that fringe group—mostly over–30 women—never stopped thirsting for it. "Tab has an intensely loyal following, albeit tiny," he said. "It's not exactly easy to find."

Tab fans who can find it have developed an informal code to help themselves and keep the brand alive.

"If you go to a store and see a six-pack, you buy it whether you need it or not to let the store know that people need it," Sheely said. "If it's not there, you tell the manager that you want it.

"But you leave one six-pack for the next desperate Tab drinker. There's honor among us."

a. Go through the story and pick out the key words. Then use those key words to write a declarative sentence below that can be the basis of a "straight news" headline.

b. Write a list of the puns, plays on words, twists of phrases, alliterations, and other techniques that could work with a feature-focused hed.

c. Write that "straight news" headline.
   • If using design software: write a 2-36-2 hed in Arial.
   • If not using design software: write a two-line hed in which each line has a count of 20 (give or take two counts on each line).

d. Write a more feature-focused headline, focusing on delivering the news to readers. Make sure the subhed and hed don't parrot by using the same words.

- If using design software: write a 3-60-1 hammerhead in Arial, with a subhed of 3-30-1 Arial italic.
- If not using design software: Write a hammer with a count of up to 13. You have up to 27 counts for the bottom deck.

e. Write another feature-focused headline with a kicker, but take a different angle not used in the first two heds.

- If using design software: write a kicker that's in 24 point Arial italic, less than five columns. The main hed is 5-48-1 Arial.
- If not using design software: write a kicker that's a count of up to 45. The main hed has a count of up to 25.

f. Write a hed that is optimized for Web search engines.

• EXERCISE 2 •

Compare the heds published in *USA Today* with the heds published in your campus newspaper. Write answers to the questions below.

1. Which has better heds? Why?

2. What could *USA Today*'s editors teach your paper's staff about writing better heds?

3. Could your paper's staff teach *USA Today* anything about writing heds for a younger generation?

Six

Typography Then and Now

Jim R. Martin

Typography concerns the design, arrangement, placement, and usage of machine-printed type. Despite the revolution in computer and printing technology, editors still realize their basic tool is the same as it has been for five hundred years: words. Even in today's profusely illustrated publications and online features, type usually dominates. And the typeface one chooses can profoundly affect the design of a publication. Although the notion of mechanical printing predates Johannes Gutenberg by at least six centuries, for all intents and purposes the history of typography begins with the German goldsmith's perfection of the letterpress around 1450. Gutenberg's invention was so well conceived that it remained the principal method of printing for more than 400 years.

Gutenberg's process for printing from movable type brought together four skills: chemistry, metallurgy, calligraphy and engraving. The key to the system was metal type.

Gutenberg used steel punches and brass molds to cast individual letters from an alloy of lead, tin and antimony. Each character was cast hundreds of times as a separate block. The thousands of individual letters were assembled into pages. After printing, the pages could be disassembled and the type cleaned and reused. The type came to be stored in compartmentalized storage cases—capital letters in an upper case and small letters in a lower case—and pulled out letter by letter to set the lines. Gutenberg also had to develop a method of holding the type in place for printing, a slow-drying ink tacky enough to adhere evenly to the metal type, and a press capable of forcing the paper down onto the type for an even impression. Gutenberg modeled his printing press after the wine and cheese presses in use at the time and formulated a linseed oil-based ink, using lead and copper compounds for pigment.

The 42-line Bible

Bringing all the elements together, Gutenberg began working on his now-famous Latin Bible. The pages of the two-volume folio-sized (11.75 × 15 inches) Bible were printed in two columns. The first nine pages had 40 lines per column, the tenth page had 41 and the remaining 1,275-plus pages had 42 lines per column. This change may have been based on the layout of the manuscript he followed, or he may have started a 40-line book and increased the number of lines per column to save time and paper. Forty-eight copies of this landmark publication, out of an estimated press run of about two hundred, are known still to exist. One can be seen at the Library of Congress. Another is housed at the New York City Public Library. Gutenberg's 42-line Bible remains a magnificent example of the printer's art.

Development of the printing process and printing the 42-line Bible were expensive. Over a period of years Gutenberg borrowed money from relatives and a considerable sum from wealthy Mainz merchant Johann Fust, putting his printing equipment up as collateral. In 1455, just as the printing neared completion, Fust foreclosed on Gutenberg for nonpayment and seized possession of the equipment and all work in progress. Fust then hired Gutenberg's chief assistant (and Fust's son-in-law), Peter Schoeffer, to finish production. It is unknown whether Gutenberg had any further hand in completing the project or reaped any financial benefits from his work. But his invention soon spread throughout Europe. It is estimated that by the year 1500 more than 1,000 printers operated out of some 200 locations in Europe. The basic printing process remained little changed for the next 400 years.

Typography, on the other hand, began to change almost immediately. Gutenberg's heavy Textura (blackletter) typeface was quickly eclipsed by more graceful, easier-to-read letterforms.

The development of typography

The 42-line Bible was designed and printed to look like a handwritten manuscript. According to early accounts, Fust tried to sell the Bibles as hand-copied originals before being found out in Paris. But during the first fifty years of printing, the so-called *incunabula* period (1450–1500), typographers such as Erhard Ratdolt and Claude Garamond started moving type design away from its dependence on calligraphic models to letterforms more in accordance with metal type and the technical possibilities of printing.

According to the best estimates, more than 10,000 different typefaces have been created since Gutenberg. Many of them are quite similar; others differ greatly. Early on, printers began to experiment with the size, shape, weight, and spacing of the letters (Figure 1). In particular, they produced typefaces with variations in:

- *Letterstrokes*, the lines that are drawn to form the letters. These can vary from hairline to quite thick or can be monotonal, with little or no variation at all.
- *Serifs*, the finishing strokes at the end of a letter's main stroke. Serifs can be rounded or flat, straight or cupped, bracketed or unbracketed.
- *Finials and terminals*, the final or ending stroke forming a hook or a ball that is attached to some curved letterforms

- *Counters*, the enclosed or partially enclosed white space within letters
- *Ascenders and descenders*, the strokes that rise above or go below the main body of some lowercase letters such as *b* and *h* and *p* and *y*. No uppercase letters have ascenders and the *Q* is the only uppercase letter with a descender.
- *X-height*, the height of the body of lowercase letters in proportion to the ascenders and descenders. The measure is actually based on the letter *x*.

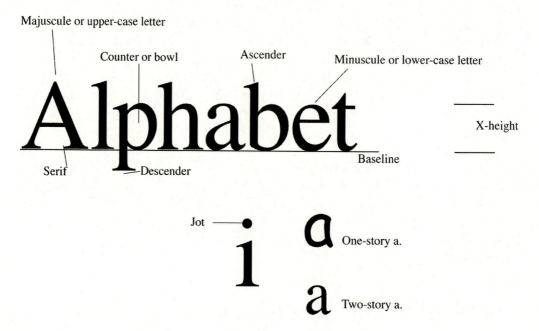

Figure 1. Type anatomy

Letterforms also vary in *posture*— whether the letter sits straight or leans; *weight*, which can range from light to extrabold; and *width*, which can expand or condense a standard shape. Over the centuries, typographers have tried in several ways to classify the multitudes of type designs. Perhaps the most common is to group typefaces according to common characteristics into races, subgroups, families, and fonts. Type dramatically sets the personality of a publication or website, and so needs to be understood by editors working in design and makeup.

Races of type

Blackletter

Gutenberg modeled his first typeface after the calligraphy of the local German monks. The race of type that developed from Gutenberg's first font is known as "blackletter" because of the heavy, compact strokes of the letters. This race is also known as "text" because of its early association with the text or body copy of printed books.

A roman typeface (Garamond old style)

A sans serif typeface (Helvetica)

An Egyptian typeface (Stymie condensed)

A script typeface (Edwardian script)

A blackletter typeface (Old English)

`A monospaced font (Courier)`

Dingbats (Zapf dingbats):

❀☐☆❋❄❊➡➹⑩❈☞✝★✩✛✫❁✂✄

Figure 2. Races of type

Today it is sometimes referred to as "Old English," although old English is actually a particular typeface of the blackletter race, and not a race itself.

The faces in this race feature pointed letters that look as if they were drawn with a broad-nibbed pen. The vertical stems are tightly spaced with pronounced stroke contrast. The terminals often have diamond-shaped finishing strokes. Because of the centuries of tradition associated with this race, many newspapers still use blackletter type for their nameplates.

Roman

Gutenberg purposely designed his type to look like the hand lettering it replaced. But within 20 years printing had expanded south to Italy, and there a new race of type soon developed that has remained dominant through five centuries. In the spirit of the Renaissance, Italian printers moved away from handwriting as a model toward the simpler, more open letterforms chiseled on Roman buildings. The first truly successful

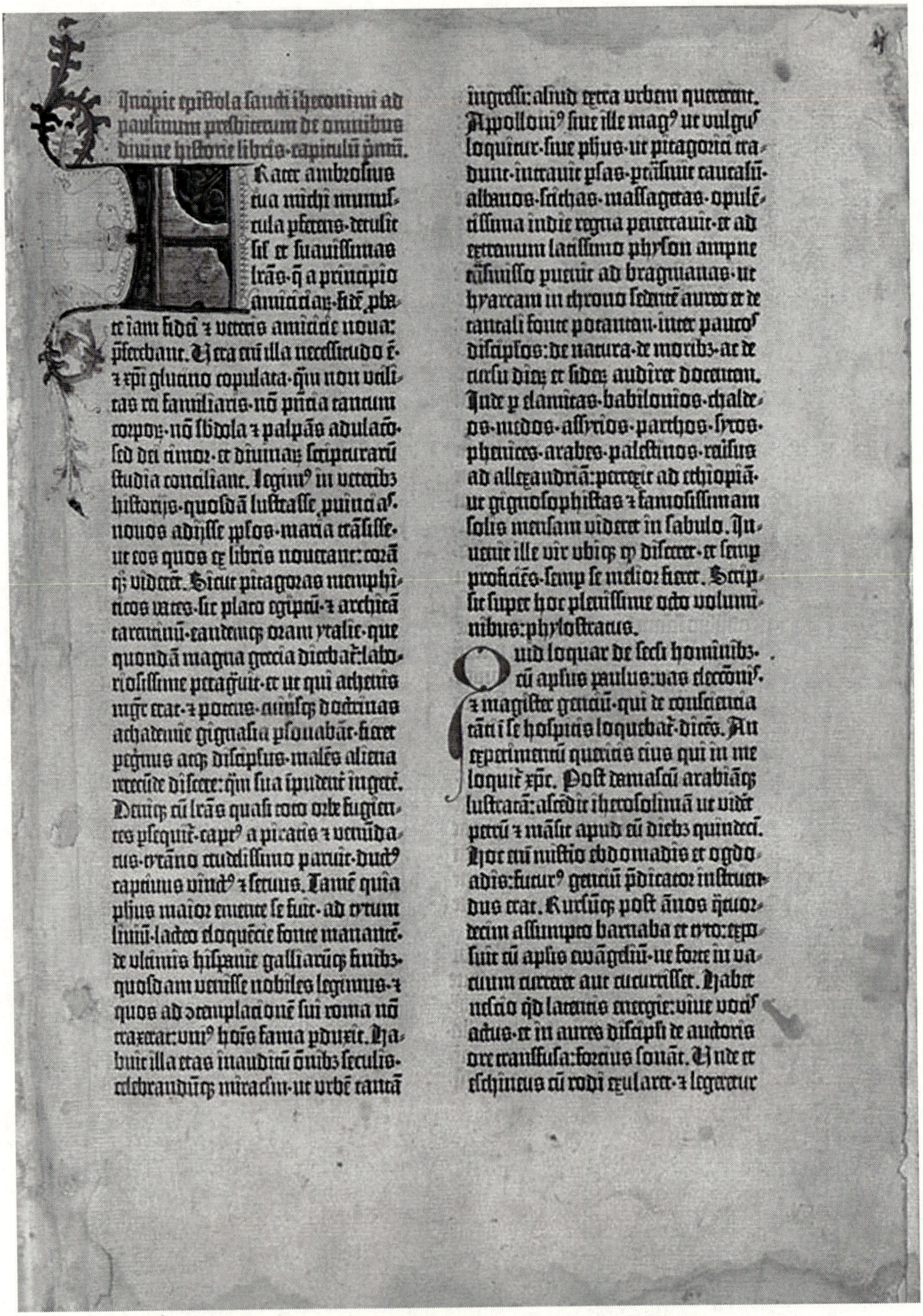

Incipit epistola sancti iheronimi ad
paulinum presbiterum de omnibus
divine historie libris-capitulu pmu.

F rater ambrosius
tua michi munus-
cula pferens-detulit
sil et suavissimas
lras-q a principio
amicicias-fide pba-
te iam fidei et veteris amicicie noua:
pferebant. Vera eni illa necessitudo e-
et xpi glutino copulata-qm non utili-
tas rei familiaris-no pntia tantum
corpou-no subdola et palpas adulacio-
sed dei timor-et divinaru scripturaru
studia conciliant. Legim⁹ in veteribus
historijs-quosda lustrasse puincias-
novos adijsse pplos-maria transisse-
ut eos quos ex libris noverant: cora
q videret. Sicut pitagoras memphi-
ticos vates-sic plato egiptu-et archita
tarentinu-eandemq oram ytalie-que
quonda magna grecia dicebat: labo-
riosissime peragravit-et ut qui athenis
mgr erat-et potens-cuiusq doctrinas
achademie gignasia psonabat-fieret
peregrinus atq discipulus-malens aliena
verecunde discere: qm sua ipudenter ingere.
Denique cu lras quasi toto orbe fugien-
tes psequit-capt⁹ a piratis et venunda-
tus-tyranno crudelissimo paruit-duct⁹
captivus vinct⁹ et servus. Tame quia
phus maior emente se fuit-ad titum
livium lacteo eloquencie fonte manante-
de ultimis hispanie galliarumq finibs-
quosdam venisse nobiles legimus-et
quos ad contemplacione sui roma no
traxerat: unius hois fama pduxit. Ha-
buit illa etas inauditu omnibs seculis-
celebrandumq miraculu-ut urbe tanta
ingressi: aliud extra urbem quererent.
Apollonius sive ille mag⁹ ut vulgus
loquitur-sive phus-ut pitagorici tra-
dunt-intravit psas-ptransivit caucasu-
albanos-scithas-massagetas-opule-
tissima indie regna penetravit-et ad
extremum latissimo phison amne
transmisso pervenit ad bragmanas-ut
hyarcam in throno sedente aureo et de
tantali fonte potantem-inter paucos
discipulos: de natura-de moribs-ac de
cursu dierum et siderum audiret docentem.
Inde p elamitas-babilonios-chalde-
os-medos-assyrios-parthos-syros-
phenices-arabes-palestinos-reversus
ad alexandriam: perrexit ad ethiopia-
ut gignosophistas et famosissimam
solis mensam videret in sabulo. In-
venit ille vir ubiq qd disceret-et semp
proficiens-semp se melior fieret. Scrip-
sit super hoc plenissime octo volumi-
nibus: phylostratus.
Quid loquar de seculi hominibs-
cu apostolus paulus: vas electionis-
et magister gentium-qui de consciencia
tanti in se hospitis loquebat dicens. An
experimentu queritis eius qui in me
loquit xps. Post damascu arabiamq
lustrata: ascendit iherosolima ut videret
petru et mansit apud eu diebs quindecim.
Hoc eni misterio ebdomadis et ogdo-
adis: futur⁹ gentiu pdicator instruen-
dus erat. Rursumq post annos quatuor-
decim assumpto barnaba et tyto: exp-
suit cu aplis evangeliu-ne forte in vacuum curreret aut cucurrisset. Habet
nescio qd latentis energie: vive vocis
actus-et in aures discipli de auctoris
ore transfusa: fortius sonat. Unde et
eschinus cu rodi exularet-et legeretur

Page from Gutenberg Bible using blackletter type

roman typeface was introduced in 1470 by Nicholas Jenson, a French-born Venetian publisher and printer. Jenson's roman face was refined by fellow Venetian publisher Aldus Manutius, and his typographer Francesco Griffo. Griffo also produced the first italic typeface, although his design had only lower case letters set with regular roman capitals. Matching italic capitals were added by another Venetian printer in 1524. The influence of Venetian printers soon made roman type dominant in all Europe outside the German-speaking areas. Development has continued through the generations, with the romans still the most numerous typefaces by far, and the most popular for text type. Most books, nearly all newspapers and at least half of all magazines use roman typestyles for body copy. One of the most popular is Times New Roman, designed in 1931 under the direction of Stanley Morison. It was designed for the exclusive use of the *Times* of London, but was released for general sale a year later. It has become one of the most widely used typefaces in the English-speaking world, not only by newspapers, but by book and magazine publishers, advertisers and printers. Its popularity seems based not so much on its design — its fine serifs ironically do not reproduce well on low-quality newsprint — but because it was adapted as the default font in common word processing programs.

Roman types are defined by contrasting thick and thin strokes and the presence of a finishing stroke or serif at the end of the major stem and hairline strokes. Because these faces are so profuse and so varied, they are usually divided into subgroups based on three characteristics: *contrast* in the thickness of letter strokes; *stress*— the angle or axis of the curves; and *serif treatment.* "Old face" or "old style" types feature strokes that make a gentle transition from thick to thin. Serifs are bracketed or molded into the terminals of the main strokes. The serifs of the ascenders in the lowercase slant, and at the bottom of the uppercase E and top of the uppercase T, extend outward. The axis of the curves is inclined to the left. Modern romans were popularized by Giambattista Bodoni, a renowned Italian type designer and friend of Benjamin Franklin, after their prototypes were introduced by French typographers in the late 1700s. In the moderns, the last vestiges of type's origin as hand-written letterforms disappeared. Rather, these faces have a distinct mechanical look reflecting a strict emphasis on form and structure. These faces have a strong contrast between thick and thin strokes. Serifs are straight, thin and unbracketed. The serifs on the lowercase ascenders are horizontal. Stress is vertical.

Many designs fall somewhere between old style and modern with characteristics of both. Contrast between thick and thin strokes is more pronounced in old style than modern. Old-style serifs are bracketed and those of the lowercase ascenders are oblique, but the slant is not as steep in modern as old style. These faces are known as transitional roman.

Some typographers would classify italic typefaces as a separate race, but it seems better to look at them as roman. Like the romans, they have strokes of various thicknesses. They have serifs or curved finishing strokes called *finials.* Their letter shapes correspond to their companion roman face. Their most striking difference is their slant to the right.

Romans come in every weight and size and are suitable for almost any application.

Sans Serif

Second only to romans in number and frequency of use are sans serif faces. "Sans" means "without" in French, and as the name implies, none of the members of this large race of type has serifs of any kind. Their variety comes from variations in stroke thickness and weight differences. Modeled after the flat, uniform strokes of ancient Greek letters, the first recorded sans serif typeface was introduced in 1816, but the designation sans serif was not applied until 1832. They had become very popular by the mid–1800s. Their stature was propelled further a century later by the German Bauhaus Institute, which emphasized functional design in furniture, architecture, product design and typography. In the last half century their popularity has increased to the point that today the use of sans serif faces rivals that of romans.

Sans serifs can be divided into two easily distinguishable subgroups: monolines and gothics. Monolines, sometimes called true sans serifs, have little or no variation in the thickness of strokes. They are geometric, precise and elegant. Their letterforms are round and lightweight as compared to gothics. Gothics have some variation in the letter strokes, although the contrast is not as apparent as in romans. Thickness variations are often found where curved and stem strokes connect, causing them to look somewhat less graceful than their monotonal counterparts.

At one time most newspapers set their headlines in a roman typeface, but now more than half use sans serif or a combination of serif and sans serif. The switch to sans serif for body type, however, has not been as pronounced. Roman typefaces are less monotonous and are considered easier to read than sans serif faces. Most newspapers still use them for text type. But sans serifs play an increasingly important role in advertising, magazines, newsletters, consumer product labeling and Web design.

Square serif or Egyptian

About the same time as William Caslon IV launched sans serif type in the early nineteenth century, a fourth race of type was introduced by another English type foundry, the Vincent Figgins Foundry in London. The first of the square serif faces (also called slab serif) was listed in the catalog as "Egyptian," and the name stuck. There was a great fascination at the time, both in England and America, with all things Egyptian, intensified by Napoleon's invasion and occupation of Egypt in 1798–99, and the discovery of the Rosetta Stone in 1799. This tablet of black basalt had parallel inscriptions in Greek and Egyptian hieroglyphic characters that provided the key to deciphering the ancient Egyptian writing. Whether Figgins wanted the shape of his letters to call to mind Egyptian architecture or to suggest the visual qualities of popular Egyptian artifacts, the race became associated with the tremendous interest in Egyptian culture.

Egyptian faces are also called "square serifs," "slab serifs" and "antiques," but the

Egyptian designation is the most prevalent, leading to names of individual typefaces such as Cairo, Karnak and Memphis.

Egyptian faces are characterized by pronounced square or rectangular serifs, uniform stroke formation and short ascenders and descenders. Serifs vary from tall serifs thicker than the stem strokes of the letters, to monoline types with little or no contrast between the serif and letter thickness, to more moderate serifs that contrast with stroke thickness.

The Egyptian faces were designed for advertising rather than for books or newspapers. Some designers feel they are monotonous and tiring when used for body copy but work well for headings and headlines. In the mid–1800s they were used extensively for theatrical posters in large sizes, often from wooden rather than metal type. Since then, they have gone through several periods of decline and revival. Today they are popular for newspaper and magazine ads, especially for reverses, white lettering on a dark background, and surprints, copy that is printed over photographic illustrations.

Hand-formed

With scripts and cursives, typography comes full circle. These forms are designed, as was Gutenberg's first typeface, to resemble handwriting. They are meant to emulate letters written with hand-held instruments—first quill pens, then fountain pens, brushes, broad-nibbed lettering pens or felt-tip markers. Together, scripts and cursives make up the hand-formed race, sometimes shortened to "hands."

Script letters generally slant to the right, and the lowercase letters connect or appear to connect. The capitals are graceful and flowing and can stand alone without connecting to the lowercase letters. Cursives also slant like handwriting, but neither the upper nor lower case letters connect. Cursive faces often include flourished capitals and may also include some alternate lowercase characters. Cursives are sometimes confused with roman italics, but italic typefaces have serifs that cursives do not. Some typographers refer to all hand-formed faces as "scripts"—those with connecting letters as "formal scripts," and those with letters that do not connect as "informal scripts."

Hand-formed faces, both scripts and cursives, have proliferated since the 1930s, but only a few examples produced before that time are still in use. These faces are much more difficult to read than serif or sans serif faces. Newspapers and magazines occasionally use them for titles, headings and subheads. Their more common use is for announcements, invitations, letterheads and in retail advertising.

Decorative

Gutenberg's 42-line Bible had blank spaces left for decorative initials to be drawn in later by a scribe. Soon afterward, printers were using two-part blocks to stamp in highly ornate capitals after the text was printed. From there it was but a short step for typographers to "embellish" existing, identifiable letterforms.

Actually this sixth race is not a race at all. Rather, it is a catchall category for the great number of miscellaneous designs that do not have the distinctive characteristics of the other races. Also known as "novelty," "specialty," "ornamental," or "mood," this category includes standard forms that have been modified with outlines, inlines, shadows and textures; faces that have been decorated with flowers, leaves or other designs; and specially created faces with letters fashioned from natural forms such as paper clips, wooden logs or smoke.

These faces are rarely used in news typography. In other places they are attention grabbers used almost exclusively for display type expressing ideas in a few words.

Interstate highway signs. Substituting Times New Roman, a serif typeface in the second example, does not work well for signage, words that must be read quickly.

How to choose typefaces

Text dominates most publications and websites. Yet many editors and graphic designers seldom stop to seriously consider their choice of body text. That choice can make a dramatic difference (Figure 3). Imagine an Interstate highway sign in Times New Roman. This serif face looks oddly ornate in signage designed to convey simple information as clearly and quickly as possible. On the other hand, a history textbook would seem peculiar set in Helvetica, an informal sans serif face.

Roman typefaces are considered graceful, austere, a voice of authority.

Old style roman faces such as Garamond and Caslon may have been designed centuries ago but still are in common use today for their dignity, trustworthy feeling and easy readability.

Modern roman faces such as Bodoni convey a dressy, formal, scientific feeling.

Sans serif faces such as Helvetica, Futura and Arial are contemporary, efficient and informal.

Egyptian faces such as Clarendon and Rockwell tend to be loud and persistent. In headlines they shout; in body text they are seldom used, although some designers are revisiting them as an interesting alternative to overused fonts. Clarendon was popular in the 1920s, and so it tends to reflect that era.

Script and decorative fonts see use mostly in advertising or announcements, sometimes in headlines, but can easily become typographic clichés. Be careful not to overuse such clichés as a blackletter font for stories about Germany, a bamboo font for stories about China, or a stars-and-stripes font for stories about Independence Day. Courier is a commonly seen slab-serif style typeface designed to look like a typewritten page. As a monospaced font, each letter takes up the same amount of horizontal space, in contrast to proportional fonts, the space of each letter calculated by a type designer to enhance readability. Courier is seldom an editor's choice today, except for special emphasis.

Families and fonts

Within races and subgroups are individual typefaces. Most have a number of closely related faces, similar in design but varying in posture, weight, or style. The collection of related designs all bear the name of their parent typeface and are known as *families*. A *font* consists of the upper and lowercase alphabet, numbers, punctuation marks and symbols in any one size of a particular typeface.

Before computerization, each font of a typeface had to be cast separately, and many faces were available in fewer than a dozen standard sizes.

Measurement was not standardized until the late 1800s, when the U.S. Type Founders group adopted the point system.

This American point system, used to measure type in *points* and *picas*, has now been the United States standard for more than a century. It is based on a system originated by French typographer Pierre Fournier in 1737 and modified by another Frenchman, Firmin Didot, in 1785.

6 pt.

8 pt.

12 pt.

18 pt.

24 pt.

36 pt.

48 pt.

72 pt.

Various point sizes

The system is based on the *pica*, a unit of measurement equal to approximately ⅙ of an inch and divided into 12 points, each point being approximately ¹⁄₇₂ of an inch. The actual measurement for a point is 0.0138 inch and for six picas is 0.9962 inch. But practically speaking we count six picas to an inch, 12 points to a pica and so 72 points to an inch.

In the days of metal type there were 16 major point sizes: 6, 7, 8, 9, 10, 11, 12, 14, 18, 24, 30, 36, 42, 48, 60 and 72. Today digital composition allows an unlimited range of point sizes, including such non-standard sizes as 17.5-point or 41.33-point. But just because such variations are possible doesn't mean using them is a good idea. Except in unusual circumstances, the editor would do well to stay with standard point sizes.

Type that is smaller than 14-point is normally used to set paragraphs of text and is known as *text type* or *body type*. Headlines, titles, subheads and ads are generally set in type sizes 14-point and larger, known as *display type*. The width of *rules* (straight lines of various thicknesses) and *borders* (decorative frames around graphics) as well as the space between lines are also measured in points.

The point size of a line of type cannot be determined by measuring any one individual letter. To get a workable reading, the type must be measured from the top of the ascenders to the bottom of the descenders, in other words from cap line to drop line. And point size alone is not a true indicator of the size of the typeface. This is because the average (or mean) size of the body, or main element of the lowercase letterform in relation to the ascenders and descenders, varies from one typeface to the next. The height of the lowercase letters exclusive of ascenders and descenders is referred to as the *x-height*. Typefaces with large x-heights are said to be "big on the body" and those with small x-heights are said to be "small on the body." Typefaces of the same point size may appear larger or smaller on the page because of different x-heights. It is the x-height, not the point size, that conveys the visual impression of the size of the typeface.

Also important to the look of type on the page are three horizontal measurements: the space required for individual letters, the space between letters and the space between words. As with x-height, *set width*—also called *set size* or simply *set*—the width of the letters themselves and the optimal space between the letters, differs from typeface to typeface. Of course the width of individual letters varies in all typefaces, with *M* and *W* being the widest, *I* being the narrowest and *X* being average. Set width is based on a unit system. The two-dimensional square of the point size—the *em*—is divided into a number of units. As the name implies, an em is about as wide as an uppercase M. So an em space in 12-point type is 12 points tall and 12 points wide. A 24-point em is 24 points tall and 24 points wide. Set width varies with x-height; it varies markedly from race to race; and it changes drastically when letterforms are expanded or condensed.

Set width is also affected by the amount of space between individual letters. Digital typesetting makes it easy to increase or decrease spacing between letters (called *letterspacing* or *tracking*) and between words (called *wordspacing*). Letterspacing is based on the unit

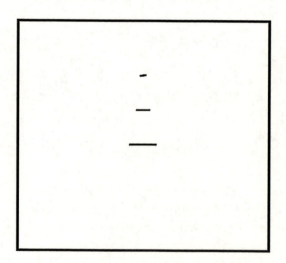

Hyphen, en-dash, em-dash in Garamond.

system, but wordspacing is based on another way of dividing the em. Even though metal type is no longer used, the terminology remains. The em (or "mut") is used to indicate paragraph indentions. Half an em is an *en* or "nut." The traditional space between words was a third of an em, referred to as a "thick space" or 3-to-the-em space, often somewhat confusingly abbreviated as "a 3-em space." A 4-to-the-em or "middle space" brings words a little closer together. A "thin space" is one fifth of an em or 5-to-an-em (5-em). One sixth an em is a "hair." For most typefaces the thin space and the hair do not provide enough space between words for the lines to be legible.

Another consideration that affects the look of type on the page is the space between the lines. This space is called *leading* (rhymes with "sledding") after the lead strips that were used to separate lines of metal type. A more modern synonym is *linespacing*. Leading is measured from baseline to baseline. When there is no extra space between lines,

Photography's roots reach back more than 150 years, with the unveiling of the Daguerreotype in France. While people had for centuries understood the principle behind the camera lens, and for many decades knew that certain chemicals were sensitive to light, these ideas were not combined into photography until much later. Nicephore Niepce in France did come up with a permanent picture (he called it a "heliograph") in the 1820s, but the first practical photography was Daguerre's highly-detailed image on a silver-coated copper plate. Daguerreotypes became the rage in Europe, and in America only a year later, introduced by Samuel Morse. (He also invented the telegraph.) Artists worried that this process designed originally as an aid to painting would destroy their livelihood. In response they turned away from realism into impressionism and other approaches—realism had been won by a picture-taking machine.

Garamond

Photography's roots reach back more than 150 years, with the unveiling of the Daguerreotype in France. While people had for centuries understood the principle behind the camera lens, and for many decades knew that certain chemicals were sensitive to light, these ideas were not combined into photography until much later. Nicephore Niepce in France did come up with a permanent picture (he called it a "heliograph") in the 1820s, but the first practical photography was Daguerre's highly-detailed image on a silver-coated copper plate. Daguerreotypes became the rage in Europe, and in America only a year later, introduced by Samuel Morse. (He also invented the telegraph.) Artists worried that this process designed originally as an aid to painting would destroy their livelihood. In response they turned away from realism into impressionism and other approaches—realism had been won by a picture-taking machine.

Bodoni

Photography's roots reach back more than 150 years, with the unveiling of the Daguerreotype in France. While people had for centuries understood the principle behind the camera lens, and for many decades knew that certain chemicals were sensitive to light, these ideas were not combined into photography until much later. Nicephore Niepce in France did come up with a permanent picture (he called it a "heliograph") in the 1820s, but the first practical photography was Daguerre's highly-detailed image on a silver-coated copper plate. Daguerreotypes became the rage in Europe, and in America only a year later, introduced by Samuel Morse. (He also invented the telegraph.) Artists worried that this process designed originally as an aid to painting would destroy their livelihood. In response they turned away from realism into impressionism and other approaches—realism had been won by a picture-taking machine.

Helvetica

Photography's roots reach back more than 150 years, with the unveiling of the Daguerreotype in France. While people had for centuries understood the principle behind the camera lens, and for many decades knew that certain chemicals were sensitive to light, these ideas were not combined into photography until much later. Nicephore Niepce in France did come up with a permanent picture (he called it a "heliograph") in the 1820s, but the first practical photography was Daguerre's highly-detailed image on a silver-coated copper plate. Daguerreotypes became the rage in Europe, and in America only a year later, introduced by Samuel Morse. (He also invented the telegraph.) Artists worried that this process designed originally as an aid to painting would destroy their livelihood. In response they turned away from realism into impressionism and other approaches—realism had been won by a picture-taking machine.

Rockwell

Four comparative typefaces. All are set the same point size, justified, with the same amount of leading between lines.

TYPE TALK: ITALIC

This slanted version of roman typefaces dates nearly to the beginning of movable type. As Venice became a center of early printing around 1500, designers reached back more than three centuries to the early medieval "humanistic hand" as a basis for typefaces reflecting a Renaissance spirit. Aldus Manutius' workshop is credited with inventing a slanted, handwritten style possibly to squeeze more text onto the costly rag-based paper. Sixteenth-century books commonly were printed in italic.

Today we avoid italics for entire pages, but keep the face on hand for emphasizing a few words. Newspaper editors using AP style do not rely on italics for titles, but editors working in many other genres do. It is grammatically correct to italicize book, magazine and newspaper titles; movie and art titles; proper names of trains and ships; foreign phrases. Italic is a font designed for a particular serif typeface. It is not simply a slanted alphabet, called "faux italics." It also is not part of sans-serif typefaces; slanted sans faces are called oblique and, in contrast to the designed italic, are simply slanted versions of a regular face.

the ascenders on one line nearly touch the descenders on the previous line. This is called "setting solid." Adding more space, or leading, between the lines does not affect type size, set width or line length. It simply moves the lines farther apart. But it does affect — greatly — the overall appearance of the printed piece. Of course the smaller the type size, the less leading needed. Eight-point type set on a 9-point line (called 8 on 9 and abbreviated 8/9) has one point of leading. Ten-point type set on a 12-point line (10/12) has two points leading. To double space, 10-point type would have to be set on a 20-point line; 12-point type would have to be set on a 24-point line. For a long time, a ratio of about 120 percent was considered standard, 10 on 12, for example. Many typesetting programs still default to that ratio, but the modern trend is to use slightly less leading.

A final consideration is line length and line arrangement. Lines can be arranged on a page in several ways: justified; unjustified, flush left, ragged right; unjustified, flush right, ragged left; centered; staggered or arranged asymmetrically. Lines can also be run around a photo or graphic in a right- or left-angle wrap or contoured around irregularly shaped art.

Staggered type is rarely used except for poetry and other specialized applications. *Asymmetrical* arrangement — no predictable pattern in the placement of lines—can be difficult to read and is usually reserved for ads, posters, book jackets, etc., where attracting attention is a major objective. A *centered* arrangement has lines of unequal lengths with both sides ragged. *Justified* copy has all the lines the same length and aligned on both the left and the right. *Unjustified* copy has the lines aligned on the left and ragged on the right or aligned on the right and ragged on the left.

Justification is accomplished using hyphenation and by adding small amounts of extra space between words to make the lines come out even. This arrangement is easy

---

TYPE TALK: FIVE TYPOGRAPHIC PITFALLS

Editors of many publications, websites or agencies often need to consider choice of typeface and type conventions. Professionally produced media stand out from amateur productions in their attention to detail—and professionalism begins with typography. Here are five common typographic mistakes, and how to avoid them.

1. Typewriter habits. One might think we'd have forgotten all about the clanky old typewriter, but not so, considering manuscript material that still relies on typewriter conventions such as:

- Two spaces after each sentence. One space is standard in published material.
- "Rabbit-ear" or "dumb" quotation marks and apostrophes. Professional typographers substitute these marks with "curly-cue" or "smart" quotes designed for the typeface.
- Two hyphens (or single hyphen) for dash. The em-dash (keystroke: shift-option-hyphen) is correct when indicating emphasis—like this. Between time and date expressions, an en-dash (keystroke: option-hyphen) is correct, such as 8–5. A hyphen separates syllables in words breaking to the next line of text.
- Open single quote (') in decade expressions, such as the '90s. Note the closed single quote, or apostrophe, should be used in these expressions (keystroke: option-shift-]).

2. Same typeface for body text and headlines. Choose a different race for each, to bring contrast into the design.

3. Widows and orphans. A widow is a single word at the bottom of a page, ending a paragraph; an orphan is a single word at the top. Adjust design to avoid these unattractive lines, if possible.

4. Overused typefaces, particularly Times, Times New Roman, and Helvetica.

5. Using typefaces designed for print on Web pages. Fonts designed for the Web are more readable on a computer screen. Two popular choices are Verdana for sans serif and Georgia for serif. Times and Times New Roman are common but less readable choices.

---

to read and gives structure to the page. But if the columns are narrow, editors run a risk of too much variation in word spacing, resulting in "rivers of white" running down the column.

Flush left/ragged right copy eliminates this problem. Lines are of different lengths, so spacing between words is uniform and there is no need for hyphenation. It produces a more informal appearance, but requires more space than justified text for the same number of words. Also, the loss of structure in unjustified copy can be disconcerting to readers. To offset a disruptive layout, vertical lines called *column rules* are often placed between columns to regain structure. Another possibility is to add an extra linespace between paragraphs and omit paragraph indentions.

Line length is also important. Line arrangement, word spacing, leading, the race

TYPE TALK: READABILITY STUDIES

Researchers have studied readability of text for more than a century, trying to establish formulas and principles to help make text as accessible as possible. Editors need to be concerned about *readability*—how the style of writing affects comprehension—but also about *legibility*—how the use of type affects comprehension. Choice of words and sentence structure affect readability. Studies of American adults' ability to read reach back to World War I.

A more recent literacy project was undertaken by the U.S. Department of Education in 1993; statistics from that year showed the 23 percent of the 191 million adults in the country were not able to read beyond basic uncomplicated texts such as flyers or brief news articles. Another 25 to 28 percent could read only simple texts. Editors need to realize that many readers may not be able to understand the more sophisticated journalism that quality news operations generally try to provide.

Comprehension can be enhanced by choice of typeface. A typeface may be legible but not readable. For example, a blackletter face such as Old English can display clean, sharp letterforms—high legibility on paper. But it is hard to comprehend, so not very readable. The typeface, its point size, its column width and its leading all contribute to readability. Editors who do not consider readability in both design and content risk losing readers.

of type, the typeface and especially the type size and x-height affect a proper line length. Copy that is set either too wide or too narrow can be difficult to read. Recommendations for optimum line length vary, but generally lines should be from 1½ to 2½ times the lowercase alphabet's length. Line length is measured in picas. Another way to estimate optimum line length is to multiply the type size (in points) by 1.5 to 3 to find a good line-length measurement. Average is 2.5. For example, a 15- to 30-pica line is fine for 10-point type. Twelve-point type requires a line length of between 18 and 36 picas.

As with all choices typographic—typeface, type size, word spacing, line arrangement and leading—editors also need to consider the esthetic dimension to line length. Some things are best done by feel. An editor who knows the rules will sense when they should be broken.

Typographical tips

1. For print publications, headlines should be set using display type—14-point and larger. Body type should be set using text type—type smaller than 14-point.

2. Headlines should get smaller as you work your way down the page.

3. Be sure the typefaces used for headlines reflect the tone and focus of the story. Do not use flippant or quirky faces over a story about a serious subject.

VOCABULARY AND JARGON FOR EDITORS

Bauhaus.

German Walter Gropius established the Bauhaus movement in Germany after World War I. Its goal was to eliminate the heavy ornamentation that had been characteristic of 19th-century design and instead adopt a simple approach, "form follows function." Sans-serif typography reflected the philosophy, as it is stripped of its ornamental serifs.

Folio.

The term dates from the dawn of printing, indicating a sheet folded in half. *Folio* today often refers to a large size book, but confusingly it has a second definition: page number. Folios on the recto (right-hand) pages are odd numbered; on the verso (left-hand) pages they are even numbered.

Fonts/typefaces.

Strictly speaking, a font (from *fount*, type cast in a metal type foundry) is one size, in one style, of one typeface. For example, 14-point Times boldface is one font; 18-point Times boldface is another font. Nowadays, however, most editors use the word "font" to mean "typeface" in all its measurements and variations.

H & J.

Hyphenation and Justification. Refers to the process of adding space between words, or hyphenating words, so that each line of type will reach to both the left and right edges of a column. Justified text used to be achieved by adding or subtracting pieces of metal between words; today it is calculated automatically by computer, but can be adjusted for the most attractive appearance based on font size and column width.

Interestingly, readers seldom notice the extensive variation in spacing between words that comes with justified text. Justified text looks more formal than unjustified (rag right).It also gives editors the opportunity to squeeze more words onto a page, as justified text reaches all the way to the right gutter.

Nib.

Scribes in the centuries before the invention of movable type copied manuscripts by hand using pens with flat ends, or *nibs*. As most scribes were right-handed, the nibs produced thin and thick areas on letters at a slight angle (oblique). Serifs had *brackets*, curves of ink attaching them to the body of the letter, based on the action of the nib pen. Variations between the thick and thin areas depended on the thickness of the nib. These features form the characteristics of old style roman typefaces still used today.

Variations.

Within a typeface may be a number of variations. Editors may choose variations to add contrast to a page. Common variations include light, boldface (bf), extrabold, italic (ital), condensed and expanded.

4. Body type (and normally display type as well) should be set in a roman or sans serif typeface. Save scripts and cursives, blackletter and specialty faces for emphasis and special occasions.

5. In general, romans are preferred for body type. A roman type exists to suit nearly every demand. A rule among old-time printers: "When in doubt, use Caslon." An exception to this rule is the Web. Studies seem to indicate a sans serif font is more readable on screen.

6. When hand-formed, blackletter or novelty typefaces are used, they should be set up and down (capitals and lowercase). Lines set in all caps in these races are difficult to read and esthetically unpleasant.

Accents:

é (acute)

è (grave)

ô (circumflex)

ü (diaresis)

ç (cedilla)

ñ (tilde)

Type accents set in Baskerville bf

7. Display type in roman, sans serif and square serif typefaces can be set in all caps occasionally but sparingly. Do not set entire paragraphs in all caps, no matter what race of type is used.

8. Do not use family variations such as italic, boldface, expanded or condensed type for a complete paragraph or an entire story. Save them for headlines, subheads and special emphasis.

9. Do not use too many typefaces on a single page. Mixing many font faces and styles looks gaudy and amateurish.

10. When using two typefaces together, make sure they are markedly different. Do not use two roman old styles, for example, or two square serifs—they do not offer enough contrast. Generally, stick to one serif font and one sans serif font.

11. It is important not to interrupt the reader when emphasizing a word or phrase. Italic type is probably least disruptive. Other possibilities for emphasis are boldface (bf), all caps, small caps, a different type size or even a different typeface. Normally, one choice is enough. Combinations such as all caps-boldface-italic are disruptive and look clumsy.

12. Do not use underlining for emphasis. Underlining is a substitute for italics in hand-written and typed copy. It can be used to indicate to the typesetter which words or phrases should be italicized. But in typeset copy it looks amateurish.

13. Initial letters and drop caps can spice up a layout. These large letters at the beginning of a paragraph are generally set bolder as well as bigger.

14. For maximum readability in most fonts, do not have more than 65 characters (two and one-half alphabets) or fewer than 26 characters (one alphabet) per line. Lines

running longer should be broken into two columns. On the other hand, justifying type in columns that are too narrow will result in "rivers of white," unpleasing gaps of unintentional white space running down the page.

15. As the length of the line is increased, leading should also be increased. Type with a large x-height needs more leading than the same size type with a smaller x-height.

16. Allow for plenty of white space. Ample white space helps the reader and gives the copy a clean, professional look. White space gives the eye a rest and calls attention to what it surrounds.

17. The indention of paragraphs should be in proportion to the width of the column. An em-space is enough for narrow lines. Longer lines may require an em-and-a-half or even a two-em space. Sometimes an extra line space can substitute for indention.

18. And while it has little to do with typography *per se*, never print anything without a quick spell check and a double check. This principle applies especially to headlines. A beautiful layout can be disgraced by a misspelled word or a typo. Well, there is a connection after all. "Typo" is short for typographical error.

Parts of this chapter are based on the author's article, "Typography," in C. H. Sterling, ed. *Encyclopedia of Journalism*. Thousand Oaks, CA.: Sage, 2009.

Know more

Arndur, D. A. (2007). *Typographic Design in the Digital Studio*. Clifton Park, NY: Thompson Delmar Learning.

Baines, P., and A. Haslam. (2005) *Type and Typography*, 2d ed. New York: Watson-Guptill.

Chappell, W., and R. Bringhurst. (1999). *A Short History of the Printed Word*, 2d ed. Point Roberts, WA: Hartley & Marks.

Craig, J., and B. Barton. (1987). *Thirty Centuries of Graphic Design*. New York: Watson-Guptill.

Meggs, P. B. (1998). *A History of Graphic Design*, 3rd ed. New York: John Wiley and Sons.

U.S. Department of Education, National Center for Education Statistics (1993). *Adult Literacy in America*. Washington, DC: GPO.

Williams, R. (2008) *The Non-Designer's Design Book*, 3d ed. Berkeley, CA: Peachpit.

Zapf, H. (1972). "The expression of our time in typography." In C. B. Grannis (ed.), *Heritage of the Graphic Arts*. New York: R.R. Bowker.

On the Web

You think type has little meaning in your life? Check out Helvetica: http://www.youtube.com/watch?v=LL60GEGjj_Q

Type anatomy and typographer's marks: http://www.ndsu.edu/pubweb/~rcollins/362design/typeanatomy.html.

Ten common typographic pitfalls: http://www.ndsu.edu/pubweb/~rcollins/362design/typepitfalls.html.

• EXERCISE 1 •

1. Prepare a brief type specimen chart using familiar typefaces available on your computer. Type the name of each typeface in 24-point and 36-point type. Type a sentence or saying in 12-point (use the same sentence for all the samples). Also in 12-point type, show variations in weight and posture. Sort the various typefaces by race. Example:

Times New Roman, 24-point

Times New Roman, 36-point

Don't believe everything you read on the Internet.

Don't believe everything you read on the Internet.

Don't believe everything you read on the Internet.

Don't believe everything you read on the Internet.

• EXERCISE 2 •

Typeset a short poem or nursery rhyme of at least four lines. Mix different races of type, different typefaces, different sizes and different weights to give a typographic inter- pretation of the poem you have chosen. You will also want to vary the line length, leading, and alignment for a more dynamic visual interpretation. (Hint: It may help to print out the type specimen chart you prepared for Exercise Number One.)

• EXERCISE 3 •

Look through old magazines to find examples of display type representing each of the races. Mount them on this page or on poster board and label each example to make a chart identifying the races of type.

SEVEN

The Visual Editor

William E. Huntzicker and *Ross F. Collins*

Photographs tell stories, and, like news and feature articles, they must be clear and focused in both content and technique.

Photos tell stories alone or as a complement to written stories, allowing readers to see events or to visualize the importance of an issue. Photos convey both information and emotion. They have power, often more power than the written word, though in recent years digital technology has removed some of the credibility that gives photographs their power.

Editors select photographers, make assignments and choose the best photos from those available at the end of each assignment. Occasionally, editors have to send reporters—sometimes known as "backpack journalists"—to assignments to write and photograph a story, sometimes with both still and video pictures for the newspaper's website. Magazine and feature editors also select photos from freelance submissions or stock agencies. Public relations and advertising professionals sometimes serve as picture editors, working with art directors to select photographs to illustrate a newsletter or build an attractive website. Media professionals working in an editing role routinely deal with visual images. And visual standards for images across the spectrum of mass media — with the obvious exception of advertising — are set by journalists.

Once the journalist returns to the newsroom or sends his or her products back to the newsroom, an editor must choose among the images, size them and place them on the page and website. Good professional photographers will do their editing on site with the camera, but editors still may have to do minor editing of images. The choices editors make are critically important to their publication's effectively competing with so many others in a visual world. Photographs, like illustrations and headlines, attract readers into the story, the page and the website. Photos increase the readability of the page and the number of people who read it. And they help readers understand the message.

The pressure to provide solid and credible photos is greater than ever, despite the decreasing specialization in both photojournalism and journalism in general. As a result, editors need a working knowledge of photojournalism, need to know how to make assignments for people with varied backgrounds, and how to edit their material for more than one platform. They work with backpack journalists assigned to provide written stories, photographs, audio and video from the scene of an event. They work with amateur news gatherers armed with cell phone cameras, an unpaid group that provides increasing numbers of important pictures used by the news media.

Fitting the photographer to the assignment

Many editors direct staffs of both writers and photographers. They know the talent and preferences of their staff. Sometimes photographers, like reporters, specialize, though photojournalism offers far fewer opportunities to specialize than reporting and writing. Photographers may cover a battle, a football game and a feature — often in the same week. Some are better at portraits and landscapes for features that require patience, and others seek out action, drawn to violent confrontations or sporting events. As convergence reworks the old newsrooms, editors know that the writer, photographer and videographer may occasionally be the same person.

When they make assignments, editors know whether the resultant photographs will speak for themselves or whether they will provide images for a written story. If the photos go with a story, the editor should send a reporter and photographer who work well as a team. Often a quick eye contact between the two can suggest to the photographer a subject that will likely complement the story. On the other hand, occasionally photographers become individualists, claiming they don't need someone telling them how to do their jobs.

The editor, however, needs photos — and possibly video — that go with the story. An in-depth story emphasizing an issue may explore some people or places as case studies. Photos should provide concrete evidence to support the story. Pictures of a different person from the one in the story can confuse the reader or distract from the theme. Regardless of the subject and its complexity, the story and photos work best if they use the same examples.

The pictures should also reflect the mood of the story. A picture of a smiling child on a story about domestic violence may not be appropriate. Photos convey emotions, and the emotion should complement the theme of the written story. Cooperation between the reporter and photographer will improve the editor's chances of getting a package that works.

Here are a few questions to ask of a photograph before using it:

- Does it tell a story?
- Does it evoke appropriate emotion?
- Does it provide information not told in the written story?
- Does it explain or elaborate on the story?
- Is it clear with a obvious message and center of interest?
- Is it simple without clutter and distracting elements?
- Can you verify its truth?
- Is its photographer credible?

Sending reporters with cameras

Long before the digital age, some tightwad editors or publishers sent reporters to the scene of an event with photo equipment, expecting little more than they'd get with a point-and-shoot snapshot camera. But as newsrooms today become leaner, photo staff often takes a hit, despite the paper's major competition coming from the visual media of television and the Web. Today's slimmer newsrooms expect journalists to do more: the printed newspaper is almost never the only product they produce. As newspapers move increasingly to the Web, print might not even be a product they produce at all. Journalists write stories, record comments, take pictures and video, and upload it all to an editor, who in a digital world must sort out more than grammar — although he or she must do that, too.

Online competition comes from around the world. For example, readers looking for exciting pictures of a Cowboys-Vikings football game could go to the websites of the various media in both Dallas and the Twin Cities. Radio journalists also provide photographs on their websites, as do the professional teams themselves. Spectators from the stands snap and upload stills and video to Facebook, linked minutes later to someone else's blog. A YouTube video goes up while the game is still in progress. Media consumers today are not limited by geography or ink and paper. The editor in a digital world knows her competition and knows how to produce visually strong material that can compete within the digital din.

Editors in the past couldn't reach some isolated corners of the world — but today they can, relying on digital pictures from folks on the street. Witnesses with cell phones in 2009 Iran transmitted pictures to the outside world after the Iranian government threw western reporters out of the country. The pictures showed government troops shooting unarmed demonstrators protesting a corrupt election. Without the covert pictures, the world outside of this insular nation would not have learned as quickly or as graphically about the violence. The public as both audience and reporter has become part of the editor's toolbox. That tool is unwieldy, difficult to control, yet powerful. Who evaluates material produced by amateurs? Maybe nobody. In a credible media operation, you as editor remain the gatekeeper to assure credibility and consistency of photography from an increasingly diverse collection of sources.

An editor needs to consider the downside of today's amateur journalism. Before the digital age, photojournalists complained that while everyone could write, few people claimed to be journalists. On the other hand, everyone who clicked a shutter claimed to be a photographer. But in the digital age photos can be created without clicking anything, except a computer mouse. In summer 2008, demonstrators calling themselves "citizen journalists" confronted police and professional journalists alike at the national political conventions in Denver and St. Paul, Minn. Editors must decide which photos are credible and which could be part of a practical joke on a news operation's credibility.

Many editors in all media have to think of the visual possibilities of stories in publication or posting. In making assignments, an editor in charge of managing staff will decide the best way to use the talent available to the news operation. For example, sending a photographer to a city council meeting for a debate may be less interesting than assigning him or her to make photos that illustrate a controversial issue on the agenda. Photographing children at the city park playground may be more valuable than photos of politicians debating playground safety. On the other hand, an editor could be embarrassed if the photographer misses a meeting at which parents and children with balloons show up to make a colorful statement about playground safety. How to choose? Knowledge and intuition based on experience serve an editor who must make difficult choices regarding staff allocation and photo usage. To gain knowledge takes time, of course. But those who will have to edit images can begin by becoming more visually sensitive.

Basics of a good photograph

Like words and graphics, pictures in journalism must tell a story or help explain a story they illustrate. To do so, the photo must have a clear message, conveying information and emotion. Photojournalists try to carefully compose pictures as they shoot on assignment, even under deadline pressure. They understand lighting, timing and identifying key subjects. These skills are built through study and practice and explains why professional photojournalists usually produce stronger images than intrepid citizens offering snapshots to the professional media. Photojournalists try to convey information quickly, relying on the simple, compelling centers of interest and uncluttered backgrounds that add power to photojournalism. Unlike amateurs, they know how to make photographs that invite viewers, convey information and evoke feelings. A successful photo on a carefully designed page will draw readers into the story and to the rest of the newspaper, magazine, website or newsletter. Photographs nowadays may be produced by everybody in minutes and by the thousands, grains of sand in an endless digital sea. Yet editors know a single photograph by an accomplished photojournalist still has the power to stir millions, perhaps even a nation. Jodi Bieber's disturbing photograph of a mutilated Afghan woman on the cover of the August 9, 2010, issue of *Time* magazine quickly reached the halls of Congress and the commentaries of world-wide social media — an exhibit of the stakes in a national debate over the country's participation in an overseas war.

And so editors prefer to hire professionals and prefer to rely on journalists who specialize in visual images, in contrast to backpackers who try to do everything. But that is not always possible. Photos come to an editor from everywhere — from reporters, from wire services, from stock agencies, from the smartphone video witness on the scene. Even professional photographers sometimes have to work fast and so they can't compose a photo as well as they would like. Editing may be up to a specialized photo or picture editor. But often it's up to a copy editor or a writer/editor putting together newsletter or website content singlehandedly. That might be you. In fact, at some point in your media career, it probably will be. So you'll need to know some basic principles.

What makes a good picture? Five photojournalism flubs.

An editor usually can't send staff back for the perfect picture. Most visual material designed for mass media is built on news events that offer fleeting opportunities for good images and few opportunities for reshoots. Professional photojournalists are trained to get the shot, and often they do. But sometimes they don't. And sometimes they weren't there. Editors generally don't fix poor images themselves, but they need to recognize weak photography when they see it. Here are a few flubs to look out for.

1. Poor image quality (Figure 1). Photos that are too dark or too light won't get any better when published on low-quality newsprint. Particularly bad are those that are dark — dot gain on halftone reproduction turns dark photos into inky blobs in print. Exposure may be fairly easy to fix using image-editing software.

Less easy to fix are out-of-focus photos. Given advanced image stabilization systems that have become part of DSLR cameras nowadays, an editor might think blurry photos are a thing of the past. Experience tells us otherwise. Some fuzziness can be fixed in the digital photo lab, but Photoshop's Unsharp Mask only goes so far, making digital edges more contrasty to give a feeling of sharpness. Truly blurry pictures can't be fixed and must be discarded — unless their content is so compelling that readers would look anyway.

Dead giveaway of an amateur photograph is the overexposed

Figure 1. This photo is both dark and out of focus. It might be improved using image editing software, such as Photoshop — but it has a long way to go. As is, it's unusable.

subject and black backgrounds produced by a snapshooter using a built-in flash on the camera (Figure 2). Professionals know how to avoid these kinds of images, and editors should avoid publishing them, unless they absolutely must. Flash-on-camera pictures can be improved using image-editing software. But that's not an editor's job, and it only can go so far.

2. No center of interest (Figure 3). Editors look for simple, compelling images that

make strong statements. Viewers should be able to draw meaning from the image in two seconds—the amount of time most readers give to a photo. Cropping may be necessary to establish this "poster effect." In fact, many photos need cropping to be suitable for publication. Extraneous information should be cropped from the background along with other elements that don't add to the meaning of the photo. Editors, as well as photographers, should remember the rule of thirds for composition. Major elements should be on lines one-third the way from an edge of

Above: Figure 2. Flash-on-camera snaps tend to overexpose the subject and underexpose the background. A good Photoshop technician can improve them somewhat — but most editors would rather find a more professionally produced photo. *Below:* Figure 3. What is the center of interest? Is it the woman in the hat? The beach chairs? The boats? Maybe even the clouds? Photojournalists look for a strong center of interest.

the frame, not centered. On the other hand, photos should not be so closely cropped that they lose context. Certainly photos can be overcropped, but generally the opposite is true.

   3. No people (Figure 4). News is about people doing things. Most editors reject photos of objects, buildings, streets, sunsets and scenery, occasionally making exceptions for travel packages or cute animals.

Figure 4. A pretty scene, but we need a human being sitting on that bench.

4. No action (Figure 5). If journalism is about people doing things, then images ought to be of people doing things. Editors of most professional news publications and websites will reject a group shot—folks standing in a line grinning at the camera. A classic photo that cries "amateur," often sadly the main fare of small-town journalism, is the grip-and-grin photo showing someone giving someone else an award, shaking hands and smiling into the camera. Why not choose photos of these people doing what they did to get the award? Mug shots—small head-and-shoulders portraits—also should be avoided if an action shot can be found. Other standard amateur clichés include dead animal pictures—photos of a hunter or angler holding a deer head or walleye on a stringer. These photos are actually offensive to some people, as are "beefcake" (men in swimsuits) and "cheesecake" (women in swimsuits). Nevertheless, editors of some nationally circulated magazines know that depicting women (and occasionally men) partially clothed on the cover will sell magazines. Probably you will not edit one of these magazines and the technique is less likely to work in, say, your corporate newsletter.

Figure 5. This photo desperately needs cropping, but even so, people should not be posing for the camera. Editors look for photos of people doing things.

5. No identification (Figure 6). This pertains mostly to news operations, in which every recognizable person in a photo needs to be identified in the caption using first and last name and some kind of further identification, such as a title, address or hometown. Journalism is a story about people. It is not a university research study in which identities are protected by research requirements. Editors used to say IDs or idents

Figure 6. Interesting picture, but an editor would need the names of the children and, in some cases, parental approval.

were needed because, if for no other reason, naming names would sell more newspapers. But reasoning goes a bit further than that. Editors presume that if a photographer asked a person to supply his name, and that person complied, the subject would be giving tacit approval to use the photo in print. These agreements may not be enough to satisfy strict legal requirements. United States law protects photographers taking photos of people in public places for non-commercial purposes. But getting the names makes editors more comfortable in a litigious society.

A reminder: clues that you're dealing with amateur photographs

- People stand in the middle of the frame and stare at the camera.
- People look directly into the camera with red eye caused by direct flash.
- People look directly into the camera while shaking hands and passing a certificate or a check.
- Background distractions cause twigs or cords to grow out of a person's head.
- Picture shows signs of obvious manipulation, with blotches showing efforts to enhance areas of light, shadow and other elements.
- Picture provides a confused message with no clear center of interest.
- Subjects in the frame are too far away, obscuring faces and details.

Placing the pictures

Once editors have pictures, they must decide on size and placement and write cutlines (captions) that explain them. Photographs can be vertical, horizontal or cut to outline the shape of the subject. Of course, newspaper pages are vertical, and vertical photographs work best to draw readers down the page. Magazine pages are vertical, but many editors prefer to work with two-page spreads, a horizontal space. Horizontal pictures reflect the shape of computer screens that display websites.

Editors may have the opportunity to use several pictures, to tell a story with photographs. If space is available for a photo story, a common mistake is to place all photos in a line, and all the same size, like a photo album. Compelling photo stories draw readers in with a dominant, theme-setting photo published larger than the rest. The largest picture could be a scene-setting long shot or a close up that draws people into the story. But it doesn't have to be. The dominant photo could be an extreme close-up, while the establishing shot could be a smaller photo that provides the overall context. Other photos can draw the reader though a visual narrative using a combination of long shots, medium shots, close-ups and details. Size should be varied and shapes should include both horizontals and verticals. Editors dealing with video material for online presentations also try to include this variety of shots.

A printed page can provide space for a variety of shapes and sizes. Online, however, a single image can include links to more photographs, often by providing a scene-setting photo and thumbnails. Nonetheless, the editor must carefully select images. Online consumers will grow tired of clicking through dozens of thumbnails, especially if they are of uneven quality.

Good editors learn what photojournalists always know: you are judged by your weakest image. Editors place pictures to attract readers, provide information, evoke an emotion and, most importantly, tell a story. Content ought to drive design. It seems common, however, for some publications to use photographs not to tell the news, but instead to embellish a graphic designer's layout. As graphic designers become more important to newspapers providing content for both print and Web, the photograph as news is sometimes giving way to the photograph as a design tool. An editor needs to assess the purpose of the photographs he or she chooses. If the purpose is to deliver news, editors should choose images worthy of advancing a newsworthy goal.

How editors choose to reach this goal is as varied as the products they produce. A different editor facing the same choices may find different solutions. A visit to *Today's Front Pages* on the Newseum website (www.newseum.org) allows viewers to see how the world's editors chose from the same day's material for their front pages. Images depicting an important national or world event dominate newspaper coverage everywhere, of course. But the manner in which editors use the same pictures differs, sometimes dramatically.

What is lying?

This chapter assumes that you wish to tell the truth by conveying facts with pictures. Photographs destined for advertising may be altered — in fact, they usually are carefully controlled — but credible editors deal with facts, whether in news operations or public relations. Editors in journalism resist the temptation to alter the content of a photograph. "Alteration" obviously means adding or removing people and objects, changing colors or moving backgrounds (Figure 7). But what else does it mean? Can an editor crop a photo to better emphasize a center of interest? Darken or lighten? Alter color balance? Sharpen focus?

Editors began to confront these ethical challenges as published photography became common at the beginning of the 20th century. Editors realized the power of the image often trumped the power of the word. While writers interpreted what they saw, photographers recorded the event with a machine. They "took a picture" from real life, apparently bypassing human interpretation.

Of course, that's not quite true. A photographer always interprets a scene by choosing one subject, by ignoring another, by choosing an angle, by setting the exposure and by composing the frame. Yet photography still set a new standard for credibility. The photograph became the final arbiter of truth.

It still maintains some of that power in a digital age. Many people would not have believed the U.S. government in 2004 apparently condoned torture in Iraq's Abu Ghraib prison — until confronted with photographic proof.

But photographs, like statistics, can lie while providing an aura of credibility. During the pre-digital age, corrupt political regimes doctored photographs to remove discredited leaders, whose memories were to be erased from the historical record. The Soviet Union was notoriously good at altering photos. The nonprofit Newseum in Washington offers examples in its feature "The Commissar Vanishes" (www.newseum. org/berlinwall/commissar_vanishes/). During the 19th century, collages were created to illustrate fairy tales, classical literature, exotic places and historical periods. Yet digital techniques today have taken photographic lying to whole new levels. Some

Figure 7. Lying with photos may be subtle — or not.

fake pictures, such as a photograph of a shark leaping toward a person climbing a ladder into a helicopter, have been distributed to millions of people as email attachments.

At the same time, digital photography reveals new truths. Like telescopes, digital cameras can provide information unavailable to the human eye. Some photographers snapping pictures of the attack on New York's World Trade Center on Sept. 11, 2001, did not know the entire value of their images until they returned to their computers and enlarged them. Within the early images of the burning towers, some photographers discovered they had pictures of people jumping or falling from the buildings. These ghastly photographs, cropped from the larger images, conveyed the terror of the moment but proved too graphic for some editors to use. Nonetheless, the digital images enhanced the photographers' ability to tell the truth about the events of 9/11— even truth both painful and shocking.

Digital photography also allows more flexibility and creativity with greater ease than film. Cropping has always been considered an editor's ethical right. But is it always done ethically? For example, a terror-stricken child stares at an unseen menace. Unseen, because an editor has cropped off a doctor giving a measles shot. Ethical cropping? Most editors would say no. In another photo, power lines intrude in the background of a public park carnival photo. Should an editor crop? Most editors would say yes. What if those power lines intruded on a scenic photo of a lake criticized for its overdevelopment? The question requires consideration of context.

Cropping decisions are among dilemmas perhaps more rightfully examined in a mass media ethics course than in an editing course. Still, editors need to consider that all changes made to an image can be questioned. Is a photo too light or dark? Most editors would adjust quality, including exposure and sharpness. But a famous case of darkening the image led *Time* magazine to apologize to readers. On the cover of the June 27, 1994, issue, editors darkened the police mug shot of celebrity O.J. Simpson, accused of murdering his wife. Editors said they made the assumption that a darker image appeared more sinister. Perhaps no one would have noticed—except rival newsmagazine *Newsweek* published the identical photo unmanipulated. (The full-sized cover is available at *Time*'s online archives, www.time.com/time/covers/0,16641,19940627,00. html.)

Still, magazine covers routinely project photographs of scenes that never existed. A magazine cover story on health care reform showed President Barack Obama in a doctor's coat with a stethoscope around his neck. *Time* magazine in 2011 commemorated the centennial birthday of President Ronald Reagan by featuring the late president standing next to Obama. Such illustrations relying on photos as a design tool have been acceptable in advertising through most of its history—but only recently seem to have become more acceptable in some magazines, even some newspapers.

Simpson in *Time* became darker and more criminal, on the apparent assumption that darker people were more evil. Through photo manipulation, news media have also done supposedly more innocuous things, perhaps removing a Coca-Cola can from a table or zipping an adolescent boy's open fly. But when *National Geographic* magazine moved an Egyptian pyramid to make a picture fit the magazine's vertical cover format, the action created a credibility crisis around a magazine venerated for the quality and accuracy of its photographs.

Credibility of photography in the digital age has been questioned as never before. Editors have a stake in preserving that credibility. They usually make the final decision regarding use of altered images.

Write intelligent cutlines

Cutlines are short descriptions of content in photographs. Sometimes they are called captions. Some editors may use both terms, regarding a caption as a short title sometimes appended to a cutline or part of a feature photo not tied to a story. But many others use the terms interchangeably. Newspaper editors seem to favor the word

PHOTOJOURNALISM ANGLES

History of the cutline.

This odd journalese for the descriptive legend under photographs shares its etymology with many words from an era when newspapers were produced by metal type using enormous, clanky Linotype machines in inky, hot composing rooms. Photographs were engraved onto metal plates that were "cut" from large sheets. A photo, therefore, was a "cut." Beneath the cut was, of course, a descriptive line of type, the cutline.

Halftones then and now.

We continue to rely on the halftone principle, even as color has made the process more complicated. Before the development of the halftone, editors couldn't print photographs directly. Instead, skilled engravers copied them onto wood or metal plates. The business of engraving became so big that some newspapers employed artists around the clock to quickly translate photos into printable blocks. But of course, engravings actually showed only a facsimile of a photo, drawn through an artist's interpretation.

At the end of the 19th century, a Cornell University technician, Frederic E. Ives, patented a way to transfer photographs to paper, the photoengraving, based on the halftone. Realizing printing presses cannot print shades of gray, Ives and others discovered he could break a continuous tone photograph into tiny dots. From a reading distance the dots were invisible. The viewer instead saw continuous tones of gray. The larger and closer together the dots, the darker the tone. Any tone could be reproduced through the spacing of dots. By the beginning of the twentieth century most publications had moved to halftones, and engravers saw their craft migrate to the world of fine art — just as today photographers who still use black-and-white film usually hang out in art departments.

One problem printing tiny dots: dot gain. Low-quality newsprint must let ink soak into the page so that it will be dry enough for quick distribution. (Well, almost dry — as anyone who fingers some newspapers know.) But tiny dots blotting into the page become smudges, leading to poor-quality photo reproduction. To combat this problem, printers use coarse screens. That is, they print fewer dots per inch, so dot gain won't mud up a photo. The tradeoff is that newspapers have somewhat lower quality images, because of fewer dots, than magazines on higher quality paper.

We see what we learn to see.

Gestalt psychologists in the early 20th century discovered that the association between what our eyes see and what our brain perceives is surprisingly different. At its most basic, the brain straightens the upside down and backward image our eye produces, just as a system of mirrors in modern Single Lens Reflex (SLR) camera viewfinders make right the image of a camera lens. But how the brain perceives visual information is more subtle than that. We see, it seems, what we are told we see, or what we learn to see, based on context and cultural background.

Sometimes we have no cultural background to perceive the meaning of a visual image. For example, in the photo at right, describe what you see.

Many of us will describe some sort of a bonfire, but what are these people doing? In fact, if you are a Muslim, you probably know. Here is the cutline:

Muslims celebrate Eid Al Adha, the feast of sacrifice, on a street in Fez, Morocco. One of the two most important Muslim holidays, it is celebrated by each family. A live sheep is ritually slaughtered in the kitchen as a symbol of sacrifice. The sheep head often ends up charred on a street-side brazier while children play in the sun with glistening sheep intestines.

You see what your culture has told you to see — and that education might be dramatically different from one culture to the next. Because photographic meaning is uncertain, editors realize every photo must have a cutline.

cutlines. Magazine editors tend to call them captions. Dictionaries seem to regard them as synonymous. You can call them either; no one will misunderstand you. This text uses the newspaper term.

Cutlines provide a vital element to help tell a story. A stand-alone picture needs an explanation that provides meaningful context. A photo that complements a story needs a cutline to tie the picture and the writing. Like a headline, the cutline draws people into the image and the written story and provides meaning. The journalists who know most about what's going on in the image should write the cutlines — the photographers. But editors also may write cutlines, and always edit them.

VOCABULARY AND JARGON FOR EDITORS

DSLR.

Digital Single Lens Reflex. SLR cameras feature a mirror system in front of the shutter that reflects the image through the lens and into the viewfinder. This system means what you see is what you snap. Most photojournalists today have replaced the film with digital image-capture technology.

Digital clip art.

Editors looking for royalty-free illustrations used to subscribe to large books of "camera-ready" line drawings. A chosen image would be cut from pages with scissors. Today that material is available by Internet download. Many editors who work for high-quality publications, however, avoid free clip art as amateurish.

Newseum.

Al Neuharth, the indefatigable South Dakotan who launched Gannett Co.'s *USA Today*, is also founder of the non-profit Freedom Forum. That group sponsors the shrine to journalism in Washington, D.C., the Newseum. Its extensive network of exhibits is complemented by a feature-rich website, www.newseum. org. Think you might be the smartest editor ever? Play the editor's knowledge section from the site's *Newsmania* game.

Paparazzi.

The Italian word for those aggressive photographers who swarm around celebrities. The name reached the world from a 1960 Italian movie, *La Dolce Vita*, and its photographer character, Paparazzo.

Rule of thirds.

Nearly all basic photography classes include the classic rule of thirds: photographers are asked to visualize the scene as divided into sections by two imaginary vertical lines and two imaginary horizontal lines. The photographer composes the scene so that the center of interest lies on an intersection.

Stand-alone photo.

A photo not tied to a story, also called an enterprise or feature photo. Editors encourage photojournalists to prowl the city in search of interesting photos, often taken in parks or at public events.

Stock agencies.

Professional photographers contribute high-quality images to agencies which sell rights to the pictures to editors. Advantages include a guarantee that people pictured have given written consent to use their image, and the photographer has given legal right to the agency to sell it. Disadvantages include cost of the image, and often a generic feeling as opposed to locally flavored images produced by staff or free-lancers.

Poster effect.

Graphic designers working on large formats such as posters know the image may flash by a viewer in just a few seconds. To make an impression, the poster must offer an uncomplicated image and simple statement. Many editors like to see a similar effect in photos produced for consumption by a distracted mass audience.

Some tips on writing meaningful cutlines

1. Write in the present tense, as you do headlines. This gives a feeling of immediacy to the photograph. A cutline might read, "Former California Gov. Arnold Schwarzenegger Tuesday unveiled a new program aimed at reducing the size of state government by reducing the size of state politicians." Note this cutline is written in the past tense. A cutline would shift to the present tense: "Former California Gov. Arnold Schwarzenegger demonstrates his famous barbell shoulder press Tuesday, saying the key to smaller government is to elect thinner politicians."

2. Provide names and identify key players by first and last name. Most editors reject photos of unidentified people. If two people appear, then name the person on the left first followed by (left) after the name. There is no need to state left to right, etc. With many subjects, you may simply write (from left).

3. Identify the same number of people as appear in the picture.

4. Don't underestimate the intelligence of your readers by stating the obvious or the inane cliché, like "John Smith looks at the new monument." Edit word clutter, such as "This photo shows…" or "Above is depicted…."

5. Provide information that is not in the story or the picture, perhaps by checking with the reporter and photographer for facts they didn't work into the story.

6. Double check facts, just as you would while editing a story.

7. When using file or stock photos, date them and check the facts. Make sure the pictured people are still living and the buildings or other landmarks still standing.

8. Provide the 5Ws, especially if the photo stands alone without an accompanying written story.

9. Describe the event as depicted, rather than the entire event as covered in the story.

10. Identify the photographer or photo agency. Readers deserve to know when pictures are taken by amateurs, stock agencies or staff photographers. Sourcing the photo is as important as identifying the sources of facts and quotations.

Sometimes the cutline provides only the name of the person pictured, if the photo is a mug shot or accompanies a story.

With an occasional exception for mug shots, people should not look directly into the camera. Direct flash also may cause red eye in people looking at the camera. Red eye can be easily repaired in Photoshop—but professional photographers make sure it's not there in the first place, by avoiding amateur flash-lit scenes.

Know more

Ang, T. (2000). *Picture Editing*. Oxford: Focal.
Harris, C. R., and P. M. Lester (2002). *Visual Journalism. A Guide for New Media Professionals*. Boston: Allyn and Bacon.
Saville, L. (2008). *100 Habits of Successful Publication Designers: Insider Secrets for Working Smart and Staying Creative*. Beverly, MA: Rockport.

• EXERCISE 1 •

Compare photos from a nearby small weekly newspaper and a large metropolitan daily, either hard copy or online versions. How are they similar? How are they different? Why? Explain your answer in writing. Include copies of the photos, if necessary.

• EXERCISE 2 •

Evaluate online and published media photography from a variety of mass media websites, news, magazine, public relations, or others. Spot five photojournalism flubs, or clues of amateur photography. Describe them in writing.

Would you as an editor choose to publish these? Why or why not? Could they be improved by cropping or other photo manipulation? Would it be ethical to do so for news presentation? In public relations material? In advertisements?

• EXERCISE 3 •

Compare daily newspaper photographs from the Newseum's website, www.newseum. org, choosing the *Today's Front Pages* link.

Why would editors choose the photos published on each newspaper's front page? Which newspapers seem to publish the best photos, and which publish the worst, based on your knowledge of quality photojournalism? Record your answers in writing.

EIGHT

Page Makeup: Beginning the Design Process

Amy Mattson Lauters

Editors whose responsibility includes placing elements on a page or on the Web usually divide themselves into two categories.

Page designers are responsible for the day-to-day chore of laying elements onto pages, and possibly onto a companion web-site. They usually are not expected to be experts in graphic design or art.

Graphic artists, on the other hand, may design publications or websites from scratch based on extensive knowledge of art principles. They may also dream up sophisticated designs for story packages or spreads. Their work rests on a larger philosophy of how a publication or website ought to look based on mission and goals of the media organization behind it.

As you might expect, the role of page designer and graphic artist can overlap, particularly in a smaller media operation. An editor as designer who usually relies on basic layout principles to move elements from a budget to a page may sometimes step past that role to produce a package of more creative dazzle. And a graphic artist might also spend the majority of her time as a basic page designer.

But one thing is certain. Unless an editor is working for a large media operation, he or she will need to understand a little of both. This chapter considers practical knowledge of basic page makeup. Chapter nine considers more overarching principles and skills behind that work.

Here the author discusses how to lay out and make up pages for multiple purposes, including newspapers, brochures and websites. She addresses the concept of *dummy sheets*, dwells on modern principles of layout, and provides organizational details, such has how to fit stories and photos to a page and how to keep track of stories. Finally, she offers five layouts beginning designers should avoid.

Two overarching principles guide all basic page makeup: Make it easy for readers to follow and understand the information presented, and be sure every element placed on a page has a purpose for being there.

A brief history of modern makeup and design

Newspaper design has evolved significantly over the last hundred years. Design styles reflect the prevailing artistic standards of their readers, and tastes change over time. A great deal of design depends upon the availability of technologies that aid in overall production. In fact, each new development in print technology over the last century ushered in short eras of innovative design that depended solely on the availability of the new technology. Some remnants of these designs remain in contemporary print, but others — perhaps deservedly — died.

The temptation with each new technology lies in the new tricks each brings to the trade. The advent of photography and the halftone process, for example, brought lurid black-and-white images to the front pages of newspapers, along with cluttered designs. Advances in typography — the art of words and type — over time also encouraged experimentation with different font types and sizes, particularly in advertising copy. The mechanical nature of the press in the 19th century encouraged a style of design that simply allowed text to flow in columns, regardless of story, each individual story headed with a single, short, column-wide headline. Stories and ads thus were placed together, running together for the length of the page. It was simply easier for typesetters to add to their work in setting the page, rather than giving thought to how it would ultimately appear.

However, in recent years, the development of pagination and graphic design software has brought a new edge to newspaper design. More tools and tricks are available than ever before; font types and styles are nearly unlimited, photographs can be cropped, modified, and illustrated in new (and sometimes unethical) ways, and full-color art, photographs and graphics now can be run with ease.

This ease has led to a challenge for fledgling editors expected to know some design: We all want to use these tools and tricks. However, the best design does not necessarily take advantage of everything these programs are capable of. Just because you can do something odd and spectacular with a design, doesn't mean you should. The primary purpose of all design today remains to provide readers with a means of reading, understanding, and retaining information in an easy-to-follow format. Every element on a page should be purposeful, and it all should enable a reader to focus on the information being presented by the document.

The advent of the World Wide Web and more recent electronic communication also has influenced modern design in interesting ways. But the key elements of a layout remain the same. And while some large publications hire professional graphic designers to put elements on a page, most of them expect editors to understand the principles of good design. Editors who find themselves working for some in-house magazines, newsletters, or smaller publications will need to know more: they'll probably need to actually use computerized pagination software to produce a publication — and perhaps to turn it into a website as well.

Page makeup; or, the purpose of each element

Regardless of the publication, the first thing every editor needs to identify is the content destined for available pages or website. For newspapers, the process means gathering all the stories, graphics and art that will be incorporated into the publication. For brochures and ads, the process means knowing the purpose of the document and identifying all the text, art, and accompanying information that must be presented within it. For the Web, the process means not only knowing what news and information will be presented within the site, but how that information will be structured, linked, and presented in a non-linear fashion. But all designs have some terms and elements in common. Below are basic principles of each format.

Newspapers

The Front Page. Page one contains all of the key identifying elements of the newspaper, and these identifying elements carry over into other pages. The most prominent of these is the *nameplate*, sometimes called the *flag*. Nameplates generally are found at the top of page one, generally span the page, and are one-and-one-half to two inches deep. The text inside the nameplate identifies the name of the newspaper. It also specifies the volume number, issue number, and date of the publication (Figure 1).

FALLS DAILY NEWS

| VOL. 15: ISS. 152 | THE NEWS STANDARD FOR A NEW CENTURY | JUNE 1, 2013 |

Falls Dairy lays off 200 workers

Figure 1

The next significant part of the page is the *headline*. Standard headlines identify the stories for readers using short sentences that have complete subjects and verbs. Headlines often determine whether readers will take time to read the story to which they are attached, so the choice of headline is important. Next are the stories with *bylines*. Bylines simply identify the writers of the stories. Page one stories nearly always have bylines. They may also have *jump lines*. Jump lines tell readers where to go to finish reading a story if the entire story will not fit on the front page. The remainder of the story is called the *jump*.

Some sort of art typically dominates page one in contemporary designs; photographers generally supply photographs to go with a main story, or feature photographs in the event the main story does not lend itself well to other art. Feature photographs stand by themselves, with separate headlines, and usually have a longer cutline, or caption, to go along with the story.

Inside pages. Inside pages generally have headlines, art, cutlines, and bylines. However, instead of nameplates, inside pages have headers at the top of each page that show readers the name and page number of the publication (Figure 2). Special inside pages will contain other elements as well. Either page two or the editorial page normally contains a box called the *masthead* (Figure 3).

| FALLS DAILY NEWS | JUNE 1, 2013 | PAGE FOUR |

Figure 2

Lorem Ipsit delorem decorum sander frommet snit.
Lorem Ipsit delorem decorum sander frommet snit.

FALLS DAILY NEWS

A wholly owned subsidiary of the Thomas Family Legacy, LLC.

Publisher: Janet Thomas
Managing Editor: Jermaine Thomas
News Editor: Kristin Blanc
Web Editor: Margo Wood
Opinion Editor: Kevin Braun
Features Editor: George Franklin
Circulation Manager: Teresa Smith
Advertising/Sales Manager: Kelly Thomas

FALLS DAILY NEWS

P.O. Box 2012
Falls, WI 55555
(715) 812-1234
On the Web at:
http://www.fallsnewspaper.com

Figure 3

The mast contains contact and identifying information for the main editorial and production staff of the newspaper, including the newspaper's publisher, circulation manager, business manager, advertising manager, production manager, and editor-in-chief. Depending upon the publication, other important information will go into the masthead, including general circulation information and U.S. Postal Service regulations information. This graphic element must be in place in each edition of the standard newspaper, and therefore is an integral part of page makeup. The editorial page also includes elements not found other pages. Specifically, a list of the editorial board or staff members usually appears on the page, along with an editorial cartoon and letters to the editor, each of which is identified by a headline.

Inside sections also will have pages that look similar to page one, with their own section nameplates (Figure 4). Other elements of pages include the stories themselves, photographs and other graphics, ads, lines, and other elements. Each of these elements makes up a total page.

Brochures

Printed brochures can come in a wide variety of styles and types, but all have elements in common with newsprint and other materials. Each contains copy, or text that imparts information; headlines, text that identifies the topic of the brochure; and art in the form of illustrations, photographs, or graphics. Often also seen in brochures are subheads, or short titles for specific sections of the brochure, a logo or other identifying information for the sponsor of the brochure, and contact information for those wanting to know more about the subject or organization that produced the brochure.

Brochures come in a wide variety of layouts and sizes. Most common is a one-page, 8½ × 11–inch wall *flyer* usually used for announcements of events, incorporating contact and event information as well as a graphic and headline meant to get attention. The next most common is the *tri-fold* brochure, often used to provide information in a format that can be easily mailed, picked up, pocketed and shared. The tri-fold has

Figure 4

MAKEUP MATTERS: GENRE

Products of mass culture attract audiences based on familiar themes. Creators know expectations of their audiences, and so they build their products within this framework. Television programs, for example, can be divided into genres such as comedy, Western, detective, horror or soap opera based on visual cues of lighting, sound and character appearance. We take these cues for granted and, in fact, recognize them almost instantly. If you channel-surf through television stations, you don't need more than a second or two in most cases to determine what kind of program you are seeing.

Within these genres creators may be able to present unexpected story lines, but the genre can't be broken without confusing an audience. For example, a producer may set a scene for a Western, and then make it humorous, but she'll still have to include the clop-clop of horses, the intense sun and the cowboys to set a genre.

Editors also work within a genre. We expect newspapers to appear in larger format, on newsprint, folded without binding, with both photos and text on the first page, and with stories tied to current events.

We expect magazines to appear on a smaller format, on coated paper stock, with a photograph or illustration on the cover, and with teasers describing content. Binding may be stitched or glued, and pages usually run to at least 12. Any fewer is a pamphlet.

Other publications also fit genres. Newsletters are expected to appear in standard page format, on wove paper, with articles and possibly an illustration on the front. A flyer is one page. A brochure is tri- or quad-fold. A website includes a banner and menu bar or tabs.

Can an editor break the genre? Of course. But the audience may not go along. An editor can produce a broadsheet on newsprint, run a large photo on the cover with teasers and call it a magazine — but that's not likely what your readers will call it. Can you include a splash page on a news-oriented website? You can — but what will your viewers presume you are trying to give them? When readers are in doubt about the product they are given, their presumptions usually run to one conclusion: advertising.

three inner panels and three outer panels that function together when folded. The three inner panels feature the specific information that needs to be shared. The three outer panels include less relevant but still important information, such as the title of the publication, contact information for the organization, and a form the reader can fill out to obtain more information. A *quad-fold* brochure has four inner panels and four outer panels, and is often used when it's important for the fourth panel to be detachable, as in the case of a donation solicitation brochure.

Menus, newsletters, and other multiple-page print publications can be included in this list, as well. The goal of all? To make it easy for readers to navigate information being presented to them.

Websites

Websites provide a space for editors to work in which the stories do not need to be told in linear fashion. That is, users of websites expect to be able to navigate through a site at their own pace, and using their own judgment. The design of an overall site, therefore, requires editors to think in terms of accessibility and usability. Additionally, editors usually have less control over the final product as viewed by the users; differences in browsers, computer platforms, speed of access and fonts available on users' machines determine what the users will ultimately see.

However, editors can adhere to structural principles that will help users navigate their sites. A gateway page, also called a *home* or index page, provides users an entrance into the rest of the site. Consider this to be a nameplate, of a sort, and use this gateway to attract attention and identify the content within the site. Once users click through to the primary index page, use a nameplate, also called a *banner* when applied in an electronic setting, at the top of each inside page to make it easier for visitors to identify the site. Each page should also include hyperlinks, or clickable "hot spots" to other locations, that connect pages to each other and back to the primary index page. This list of links can be included at the top, bottom, left or right of the main content page. Contact information should also appear on each page, usually at the bottom, and editors may consider creating a "contact us" page that includes a special form to submit their questions via e-mail.

Beyond these basics, Web pages have distinct design advantages in that each can host not only text and graphics, but also animation, audio and video. The key to their usage is, again, purpose: Each element included on the page should be a purposeful part of overall storytelling.

Every publication, whether electronic or print, begins with these elements.

Fitting stories and photos to the page

Regardless of media, most editors begin with a *budget* for the page they are editing. The budget is a list of all content that will appear on that page; in a newspaper, this includes a list of stories, art and graphics.

Each budget item will be ranked for importance. Ranking will reflect values of the publication. The most important newspaper story of the day probably will see placement at the top of page one, the "top story" of the day. The story will be identified with a larger headline, to cue the reader that an editor deems the story to be significant.

Other newspaper stories on page one should be set on the page in order of their importance. An exception to this rule lies in the availability of art, such as a photograph, to go with one of the stories. Major art should be placed toward the center of the page, under the headline for that piece, and accompanied by the story itself to the left and/or under it. Editors aim for three to four stories on the front page of a broadsheet newspaper, and for one to two on the front page of a tabloid sized newspaper.

Once top stories have been established, the budget ranking helps identify stories available for subsequent pages. Local stories loom large based on the news value of proximity. Many newspaper editors nearly always believe local news ought to come first, and presume national and international events will have less direct impact on a community — and so will attract fewer readers. Contemporary editors, in fact, have tried to compete with the worldwide reach of the Web by pulling back to a more intense devotion to local news. Critics, however, have contended that such gatekeeping produces a parochial and narrow-minded newspaper. Choice of publication design and makeup reflects news philosophy as much as it reflects design principles.

Editors working on the Web may take a similar approach. Placement of stories and other content on line will coincide with the information's budget rank. A key difference, however, between editing for the Web and for print is the element of time; most timely stories should appear on the primary index page of a Web news site, with links to further information included elsewhere on the site. Of course, because the Web is non-linear, readers will set their own priorities. Editors guide this choice as best they can by placing links to stories they believe most important at the top of the website.

In designing a brochure, an editor will have a budget that includes a list of information, art and text to be included. Inside placement will be determined by what is most important to the brochure's purpose. Placement on the first panel often will focus on a graphic element likely to draw attention. What is inside might be critical, but if the outside can't grab attention of readers, that information won't reach them.

Dummy sheets

To build a layout, some editors take that budget and start sketching dummy sheets. Dummy sheets are working plans for overall design of a page (Figure 5). Several cues are used to help editors plan the overall layout of a page. Each represents a different graphic element.

Box with an X: art or graphic drawn to scale.

Wavy arrow: text; when ended with "END," indicates that text will end at that place. Could also end with a "JUMP."

Headlines: written in boxes at the top of stories.

Large quotation marks: pull quotes.

In some news organizations, dummy sheets will come from the advertising staff with ad space already defined, leaving a *news hole* for editors to fill (Figure 6). Editors then use these sheets to determine preliminary layout for the final pages. In other organizations, it's up to the editor or designer to create dummies. Dummies can also be useful tools for the creation of certain brochures, such as tri-folds, which require a bit of visualization to work effectively.

Important points as preliminary sketching on dummy sheets begins:

• Prioritize important stories. Make headlines for those stories bigger than others, and place them higher on the page.

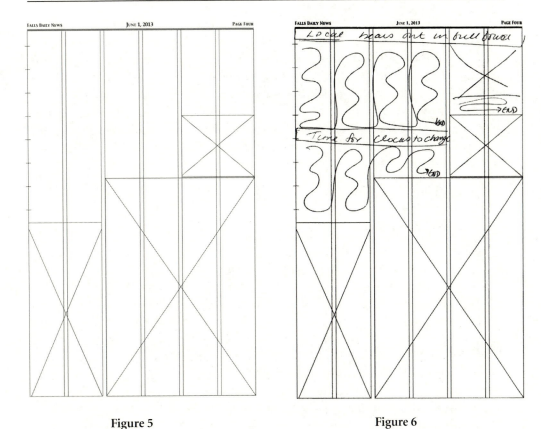

Figure 5   Figure 6

• Make sure all parts of a package —copy, art, cutlines, headlines, and other elements— are placed together on a page.

• Limit jumps. Note: readers often don't bother to pursue a jumped story. If a newspaper story must be jumped, jump only once. If possible, jump multiple stories to the same page, and note jumps always move to a subsequent page, never to a previous page. If an editor is left with just a column inch or two to jump, a better choice is to cut the story. Readers who decide to follow the jump to discover it consists of only a few words will mildly resent having made the effort.

Newspaper design styles

Designs styles may vary widely within a single publication. Ads contrast editorial material, and often dominate inside pages. In fact, in recent years, the newspaper news hole, or space left over for news stories, has shrunk, and sometimes it's a lucky editor who has more than a few column inches in which to place stories on inside pages.

When advertisements create an awkward ladder on an inside page, an editor is left with few options in an effort to attractively squeeze in copy and heds. A typical newspaper layout places a headline across four or six columns at the top. Copy flows down to the borders of the ads. If possible, a photo may be placed over columns five and six.

A section front, however, allows editors some freedom to work with ad-free layouts. Page design helps to guide eyes of readers to the stories on the page, taking advantage of classic eye pattern research. In Western societies most people read from left to right; on a well-designed page, those same readers will look at the design from left to right, following a Z pattern down the page that focuses in on headlines and art along the Z. In Eastern societies, some read from right to left, or up and down, on a page.

To take advantage of eye-tracking patterns, three design styles have evolved for modern newspapers:

- modular design;
- non-modular design;
- modified modular design.

Modular design

This standard emerged in the 1980s. Modular design makes each story a complete package; no stories are jumped, but are ended in the space designated for them (Figure 7). We know from eye-tracking studies that readers primarily see photographs and headlines first, and afterwards focus on stories that attract interest. Rarely do readers find the energy or interest to follow a story into subsequent pages. In modular design, too, photographs are cropped to strong vertical or horizontal shapes that run in the space directly adjacent to the stories. Each complete story package forms a rectangular shape; modular design tolerates no laddering. Editors who choose strict modular design often must cut stories to fit designated space.

Non-modular design

Non-modular editors, reflecting an older newspaper standard, run stories in succession along columns, jumping stories when they run out of room. Readers are meant to start at the first column and continue until all stories are read, turning pages as they go. This style borrows heavily from early printing developments and their concept of linear books, which require readers to start on page one and move through the text. Such design primarily accepts that readers will, in fact, go through the work linearly. While this may have been the case before the advent of electronic media and electronic design, editors today know most readers do not start at the beginning.

Modified modular design

Most newspapers today use a modified form of modular design. Stories are packaged as completely as possible, but jumps are permissible, with the caveat that jumps go to one designated page. Additionally, since the advent of the Web, readers expect branching; art, graphics and sidebars can be packaged with materials in one boxed decorum sander frommet   decorum sander frommet   snit. Lorem Ipsit delorem   snit. Lorem Ipsit delorem   decorum sander frommet

Girl Scouts take over City Hall

By Joe Thomas
Staff Writer

Lorem Ipsit delorem decorum sander frommet snit. Lorem Ipsit delorem decorum sander frommet snit. Lorem Ipsit delorem decorum sander frommet snit. Lorem Ipsit delorem decorum sander frommet snit. Lorem Ipsit delorem decorum sander frommet snit. Lorem Ipsit delorem decorum sander frommet snit. Lorem Ipsit delorem decorum sander frommet snit. Lorem Ipsit delorem decorum sander frommet snit. Lorem Ipsit delorem decorum sander frommet snit.

Lorem Ipsit delorem decorum sander frommet snit. Lorem Ipsit delorem decorum sander frommet snit. Lorem Ipsit delorem decorum sander frommet snit. Lorem Ipsit delorem decorum sander frommet snit. Lorem Ipsit delorem decorum sander frommet snit. Lorem Ipsit delorem decorum sander frommet snit. Lorem Ipsit delorem decorum sander frommet snit. Lorem Ipsit delorem decorum sander frommet snit. Lorem Ipsit delorem decorum sander frommet snit. Lorem Ipsit delorem decorum sander frommet snit. Lorem Ipsit delorem decorum sander frommet

Photo by Joe Thomas

Lorem Ipsit delorem decorum sander frommet snit. Lorem Ipsit delorem decorum sander frommet snit. Lorem Ipsit delorem decorum sander frommet snit. Lorem Ipsit delorem decorum sander frommet snit. Lorem Ipsit delorem decorum sander frommet snit. Lorem Ipsit delorem decorum sander frommet snit. Lorem Ipsit delorem decorum sander frommet snit. Lorem Ipsit delorem decorum sander frommet snit.

snit.

Lorem Ipsit delorem decorum sander frommet snit. Lorem Ipsit delorem decorum sander frommet snit. Lorem Ipsit delorem decorum sander frommet snit. Lorem Ipsit delorem decorum sander frommet snit. Lorem Ipsit delorem decorum sander frommet snit. Lorem Ipsit delorem decorum sander frommet snit. Lorem Ipsit delorem decorum sander frommet snit. Lorem Ipsit delorem decorum sander frommet

snit. Lorem Ipsit delorem decorum sander frommet snit. Lorem Ipsit delorem decorum sander frommet snit. Lorem Ipsit delorem decorum sander frommet snit. Lorem Ipsit delorem decorum sander frommet snit.

Lorem Ipsit delorem decorum sander frommet snit. Lorem Ipsit delorem decorum sander frommet snit. Lorem Ipsit delorem decorum sander frommet snit. Lorem Ipsit delorem

snit. Lorem Ipsit delorem decorum sander frommet snit. Lorem Ipsit delorem decorum sander frommet snit. Lorem Ipsit delorem decorum sander frommet snit. Lorem Ipsit delorem decorum sander frommet snit. Lorem Ipsit delorem decorum sander frommet snit. Lorem Ipsit delorem decorum sander frommet snit. Lorem Ipsit delorem decorum sander frommet

decorum sander frommet snit. Lorem Ipsit delorem decorum sander frommet snit. Lorem Ipsit delorem decorum sander frommet snit.

Lorem Ipsit delorem decorum sander frommet snit. Lorem Ipsit delorem decorum sander frommet snit. Lorem Ipsit delorem decorum sander frommet snit. Lorem Ipsit delorem decorum sander frommet snit.

Figure 7

shape. Editors start with the largest art, and build the package around it. The style an editor chooses will depend on the availability of space, number of stories, and available art and sidebars.

Editors who design for smaller formats may be faced with choices both easier and more difficult. On the easy side, a typical magazine or newsletter page is too small to display more than two or so stories and illustrations— many times a single story package will fill the page. The editor faces fewer choices in selection of elements and makeup packages. Small-format makeup becomes more difficult, however, as readers handling the higher-quality paper usually used for magazines tend to expect more sophisticated design packages. Editors are not expected to be trained graphic designers, and so may need to work more closely with artists on smaller formats.

MAKEUP MATTERS: ACCESSIBILITY STANDARDS ON THE WEB

Editing students are usually young and healthy, and we hope you're both of those. But some are physically or mentally challenged. And many adults who use the Web bring a variety of disabilities to their screens, problems many editors never recognize — unless they have the same problem. Disabilities editors need to consider cover motor skill problems, cognitive impairment, hearing impairment or visual impairment. For example, visually impaired people rejoiced with the development of the Web. Finally, a computerized text reader could quickly and easily read and voice the myriad publications that once were available only on paper or laboriously transferred to Braille. But elation turned to caution as some content providers did not understand how the Web works for people with this disability. Text readers rely on HTML-based text. They cannot easily read pdf files or jpeg picture-like text. Designers who try to control every last pixel of their web page by pdf or jpg effectively deny content to the sight-impaired.

The World Wide Web Consortium (W3C) Web Accessibility Initiative (http://www.w3.org/WAI/) helps content providers to make websites accessible to everyone. The Web can revolutionize accessibility for the disabled — but only if editors and designers keep their special needs in mind.

Beyond these differences, most editors also choose a modular design formula for newsletters and magazines. Newsletter editors usually lay out page one with copy and art, a miniature version of a newspaper front page. Magazine covers usually feature illustrations and teasers, with little copy. But unlike newspapers and newsletters, magazine editors usually work with spreads — two adjacent pages that form one horizontal rectangle. The horizontal feature of a spread, something seldom available to newspaper editors, gives magazine editors an opportunity to run larger art across the space between pages to make a more varied and interesting layout. Also common in magazines are jumps to several subsequent pages.

Style on the Web continues to evolve with new technologies, tools and tricks. The key to design style on the Web begins with hyperlinks. Use links from the primary index page to direct readers to pages that include longer stories, graphics and other elements in a package. Longer pages, which require users to scroll to read all the information, may not be followed. Keep index pages short, don't force readers to scroll, and choose graphics and fonts common to all computers to ensure ease of navigation and use by text readers.

Working by example: Layouts that work, and layouts that don't

For the following examples, editors of a local news organization have a news budget that includes the material below.

Breaking news: Layoffs at a local cheese factory; no art.

News feature: Girl Scouts take over city hall for a day; two large photos of the group in varied tasks, one vertical, one horizontal.

Hard news: City council agrees to increase taxes; bar graph showing yearly increases over the last five years.

Commentary: Increase in taxes will mean bad things for city; mug shot of editor.

It appears the top story should be the breaking news: Layoffs at a local cheese factory. Top stories should appear above the fold of a broadsheet newspaper, and should be identified with larger headlines—60 pt. or more—that alert the reader to the editor's choice of significant story. The second most important story may be the city tax increase, which can be run with a bar graph. Because the fourth story on the list, a commentary from the editor about the increase, is related to the council story, the rule of proximity tells us it should be run adjacent to it. Principles of modern journalism indicate the opinion piece be clearly identified as commentary or news analysis.

The soft news feature about a local Girl Scout troop at city hall for a day offers a glimpse of a timely story that includes photographs. Either the horizontal or vertical could anchor the page, an opportunity to package the story in a modular box.

A popular layout would look like this: The main story could run across six columns at the top, with a sizeable headline; the Girl Scout story could be packaged below it to the left, in five columns (including one or both photos); the tax increase story could be to the right, flowing down the sixth column to the bottom of the page, and the commentary, with bar graph, could be immediately to the left and under the Girl Scout story (Figure 8).

Here's why: Visually, we're telling readers they need to know about the layoffs at the local cheese factory first. Their eyes will move down and back to the left after they see that headline, and should immediately see the Girl Scout photos that anchor the page, then move to the right to see the city tax story. The natural movement of the eye to the left and down will then take readers to the commentary, with mug shot and bar graph, and the tax story.

It's simple. It's clean. And it's effective.

What won't work

The point of the layout is to prioritize the stories that readers should see first. A layout that leads with the commentary, or the feature story, would not work as well. The order in which stories appear makes a difference. This is why news judgment remains a key skill, even at the editor-as-designer's desk. The editor's job is show by placement which stories are important. Top stories always go at the top. Important stories with art get preferential treatment, because art, in addition to the headline, helps call attention to the piece and underline its importance. If possible, stories should be placed in order from most important to least important on the front page, but all

FALLS DAILY NEWS

VOL. 15: ISS. 152   THE NEWS STANDARD FOR A NEW CENTURY   JUNE 1, 2013

Falls Dairy lays off 200 workers

By Joe Thomas
Staff Writer

Lorem Ipsit delorem decorum sander frommet snit. Lorem Ipsit delorem decorum sander frommet snit. Lorem Ipsit delorem decorum sander frommet snit. Lorem Ipsit delorem decorum sander frommet

snit. Lorem Ipsit delorem decorum sander frommet snit. Lorem Ipsit delorem decorum sander frommet snit. Lorem Ipsit delorem decorum sander frommet snit. Lorem Ipsit delorem decorum sander frommet snit. Lorem Ipsit delorem decorum sander frommet snit. Lorem Ipsit delorem decorum sander frommet

snit. Lorem Ipsit delorem decorum sander frommet snit. Lorem Ipsit delorem snit. Lorem Ipsit delorem decorum sander frommet snit. Lorem Ipsit delorem decorum sander frommet snit. Lorem Ipsit delorem decorum sander frommet snit. Lorem Ipsit delorem decorum sander frommet

decorum sander frommet snit. Lorem Ipsit delorem decorum sander frommet snit. Lorem Ipsit delorem decorum sander frommet snit. Lorem Ipsit delorem decorum sander frommet snit. Lorem Ipsit delorem decorum sander frommet snit. Lorem Ipsit delorem

decorum sander frommet snit. Lorem Ipsit delorem decorum sander frommet snit. Lorem Ipsit delorem decorum sander frommet snit. Lorem Ipsit delorem Lorem Ipsit delorem decorum sander frommet snit. Lorem Ipsit delorem decorum sander frommet snit. Lorem Ipsit delorem decorum sander frommet

snit. Lorem Ipsit delorem decorum sander frommet snit. Lorem Ipsit delorem decorum sander frommet snit. Lorem Ipsit delorem decorum sander frommet snit. Lorem Ipsit delorem decorum sander frommet snit. Lorem Ipsit delorem decorum sander frommet

Girl Scouts take over City Hall

By Joe Thomas
Staff Writer

Lorem Ipsit delorem decorum sander frommet snit. Lorem Ipsit delorem decorum sander frommet snit. Lorem Ipsit delorem decorum sander frommet snit. Lorem Ipsit delorem decorum sander frommet snit. Lorem Ipsit delorem decorum sander frommet snit. Lorem Ipsit delorem decorum sander frommet snit. Lorem Ipsit delorem decorum sander frommet snit. Lorem Ipsit delorem decorum sander frommet snit. Lorem Ipsit delorem decorum sander frommet snit.

Lorem Ipsit delorem decorum sander frommet snit. Lorem Ipsit delorem decorum sander frommet snit. Lorem Ipsit delorem decorum sander frommet snit. Lorem Ipsit delorem decorum sander frommet snit. Lorem Ipsit delorem decorum sander frommet snit. Lorem Ipsit delorem decorum sander frommet snit. Lorem Ipsit delorem decorum sander frommet snit. Lorem Ipsit delorem decorum sander frommet snit. Lorem Ipsit delorem decorum sander frommet snit. Lorem Ipsit delorem

Photo by Joe Thomas

Lorem Ipsit delorem decorum sander frommet snit. Lorem Ipsit delorem decorum sander frommet snit. Lorem Ipsit delorem decorum sander frommet snit. Lorem Ipsit delorem decorum sander frommet snit. Lorem Ipsit delorem decorum sander frommet snit. Lorem Ipsit delorem decorum sander frommet snit.

snit.

Lorem Ipsit delorem decorum sander frommet snit. Lorem Ipsit delorem decorum sander frommet snit. Lorem Ipsit delorem decorum sander frommet snit. Lorem Ipsit delorem decorum sander frommet snit. Lorem Ipsit delorem decorum sander frommet snit.

Lorem Ipsit delorem decorum sander frommet snit. Lorem Ipsit delorem decorum sander frommet snit. Lorem Ipsit delorem decorum sander frommet snit. Lorem Ipsit delorem decorum sander frommet snit. Lorem Ipsit delorem decorum sander frommet snit. Lorem Ipsit delorem decorum sander frommet snit.

snit. Lorem Ipsit delorem decorum sander frommet snit. Lorem Ipsit delorem decorum sander frommet snit. Lorem Ipsit delorem decorum sander frommet snit. Lorem Ipsit delorem decorum sander frommet snit. Lorem Ipsit delorem

decorum sander frommet decorum sander frommet snit. Lorem Ipsit delorem decorum sander frommet snit. Lorem Ipsit delorem decorum sander frommet snit. Lorem Ipsit delorem decorum sander frommet snit. Lorem Ipsit delorem decorum sander frommet snit.

City raises taxes

News Staff

Lorem Ipsit delorem decorum sander frommet snit. Lorem Ipsit delorem decorum sander frommet snit. Lorem Ipsit delorem decorum sander frommet snit. Lorem Ipsit delorem decorum sander frommet snit. Lorem Ipsit delorem decorum sander frommet snit. Lorem Ipsit delorem decorum sander frommet snit. Lorem Ipsit delorem decorum sander frommet snit. Lorem Ipsit delorem decorum sander frommet snit. Lorem Ipsit delorem decorum sander frommet snit.

Lorem Ipsit delorem decorum sander frommet snit. Lorem Ipsit delorem decorum sander frommet snit. Lorem Ipsit delorem decorum sander frommet snit. Lorem Ipsit delorem decorum sander frommet snit. Lorem Ipsit delorem decorum sander frommet snit.

Lorem Ipsit delorem decorum sander frommet snit. Lorem Ipsit delorem decorum sander frommet snit. Lorem Ipsit delorem decorum sander frommet snit. Lorem Ipsit delorem decorum sander frommet snit. Lorem Ipsit delorem decorum sander frommet snit. Lorem Ipsit delorem decorum sander frommet snit. Lorem Ipsit delorem decorum sander frommet snit. Lorem Ipsit delorem decorum sander frommet

Tax increase means better services

Lorem Ipsit delorem decorum sander frommet snit. Lorem Ipsit delorem decorum sander frommet snit. Lorem Ipsit delorem decorum sander frommet snit. Lorem Ipsit delorem decorum sander frommet snit. Lorem Ipsit delorem decorum sander frommet snit. Lorem Ipsit delorem decorum sander frommet snit. Lorem Ipsit delorem decorum sander frommet snit. Lorem Ipsit delorem decorum sander frommet snit. Lorem Ipsit delorem decorum sander frommet snit. Lorem Ipsit delorem

decorum sander frommet snit. Lorem Ipsit delorem decorum sander frommet snit. Lorem Ipsit delorem decorum sander frommet snit. Lorem Ipsit delorem decorum sander frommet snit. Lorem Ipsit delorem decorum sander frommet snit. Lorem Ipsit delorem decorum sander frommet snit. Lorem Ipsit delorem decorum sander frommet snit. Lorem Ipsit delorem decorum sander frommet snit. Lorem Ipsit delorem decorum sander frommet snit. Lorem Ipsit delorem

decorum sander frommet snit. Lorem Ipsit delorem decorum sander frommet snit. Lorem Ipsit delorem decorum sander frommet snit. Lorem Ipsit delorem decorum sander frommet snit. Lorem Ipsit delorem decorum sander frommet snit. Lorem Ipsit delorem decorum sander frommet snit. Lorem Ipsit delorem decorum sander frommet snit. Lorem Ipsit delorem decorum sander frommet snit. Lorem Ipsit delorem

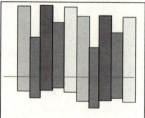

Graph by Margo Wood

Figure 8

MAKEUP MATTERS: THE NEWS HOLE

A classically crusty editor teaching a group of aspiring journalists asked the class: "What is the first duty of a newspaper?" Answers ranged from "protect democracy," to "cover politics," to "afflict the comfortable"—that last one from a student fresh from a journalism history class. "No, no, *no*," responded the editor. "The first duty of a newspaper is to make money. Because without that, there will be no newspaper."

Online competition today has sent the old paper-heavy newspapers scurrying to the Web, or alas, sometimes to bankruptcy court. But the reason is exactly as the old editor proposed. Most editors work in a for-profit operation. While journalism ideals presume a wall of separation between editorial and advertising, some publications let that wall become porous. And most editors know one thing is certain: the copy on their news budget may or may not end up finding space, but the advertising will always be exactly what the advertiser has paid for. That's because the advertising usually gets laid in first. Editors receive pages from advertising staff who has placed ads calculated to pay for the product by having a set percentage of advertising to non-advertising copy. This number is called the *advertising ratio*, and the space left over after ad placement is called the *news hole*. Editors are responsible for filling the news hole.

Publication ad ratios are measured in percentages. A 25 percent ad ratio means 25 percent of the surface area in a publication will be paid for, that is, will be advertising. Many newspapers traditionally tried to maintain an ad ratio of 50 percent—although that is creeping up. Today's newspaper usually contains slightly more advertisements than editorial copy, up to 60 percent advertising. A publication that reaches an ad ratio of 80 percent and up is called a *shopper*. Even if the editor doesn't think she or he is working for a shopper, if the publication is stuffed to more than three-fourths with advertising, readers will consider it one regardless.

Web-based media have re-thought the old ad ratio, as consumers won't accept full-page commercial material, and can more easily ignore online rail ads. Click-through advertising and targeted advertising based on user preferences seem to give media new ways to generate income.

---

stories on the front page should adhere to established news values. This visual prioritization continues on the inside pages, with local stories gaining prominence over national stories, as national stories are easily accessible online or on a 24-hour news channel.

A layout that does not emphasize related art and text will fail. In the example, pictures that go with the Girl Scout story should be placed with that story, not elsewhere. The bar graph indicating tax increases could be—and should be—placed with either story about those tax increases. Art that floats in the middle of text without being anchored to its story doesn't make sense to readers. The rule of proximity tells us that readers need to see everything related to the central story appear adjacent to that story.

MAKEUP MATTERS: BASIC COMPOSITION

Each period of design history has been influenced by new technologies introduced in each era. Through each era, however, some design principles have remained the same. The chief principles influencing newsprint layout — and thus, other publications — surround a set of two large concepts: *proximity* and *repetition*. Both allow readers to feel comfortable reading the publications, and enhance unity of the overall design.

The principle of proximity.

Simply put, proximity asks editors to group related items together. At its core, this principle makes intuitive sense; photos and art that go with a related story should be placed adjacent to that story, and headlines, cutlines, and bylines that go with these elements should also be placed with that story. The principle can be extended to the overarching organization of the publication. A newspaper editor's choice for prominent news, for example, will be displayed on page one. Editorials, letters to the editor, and other opinion pieces will be grouped on a single page or section. Sports stories will be grouped in the sports section, feature stories in the feature section, and so on.

On the Web, proximity becomes even more critical as designers organize their pages to be comfortably linked by category. Each page should house information that goes together. Proximity allows editors to help guide readers through the stories that go together, and allows readers to comfortably find information they are looking for in the places they expect to see it.

The principle of repetition.

Within each publication, items are repeated throughout the document to bring a sense of unity to the finished product. This sense of repetition achieves an overall look for the publication and allows editors to consistently use elements that go with the overall product design.

Repeating specific design elements throughout a product helps to "brand" it in such a way as to make it instantly recognizable. Examples include the fonts used in each document for headlines, text, cutlines and bylines. A list of the fonts and sizes available throughout the document, called a style sheet, aids in the creation of consistent design from section to section.

Repetition is especially key for Web designers. Style sheets on the Web take on a technical purpose; a Cascading Style Sheet, or CSS script, asks designers to designate fonts, styles, and other repeatable elements once, then apply them to all the pages on a site. Repeated graphic elements and text on each page will help cue readers to their positioning on the site, and alert them to when they've left the site.

Consistency of order helps orient readers from issue to issue: opinions may appear invariably on page four, for example and comics may always appear on the back page. Editors working on the Web may establish consistent placement of contact information on the bottom of each page; in an ad or brochure, editors might set up consistent placement of a logo at the top.

A layout that requires multiple jumps fails. Readability research shows readers not only don't often follow jumps; they're irritated by them. Your job in layout is to make sure readers stay with a story until it's finished. Your reporters may have written masterpieces, but unless readers follow, those masterpieces will not get the attention they deserve. A designated jump page helps readers when a jump is absolutely required. The rule of repetition helps us to understand that readers will grow to expect that jumped stories will appear on the same page from issue to issue.

How does this approach apply to small-format publication design? It's similar, in that the editor again prioritizes stories to feature. Priorities, however, may be different. Magazine and newsletter editors seldom face daily deadlines, and seldom include in their budgets stories we'd consider "hard news"—such as a cheese factory layoff. They do, however, consider news values based on mission of the publication, strength of the writing, and quality of the illustrations. Good packages deserve spreads, and so pages should be reserved for these features. Jumps may be inevitable on a smaller format— but readers will be more likely to follow jumps to pages immediately following the spread, book-style.

Taking this budget to the Web

Because the Web offers designers an opportunity to use audio, video, animation, and other graphic devices to enhance storytelling, the layout incorporating the same news budget will be slightly different. In this example, we'll assume the same news organization runs both the printed and the online versions of the news site.

The key to a good news website is not to simply upload stories from the day's newspaper, ("shovelware") but to add to those stories, taking advantage of Web capabilities. In the case of the cheese factory layoffs, the announcement could be run on the primary index page, including just the heading (SEO enhanced), a short lead highlighting the announcement, a graphic, and possibly audio or video of the actual press conference. This could be linked to another page on which the full story, along with links to other information, would be available.

In smaller type, other stories could be listed by heading, with short leads, and links to pages for full pieces. For the Girl Scout story, that page would include not just the graphic, but perhaps audio of interviews with the Girl Scouts. Quotes can be linked to sound bites. For the city council story, the bar graph could become interactive. Commentary could include not just the mug shot, but could be set up as a blog, allowing response from readers.

What won't work?

Just moving the stories over from the printed paper to a newspaper layout on the Web shows a lack of creativity and a lack of sensitivity to what Web readers are looking for in their stories. websites should provide added value to news organizations.

MAKEUP MATTERS: THE WEB AND DEAD-TREE MEDIA

The Web appears to be a marvelous way for an editor to reach consumers of mass media products. Readers can merely open their browser, smartphone or wireless reading device and enjoy text, photos, sound and video. Sometimes they can respond and become part of the content. And think of the trees saved. Twelve average trees produce one ton of low-quality newsprint (and 24 trees for the higher quality wove paper you use in your printer). This means, according to recycling advocates, that 75,000 trees sacrifice themselves for a single Sunday edition of the *New York Times*. But don't blame that gray lady — it's just a fraction of the 25 million trees cut each year to produce the nation's newspapers (http://www.recycling-revolution.com/recycling-facts.html). Newspaper editors sometimes joke about a bad story in print, saying "it's a shame they killed trees to print that." But it's a joke with a vein of truth.

That said, the Web is not always the best way to reach consumers. Perhaps ancient cultures loved to read long articles on a scroll, but Web fans generally don't like scrolling. Computer screens usually do not match the resolution quality of the printed word, making online reading of long texts more tedious. And non-linear Web presentation doesn't always enhance learning. Sometimes, particularly in textbooks, a reader needs to follow an extended argument from beginning to end. This need may better be met by paper-based technology. Also beyond an editor's control on the Web are technical details that can make it difficult to stabilize matters of text font and cutlines that serve to enhance a reader's experience.

A word about color

The extensive use of color in publication design, a relatively recent development, offers editors an opportunity to further highlight more important stories. The mechanical process for allowing full-color front pages requires a press that can print using four different inks: cyan, magenta, yellow and black. These four *process colors*, when blended together, can create in ink any other color of the rainbow.

Used to emphasize stories, color can be an asset to an editor. It can also be a source of tasteless connotation certain to alienate some readers. An example? An editor might be tempted to create a red graphic to go with a headline about city violence, a dramatization for a bloody murder story. Conversely, a good example of color use might choosing green for a recyclables symbol, to accompany an environmental story about recycling. That adds emphasis without overdoing.

Editors should be careful in their use of multiple colors. Colors take on meaning when placed adjacent to stories. We observe the color red can denote blood. In western society it also may connote passion, anger, caution, even healing. Blue can denote peace, water, calm, or cool. Green can denote money or nature, and it has become associated with environmental causes. But not all colors mean the same things to all audiences. In some Eastern cultures, red means "good luck," while white is the color of mourning and black is the color of joy. Purple in many cultures traditionally has been associated with royalty, but in recent years, it also has become associated with young girls.

Also worth an editor's consideration? The mechanical process of printing ink on a page differs from the electronic process used to display color on a computer screen. Television and monitors begin with black and project red, green and blue pixels (RGB) additively to display color on a screen; printing presses begin with white and apply process colors subtractively to produce color on paper. Because each system uses different color schemes to calculate percentages of color proportions, what is seen on a computer screen may not be what prints. This variance in color can be minimized by ensuring the color schemes in your layout program are set to "CMYK" (cyan, magenta, yellow, black), and that values of each color for daily use are recorded on the newspaper's style sheet. This will ensure consistency in color from one publication to the next, again adhering to the rule of repetition. Conversely, Web pages can be designed using colors in the RGB color scheme, because the final product will be electronic.

Full-color photographs on front pages have become the norm in most daily and some weekly newspapers. Many magazines rely on full color throughout. The use of spot color, or one specific ink mixed like paint and used throughout a design, also has become a norm, and a frequent selling point for advertisers. Despite its additional cost, readers have come to expect color in their designs, and editors should use it when available. But carefully, and with purpose.

All design should be purposeful. Every element on the page should have a reason

---

MAKEUP MATTERS: PROXIMITY, REPETITION AND PSYCHOLOGY

Analysis of visual images has fallen in the past century as much to psychologists as to artists or art historians. Early researchers examining visual perception discovered the perhaps surprising principle that it is our mind that sees; our eyes are simply the living lenses that transmit the image, as objective as a camera lens that sometimes blinks. Yet because we generally don't understand how our brain perceives what we see, we distrust analysis of visual perception in favor of the touchstone of words printed and spoken. "We have neglected the gift of comprehending things through our senses," wrote visual psychologist Rudolf Arnheim. "We suffer a paucity of ideas that can be expressed in images and an incapacity to discover meaning in what we see."

Yet we do see, and our brain does perceive, whether we understand the process or not. The brain tries to make patterns, tries to find meaning in simple shapes. The principle of proximity works because the brain tries to make connections by relating things close to each other. We find repetition pleasing as the brain tries to find order in a visual cacophony of our world. Most editors are not artists, hardly so. But even basic study of visual literacy within a predominantly word-based curriculum can offer an editor a more sophisticated view of a mass media world increasingly build atop visual images.

VOCABULARY AND JARGON FOR EDITORS

Art.
Editor's journalese for photographs and illustrations.

Broadsheet.
Most newspapers print on newsprint of a fairly unwieldy size, the broadsheet. Actual broadsheet size varies, but usually is about 22 inches high. Broadsheet-sized newspapers trace their history back at least two centuries.

Traditionally they matched the printer's standard of 17 inches wide — the standard size of two 8½ × 11–inch sheets side by side — but many newspapers today have slimmed to save paper cost.

Column-inch.
A measurement of space one column wide by one inch deep. Editors measure story size in column inches, and advertising staffs often sell space by column inch.

Columns and grids.
Grids are nonprinting lines that divide space on a page. Most editors work with grid sheets indicating the number of columns on the page. Copy is set within these columns. Newspaper columns seldom vary in width. In magazines or books, however, designers sometimes combine wider and narrower columns, such as the 2+1: two columns for text, and one smaller column for illustrations or notes. This book is laid out using a 2+1.

Graphic.
An illustration adding information to a story, such as a graph or chart.

Gutter/alley.
Usually the space between columns is the *gutter*, while the space between pages on a spread — two facing pages— is the *alley*. The alley on books and magazines must be wide enough to allow binding without burying text. Some editors confuse the terms; an editor who calls for a headline across an alley may be referring to a multicolumn hed.

Laddered placement.
Advertising staff on most quality publications avoids sprinkling advertisements around a large-format page, but group them into one area. Editors make a clear distinction between display ads and editorial copy by repeating the word *advertisement* in small type above a large ad. Several ads placed together toward the bottom inside and outside of each page are *laddered* up to the top, creating a *well* of space for editors to fill.

Non-linear information presentation.
Mass media before the Internet presented information linearly. Consumers were expected to progress through a publication or broadcast from first to last, in arbitrary sequence. But cognitive psychologists say this layout does not reflect human's innate

learning style: active, wide-ranging, visual, quick and non-linear. The Web usually reflects this need with link-based information presentation. The reader, and not the editor, chooses the sequence.

Splash page.

An entry video or artistic presentation, often done using Flash software, that Web viewers see before heading to the index page. Splash pages usually are not used on news websites, as most viewers prefer to go directly to the information they're looking for.

Teaser.

Short sentence aimed at attracting readers into a publication. Newsstand magazines and tabloids almost always use cover teasers to attract readers Newspapers often use them on the *ears*— the top edges— or elsewhere on a front page to draw readers.

---

for being there, and every editor working to lay out a page should never forget needs of readers. Wild and clever layouts may impress colleagues. But do they attract readers? Bear in mind that the purpose of good layout is to attract readers to the information they need in an easy-to-follow format, and to ensure that the most important information gets the most attention.

To that end, layout relies on two primary rules: proximity and repetition. The rule of proximity tells us that related story parts should be placed together on a page. The rule of repetition tells us that elements of design and organization should be repeated throughout to enable readers to quickly and easily find information. Both rules encourage layout as secondary to stories. No one notices a good layout. But everyone notices a bad one.

Know more

Lester, P. M. (2006). *Visual Communication: Images with Messages*, 4th ed. Belmont, CA: Thomson Higher Education.

Parker, R. C. (1998). *Looking Good in Print*, 4th ed. Scottsdale, AZ: Coriolis Group.

Siebert, L., and Ballard, L. (1992). *Making a Good Layout: A Hands-On Guide to Understanding and Using Basic Principles of Design and Layout.* Cincinnati, OH: North Light.

Williams, R. (2008). *The Non-Designer's Design Book: Design and Typographic Principles for the Visual Novice.* 3d ed. Berkley, CA: Peachpit.

• EXERCISE 1 •

Choose any newspaper's front page. Try to reproduce that front page within your design program, paying special attention to the layout of the stories, the fonts used for headlines, cutlines, body, and byline text, and the use of color. Finally, on the front and

The Daily Gazette

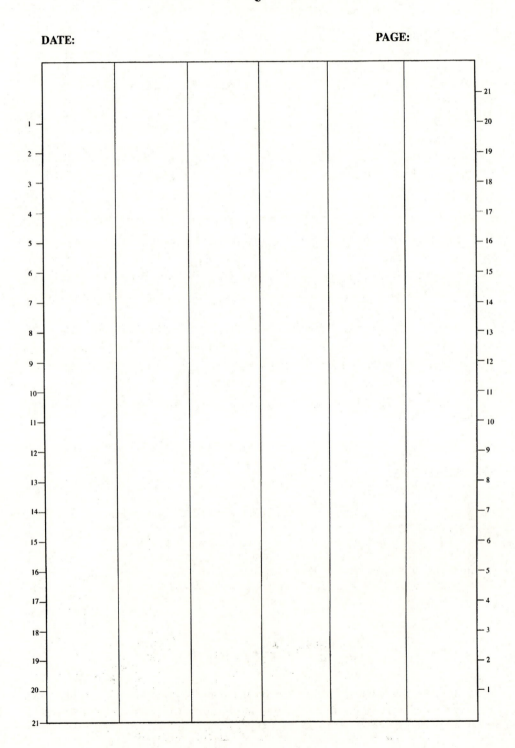

back of the page below, or on a separate sheet, discuss how that newspaper's page designer adhered to the rules of proximity and repetition for the design.

Based on your design, consider how an editor would convert the work into a website. How would it differ? What stories will be placed, and where will they go? What other elements could you use to enhance the website? Describe in writing.

• EXERCISE 2 •

Put yourself in the role of the editor working on page design. You are given the following stories and art:

Feature: Lutefisk as a holiday tradition, with photographs of a local family preparing and eating lutefisk. (Don't know what lutefisk is? Good editors must be informed: http://dare.wisc.edu/?q=node/115.)

Hard news: Two suspects sought in Tasty Treat murder, no art.

Hard news: City council passes sales tax increase to support new stadium building, with an artist's rendering of the proposed new stadium.

Hard news: County board agrees to cut property taxes for the following year, no art.

Rank order these stories in terms of news value, referring to Chapter One, if necessary.

Using a standard dummy sheet (see facing page), sketch out a layout that visually prioritizes the stories in order of importance and works with the rules of repetition and proximity.

Using a Web dummy sheet, determine where the stories will be placed and in what order on the website.

• EXERCISE 3 •

You have been asked to redesign a local newspaper.

Begin by defining a new style sheet for the publication. What fonts, styles and colors will be standardized for your redesign? In writing define each element of the page and identify a standard for each, then justify your choices. Finally, add suggestions for how that newspaper could incorporate the style sheet into a new website design.

NINE

Page Design on Paper and Screen
Therese L. Lueck and *Val Pipps*

In the last chapter we covered basic page makeup. Many editors are expected to place material on pages or on websites designed by someone else. But sometimes editors also are expected to apply some design concepts, and show some basic pagination software skills. This chapter covers that.

A rapidly shifting media marketplace makes it critical for publishers to consider product branding. This requires sophisticated design, and most editors are acutely aware of that need. They want their publication to represent their mission while at the same time speak for itself, to fit into the community conversation as a familiar acquaintance while standing out among the competition. Good publication and web design can accomplish these seemingly disparate goals. Editors today are becoming visual journalists who need to understand design across media. This chapter will focus on the importance of design, assessment of good design and the application of design principles.

The traditional newspaper, or broadsheet, is downsizing, often trimming its page size by using smaller pieces of newsprint, the paper on which the news is printed. This physical resizing is changing the space that designers have to work with, squeezing the rectangle-shaped page from the sides as well as from the top and bottom. The available design space is also being reduced by the introduction of advertising onto pages that had typically not been available for ad placement. The advertising might be stripped across the top of the page, the bottom or both. These reductions of the available design space often alter the proportion of the page as well as its size. A designer needs to maintain flexibility and retain the vision and purpose of the design when confronted with changes in the physical production dimensions and the encroachment of advertising into the editorial design space.

Regardless of whether you're designing a page for a newspaper, magazine or newsletter, you want to recognize that the original vehicle for your initial design may not be the final destination of the design you create. Transferability, or the ability of your design to be translated across media, is an important consideration for you to keep in mind. As the news industry is moving increasingly in the direction of cross-platform design as the media converge, a 2008 study noted that print and Internet Web staffs need to work together better in order to successfully negotiate content and design application across the various media platforms.

One famous designer, Mario Garcia, has been urging newspapers to "downsize" physically for years. However, advertisers often balk when they are accustomed to the large broadsheet, which offers more space for their displays. Nevertheless, spurred by the economic downturn and audiences' changing media habits, some newspapers have converted from their traditional broadsheet to tabloid format in order to attract readers and cut production costs. Although the word "tabloid" has become synonymous with sensationalized journalism, the label actually refers to the format of the newsprint magazine, which is about half the size of a broadsheet.

Not all newspapers in tabloid format are worried that they will be mistaken for the sensationalized supermarket publications. In fact, one Oregon newspaper publicized the fact that it bases its design elements on one of the more widely read tabloids. In addition, students have found inspiration for creating their own designs by looking at the tabloids. Some publications are taking physical downsizing a step further than the move from broadsheet to tabloid in moving from tabloid to magazine. For example, in 2007, *Computerworld* made the transition from its tabloid format to become a magazine. Several years earlier, the trade magazine *Advertising Age* unveiled its redesign, stating that the publication was able to retain the look of an industry leader while maintaining the mission of the long-standing publication. In considering page design, you want to keep this big picture in mind, which means you need to consider the overall look and feel of the page and how it fits into the publication as a whole. Make sure you understand the mission statement, so that the vehicle you design works with the publication's content to communicate that mission through an appropriate tone for the intended audience. Familiarizing yourself with the publication's editorial mission and the intended audience is an essential first step, but it is not the end of the process. In determining what the big picture is, you have a wide variety of resources and contexts available. When you think about the design, consider aspects of the larger culture and the publication's intended impact as well as the culture of the publication's working environment. Popular culture, art movements, particular artists, or pieces of music, literature or visual art may be significant to the enterprise that the publication represents, the context from which it operates or the audience it hopes to engage. For example, consider the design of the building that houses a publication's headquarters, the architecture of its surrounding community, or a bygone or future era the enterprise addresses that you could evoke through publication design. Draw on your own background to capture the big picture. Recall the art classes you have taken, particularly those in which you learned about composition and perspective.

Once you have tapped into your rich array of background, popular culture and powers of observation, you're ready to define the big picture in terms of the design you want to create for your publication. This chapter points out best practices in bringing the big picture into practical terms in order to achieve good page design, and it invites you to apply these practices to the creation of your own page design.

You'll want to keep four principles in mind throughout the design process: **balance,**

contrast, **focus** and **unity**. These principles govern the placement of elements on the page, in particular photographs, headlines, story copy and cutlines, or captions. Working with these principles will allow you to achieve the look and feel you desire, and to communicate that big picture that your page design represents. **Balance** is the perceived optical weight of the arrangement of elements in any design. Perceived weight is created when an element such as a photograph is positioned on a page; that placement gives "weight" to that portion of the page. In achieving a balanced design, weight should be distributed throughout the page, not concentrated in only one place. Therefore, when a weight such a photograph is part of the design for one portion of the page, another portion of the page should also contain a similar weight. The balance of a page can be either symmetrical or asymmetrical.

Formal symmetry is created when both sides of the page look the same. If a vertical line were drawn down the middle of the page and that page was folded in half, both sides would match (Figure 1). Asymmetrical design is the opposite of symmetrical design. With that imaginary line, when the page is folded in half, the sides do not match, but they do provide a counter weight to each other (Figure 2). Asymmetrical design often allows the designer more flexibility than formal symmetry, and it can facilitate visual movement around the page, which is desirable.

Contrast, meaning difference, helps move the reader around the page visually. While you may be familiar with the concept of contrast as it pertains to photographs, the design-based use of the term encompasses more than the density of elements in a photograph, although it does include that concept. Much like you adjust the lightness and darkness in a photograph for contrast among its elements, contrast in page design is desirable and is created by establishing difference among the elements on a page. The designer should create a page that has elements of different sizes and shapes, as well as density. A page that is easily "read" is one that draws the reader's eye to one portion and encourages the flow of viewing from that section to another point on the page and around the rest of the page (Figure 3).

Focus, which includes proportion, denotes the relationship among the elements. The focus of the design is the point of visual entry at which the reader starts to scan the page (Figure 4). One element that is often used to draw the first focus of the reader is a large photograph. Newspaper and web designer Mario Garcia calls the focus of the page the *Center of Visual Impact*.

Unity is as essential to the big picture as it is to the detail of the design. In Chapter Eight we considered the visual principle of repetition. Such repetition has as its goal unity. When a publication itself has unity, it has coherence throughout. The design permits the reader to understand that each page or section is part of the whole. The typographical treatment is the same no matter which section of the publication is being read. For instance, in newspapers the same typeface is used for body text throughout the publication. Likewise, the same logos for sections and columns are used throughout the publication, and the same type families are maintained for headlines (Figure 5).

The same idea with regard to using unifying devices for coherence in the publication as a whole should also be employed on the smaller levels of design. For unique

Xjdfna lasxsdl sdlflj dlfjalls.
C1

Xlsd aldkja lsdk aladl ladk. Xlsd aldkja lsdk aladl ladk lala dl.
B1

Vea ldk lakd ladk ladkf.
A4

Editing Eagle

April 13, 2013   www.editingeagle.com   Volume 1, No. 1

72-pt. headline at top of page

Lectia. Id quia doles erae nonne quam doluption rerum nempore volupta tecat.

Gent il inimenimus, velicta tasiecae sent vendunt resiota corporio ma dolorem porendi tectest, omnimi, edis audipsa menducias quis adis voluptae soluptist, il il inimusam, status doluptate dolorro bea con ne moluptatur solor.

Arum ad quisiti ipsae consodisitat accus, omnis ea sim nis sit, omnietaq nitibus volupid quibus coresu nfiate iantibus arionet quis cici ut et, ediona cusdam, que et acea dit, sequos doluptatiume occum ide nis voluptati ditibus minullu ptatur accus.

Re doluptatur, optiist aut as sum voluporsant, cullaborae de od es reri iur? Cium in exerum is conem inction conseruntin nam nobis ut vel incris non providitius cum lantiae et ut vent, incidit

plam aut et et qui re nonsequat preptas piciis nus, nis sequide nietuscis qui qui debitiis dio ilique quue vendit parum eatus, optatem ipounducis volupti beatectur aut ut aut voles cum ut undit.

Haribusciamus sam, tem qui consed eiusame eos voluptatis coresdi si cullupt atione pro dolesrequin que nonsequos et ees ex eatetur serovid qui in jeratem fagiati sciatur?

Ceperch icipsum sin ent ea volensitatur albuscid que sequi voluptur accaborum etur, qui refferi aectem nsiparunt eribus, qui vidella veria voluptis non con nes et et maximporemldebit quatio porem nisto.

Maximet que nectius volupta conrectur sapis exematecte sinvell audiscias quaeri rationis ectem rem init harum ea descris aut and optatis ciust, quis ditias dicrum quibus et odipidellore reicabo.

Sin cus volaptiorem dolsptaque fictate quam renique voluptate et, evelita spella duntis cus magnatur sim dollores et, secab iducide mquatus estiam, exped et fugiatur, aut qui at alite audipis postio est, aribus aliciatur maio.

Hene none volorum endist

occabor istorum rehontis ssodita volorporum asped modit dolaremqut dollat elessit quibus.

Non non re exeest, iminetia soluptatur mi, cuptaturion endaectae voluptatur apera verum volupta tebusam asspedstiat omnima doluptatus sus undae peratusda ni a cumquamus aut rein.

Delit in peremolupici autectur, nullita tiandior resuequanto

Balance: Symmetrical or formal balance has the same weight on each side of an imaginary line drawn down the middle of the page.

Ibus sinvendita quodi doluptas inctendignam sit quiasinverit verspellabor aut omnimpe rierundi sit utectia quidento

48-pt. headline over this story

Lectia. Id quia doles erae nonne quam doluption rerum nempore volupta tecat.

Gent il inimenimus, velicta tasiecae sent vendunt resiota corporio ma dolorem porendi tectest, omnimi, edis audipsa menducias quis adis voluptae soluptist, il il inimusam, status doluptate dolorro bea con ne moluptatur solor.

Arum ad quisiti ipsae consodisitat accus, omnis ea sim nis sit, omnietaq nitibus volupid quibus coresu nfiate iantibus arionet quis cici ut et, ediona cusdam, que et acea dit, sequos doluptatiume occum ide nis voluptati ditibus minullu ptatur accus.

Re doluptatur, optiist aut as sum voluporsant, cullaborae de

od es reri iur? Cium in exerum is conem inction conseruntin nam nobis ut vel incris non providitius cum lantiae et ut vent, incidit plam aut et et qui re nonsequat preptas piciis nus, nis sequide sietuscis qui qui debitiis dio ilique quue vendit parum eatus, optatem ipounducis volupti beatectur aut ut aut voles cum ut undit.

Haribusciamus sam, tem qui consed eiusame eos voluptatis coresdi si cullupt atione pro dolesrequin que nonsequos et ees ex eatetur serovid qui in jeratem fagiati sciatur?

Ceperch icipsum sin ent ea volensitatur albuscid que sequi voluptur accaborum etur, qui re-

vidella veria voluptis non con nes et et maximporemldebit quatio porem nisto.

Maximet que nectius volupta conrectur sapis exematecte sinvell audiscias quaeri rationis ectem rem init harum ea descris aut and optatis ciust, quis ditias dicrum quibus et odipidellore reicabo.

Sin cus volaptiorem dolsptaque fictate quam renique voluptate et, evelita spella duntis cus magnatur sim dollores et, secab iducide mquatus estiam, exped et fugiatur, aut qui at alite audipis postio est, aribus aliciatur maio.

Hene none volorum endist

occabor istorum rehontis modita volorporum asped modit dolaremqut dollat elesit quibus.

Non non re exeest, iminetia soluptatur mi, cuptaturion endaectae voluptatur apera verum volupta tebusam asspedtiat omnima doluptatus sus andae peratunda ni a cumquamus aut rein.

Delit in peremolupici autectur, nullita tiandior resuequanto bea recabo. Itatur autas endi quas magnam rehenti bneciduat, ipsum re sequos molenim ex cerunt fugit quam dolendis ndndis dndad run

36-pt. headline at bottom of the page

Lectia. Id quia doles erae nonne quam doluption rerum nempore volupta tecat.

Gent il inimenimus, velicta tasiecae sent vendunt resiota corporio ma dolorem porendi tectest, omnimi, edis audipsa menducias quis adis voluptae soluptist, il il inimusam, status doluptate dolorro bea con ne moluptatur solor.

Arum ad quisiti ipsae consodisitat accus, omnis ea sim nis sit, omnietaq nitibus volupid quibus coresu nfiate iantibus arionet quis cici ut et, ediona cusdam, que et acea dit, sequos doluptati

ume occum ide nis voluptati ditibus minullu ptatur accus.

Re doluptatur, optiist aut as sum voloporsant, cullaborae de od es reri iur? Cium in exerum is conem inction conseruntin nam nobis ut vel incris non providitius cum lantiae et ut vent, incidit plam aut et et qui re nonsequat preptas piciis nus, nis sequide sietuscis qui qui debitiis dio ilique quue vendit parum eatus, optatem ipounducis volupti beatectur aut ut aut voles cum ut undit.

Haribusciamus sam, tem qui consed eiusame eos voluptatis

Ibus sinvendita quodi doluptas inctendignam sit quiasinvert verspellabor aut omnimpe rierundi sit utectia quidento

36-pt. headline at bottom of the page

Lectia. Id quia doles erae nonne quam doluption rerum nempore volupta tecat.

Gent il inimenimus, velicta tasiecae sent vendunt resiota corporio ma dolorem porendi tectest, omnimi, edis audipsa menducias quis adis voluptae soluptist, il il inimusam, status doluptate dolorro bea con ne moluptatur solor.

Arum ad quisiti ipsae consodisitat accus, omnis ea sim nis sit, omnietaq nitibus volupid quibus coresu nfiate iantibus arionet quis cici ut et, ediona cusdam, que et acea dit, sequos doluptati

ume occum ide nis voluptati ditibus minullu ptatur accus.

Re doluptatur, optiist aut as sum voloporsant, cullaborae de conem inction conseruntin nam nobis ut vel incris non providitius cum lantiae et ut vent, incidit plam aut et et qui re nonsequat preptas piciis nus, nis sequide sietuscis qui qui debitiis dio ilique quue vendit parum eatus, optatem ipounducis volupti beatectur aut

Haribusciamus sam, tem qui consed eiusame eos voluptatis

Figure 1

Xjdfna lasxsdl sdlflj dlfjalls.
C1

Xlsd aldkja lsdk aladl ladk lala dl.
B1

Vea ldk lakd ladk ladkf.
A4

Editing Eagle

April 13, 2013   www.editingeagle.com   Volume 1, No. 1

72-pt. headline at top of page

Lectio. Id quia doles erae nonse quam doluption renum nempore volupta tecat.

Gent il itumenimus, velicta tasceae sent vendunt restota corporio ma dolorem porendi tectest, omnimi, odis audipsa menducias quis adis voluptae soluptsi, il il inimusam, sitatus doluptate dolorro bea con ne molupttatur selor.

Arum ad quisiti ipsae consodisitat accus, omnis ea sim nis sit, omnimag nitibus volupid quibus coresu ntiate suntibus arionet quis eici ut et, odioria cusdam, que et acea dit, sequos doluptatiume occum ide nis voluptati dinbus minulla ptatur accus.

Re doluptatur, opislat aot as sum volueposant, cullaborae de od es reri iur? Cium in exerum is conem inction conserunto tum nobis et vel inctis non providitus cum luntiae ut us vent, incidi

plam aut et et qui re nonsequat preptas picius eus, nia sequide nietusciis qui qui debitiisi dio ilique quae vendit parum eatus, opatem ipsunduciis volupti beatectur aut ut aut veles cum ut undi.

Haribuscimus sam, tem qui consed einsaene eos voluptatus consedi si cullupt atiore pro dolesequis qua nonsequos et eos exeatetur serovid qui in peratem fugiati seiuur?

Ceperch icipsum sin ent ea volessitatur alibescid que sequ voluptur accaborum etur, qui refen aectem nulparum eribus, qui vidella veria voluptis non con nes et et maximporemldebt quatio corem nisto.

Maximet que nectius volupta conrectur sapis exernatecte sinvell andestiss querri ratoris ocatem rem init harum ea descis aut aut optatlis eiust, quis ditias denum quodus et odipidellore reicabo.

Hene none volorum endist

denum quidus et odipidellore reicabo.

Sin eus voluptiorem doluptique licitate quam resequue voluptate et, evelita spella duntis eus magnatur sim dollores et, secab iducide mquatus estium, exped et fugiatur, aut qui ut alite et qui in res ma si odit pratem ut audips postio est, aribus alciatur

Hene none volorum endist occabor istorum rehentis media voloriporum asped modit dolorempui dollut clessiti quibus.

Non non re exorst, ininctia soluptatur mi, cuptaturion endacstae voluptatur apera verum volupta volupta tibusam aspeditiat omnima doluptatus sus andae peratusda ni a cumquamus aut rem.

Delit in poremolupici autectur, nullita tiandiur ressequunto

Balance:
Imagine a dotted line running down the middle of the page. The balance should be asymmetrical, meaning that each side of the dotted line should be different.

Notice how the visual weight on the left side is balanced by the visual weight on the right side in the lower right portion of the page.

36-pt. headline at bottom of the page

Lectio. Id quia doles erae nonse quam doluption renum nempore volupta tecat.

Gent il itimenimus, velicta tasceae sent vendunt restota corporio ma dolorem porendi tectest, omnimi, odis audipsa menducias quis adis voluptae soluptsi, il il inimusam, sitatus doluptate dolorro bea con ne molupttatur selor.

Arum ad quisiti ipsae consodisitat accus, omnis ea sim nis sit, omnimag nitibus volupid quibus coresu ntiate suntibus arionet quis eici ut et, odioria cusdam, que et acea dit, sequos doluptatiume occum ide nis voluptati dinbus minulla ptatur accus.

Re doluptatur, opislat aot as

sum voleuposant, cullaborae de nobis et vel inctis non providitus cum luntiae ut us vent, incidi plam aut et et qui re nonsequat preptas picius eus, nia sequide nietusciis qui qui debitiisi dio ilique quae vendit parum eatus, opatem ipsunduciis volupti beatectur aut ut aut veles cum ut undi.

Haribuscimus sam, tem qui consed einsaene eos voluptatus consedi si cullupt atiore pro dolesequis qua nonsequos et eos exeatetur serovid qui in peratem fugiati seiuur?

Ceperch icipsum sin ent ea volessitatur alibescid que sequi

voluptur accaborum etur, qui refen aectem nulparum eribus, qui vidella veria voluptis non con nes et et maximporemldebt quatio corem nisto.

Maximet que nectius volupta conrectur sapis exernatecte sinvell andestiss querri ratoris ocatem rem init harum ea descis aut aut optatlis eiust, quis ditias denum quodus et odipidellore res

Sin eus voluptiorem doluptaque licitate quam resequue voluptate et, evelita spella duntis eus magnatur sim dollores et, secab iducide mquatus estium, exped et fugiatur, aut qui ut alite et qui in res ma si odit pratem ut

audips postio est, aribus alciatur maio.

Hene none volorum endist occabor istorum rehentis media voloriporum asped modit dolorempui dollut clessiti quibus.

Non non re exorst, ininctia soluptatur mi, cuptaturion endacstae voluptatur apera verum volupta volupta tibusam aspeditiat omnima doluptatus sus andae peratusda ni a cumquamus aut rem.

Delit in poremolupici autectur, nullita tiandiur ressequunto bea necabo. Itatur autas endi quas magnam rehenti buscibint, ipsum re sequos molenim ex errunt fugit quiam dolendis nduda dladnd mm

Ibus sinvendita quodi doluptas inctendignam sit quiasinverit verspellabor aut omnimpe rferundi sit ufectia quidento

Figure 2

Xjdfna lasxsdl sdlflj dlfjalls. **C1**

Xlsd aldkja lsdk aladl ladk lala dl. **B1**

Vea ldk lakd ladk ladkf. **A4**

Editing Eagle

April 13, 20103   www.editingeagle.com   Volume 1, No. 1

72-pt. headline at top of page

Lectio. Id quia doles erae nonse quam doluption rerum nempore volupta tecat.

Gent il iminemimus, velicta tassecae sent vendunt restota corporio ita dolorem porendi tectent, omnimi, odis audipsa menducias quis adis voluptae soluptsi, il il inimenum, sitatus doluptate dolorro bea con ne moluptatur soler.

Anmi ad quisiti ipsae connse distat accus, omnis ea sim nis sit, omnimag nitibus volupid quibus ccessvo ntiate iumibus aroneri quis eici ut et, odioria cusdam, qae et acea dit, sequos doluptati ume occum ide nis voluptati ditbus minullu ptatur accus.

Re doluptatur, optist aut as sum voluerponant, cullaborse de ed es reri iur? Cium in exerum is conem inction conseruntin num nobis et vel inciis non providitas cum lantiae et ut vent, inedit plam aut et et qui re nonsequat preptas picus nus, nia sequde naetascin qui qui debitini dio iliqae quae vendit parum catus, optatem ipsunducis volupti beatectur aut ut aut voles cum ut undit.

Haribuscimus sam, tem qui consed eiusame ers voluptatus comedi si cullupt atiore pro dolesequis que nonsequor et eos ex eatetur seravid qui in peratem fugiati sciatur?

Ceperch icipsum sin est ea volesitatur albiuscid que sequi voluptur acceaborum etur, qui reriferi arctem nulparent eribus, qui vidella veria voluptis non con nis et et maximporemldebit quatio corem nisto.

Maximet que nectius volupta conrector iapis exemstecte sinvell andiscias quaeri rations eca tem rem init harum ea desciis aut ant optatiis eiust, quis ditias aut ant optatiis eiust, quis ditias

derum quidus et odipidellore reicabo.

Sin cus veluptiorem doluptaque lictate quam resequae voluptate et, evelita spella duntis cus magnatur sum dollores et, secab iducide mgnatus entium, exped et fugiatur, aut qui ut alite et qui in res ma si odit pratem in audipis postio est, aribus aliciatur maio.

Hene none volorum undist

occabor istorum rehentis modita veloeporum aspcd modit doloremigo dollut eleusi quibus.

Non non re excest. inimctu soluptatur mi, cuptaturion cndacctae voluptatur apera venum volupta volupta tibusam aspediat omnima deluptatus us andae peratousda ni a cumspianus aut rem.

Delii in poremolupici antectur, nullita tiandior resnequntto

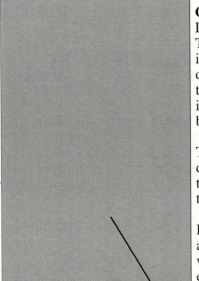

Contrast:
Large versus small. The larger headline is bold and at the top of the page versus the smaller headline in regular style at the bottom of the page.

The larger photo dominates and is near the visual middle of the page.

Both of these are examples of contrast, which helps create eye movement.

36-pt. headline at bottom of the page

Lectio. Id quis dules erae nonse quam doluption rerum nempore volupta tecat.

Gent il iminemimus, velicta tassecae sent vendunt restota corporio ita dolorem porendi tectent, omnimi, odis audipsa menducias quis adis voluptae soluptsi, il il inimenum, sitatus doluptate dolorro bea con ne moluptatur soler.

Anmi ad quisiti ipsae connse distat accus, omnis ea sim nis sit, omnimag nitibus volupid quibus conessu ntiate iumibus aroneri quis eici ut et, odioria cusdam, qise et acea dit, sequos doluptati ume occum ide nis voluptati ditbus minullu ptatur accus.

Re doluptatur, optist aut as

sum volerponant, cullaborse de ed es reri iur? Cium in exerum is conem inction conseruntin num nobis et vel inciis non providitas cum lantiae et ut vent, inedit plam aut et et qui re nonsequat preptas picus nus, nia sequde naetascin qui qui debitini dio iliqae quae vendit parum catus, optatem ipsunducis volupti beatectur aut ut aut voles cum ut undit.

Haribuscimus sam, tem qui consed eiusame ers voluptatus comedi si cullupt atiore pro dolesequis que nonsequor et cos ex eatetur seravid qui in peratem fugiati sciatur?

Ceperch icipsum sin est ea volessitatur albiuscid que sequi

voluptur acceaborum etur, qui reriferi arctem nulparent eribus, qui vidella veria voluptis non con nis et et maximporemldebit quatio corem nisto.

Maximet que nectius volupta conrector iapis exemstecte sinvell andiscias quaeri rations eca tem rem init harum ea desciis aut ant optatiis eiust, quis ditias derum quidus et odipidellore reicabo.

Sin cus veluptiorem doluptaque lictate quam resequae voluptate et, evelita spella duntis cus magnatur sum dollores et, secab iducide mgnatus entium, exped et fugiatur, aut qui ut alite et qui in res ma si odit pratem in

audipes postio est, aribus aliciatur maio.

Hene none volorum endist occabor istorum rehentis modita veloeporum aspcd modit doloremigo dollut eleusi quibus.

Non non re excest. inimctu soluptatur mi, cuptaturion cndacctae voluptatur apera venum volupta volupta tibusam aspediat omnima deluptatus us andae peracousda ni a cumspianus aut rem.

Delii in poremolupici antectur, nullita tiandior resnequntto bea necabo. Itatur astas endi quas magnam rehenti buscident, ipsum re sequos molenium ex errunt fugit quiam doleodis

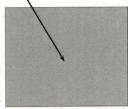

Ibut sinvendita quodi doluptas inctendignam sit quiasinverit verspellabor aut omnimpe rferund sit utiectia quidento

Figure 3

Xjdfna lasxsdl
sdlflj dlfjalls.
C1

Xlsd aldkja lsdk
aladl ladk lala dl.
B1

Vea ldk lakd
ladk ladkf.
A4

Editing Eagle

April 13, 2013   www.editingeagle.com   Volume 1, No. 1

72-pt. headline at top of page

Lectio. Id quia doles erae nonse quam doluption renum nempore volupta tecat.

Gent il immenimus, velicta tassecae sent vendunt restora corporio ma dolorem porendi tectest, onmimi, odis audipsa menducias quis adis voluptae soluptat, il il imimusam, sitatus doluptate dolorru bea con ne moluptatur sofor. Anum ad quositi ipsae consedistat accus, omnis ea sim res sit.

omnimag nitibus volupid quibus coressu ntiate nutilbus arionet quis eici ut et, odioria cusdam, que et acea dit, sequos doluptatiune occurr ide nis voluptati daibus minulle ptatur accus.

Re doluptatur, optist aut as sum voloeposant, collaborae de od es reri int? Cium in exeram is conem inction conserunim num nobis et vel inciis non providitius eum lautiae et ut vent, incilit

plam aut et et qui re nonsequat preptas piciis nus, nia sequide nienucsis qui qui debitisi dio ilique quae vendit parum eatus, optatem ipsunduciis volupti beatectur aut at aut voles cum ut endit.

Harihuscimus sam, tem qui consed einsame eos voluptatus consedi si cullupt atiore pro dolesquis que nonsequos et eos ex eatetur servoid qui in peratem fugiati sciatur?

Ceperch icipuum sin ent ea volessitatur alibuscid que sequ voluptur accaborum etur, qui rerfen aectem nulparum eribus, qui vidella veria voluptis non con nes et et maximporemldebit quatio corem nisto.

Maxumet que nectius volupta conrector sapis evernatecte sinvell andiscias quaeri ratem rem init harum ea desciis aut at optatiis eiust, quis ditias

derum quidus et odipideflore reicubo.

Sin cus voluptionem doluptaque lictate quam reseque voloptate et, evelita spella duntis cus magnatur siin dellores et, secab iduiche mqeatus estium, exped et fugiatur, aut qui at alate et qui in res ma si odit pretem ut audipis postio est, aribus alieiatur maio.

Hene none volorum endist

occabor istorum rehentis media voloeporum asped modit dolorenqui dollut elessit qaibus.

Non non re excesti, immetia soluptatur mi, cuptation endiscetae voluptatur apera verum volupta volupta tibusam aspeditat onmima doluptatis sus zudae peratnuda ni a cumqutanus aut rem.

Delit in poremolupici autectur, nullita tiandiur ressequnto

Ibus sinvendita quodi doluptas inctendignam sit quiasinverit verspellabor aut omnimpe rferundi sit utectia quidento

48-pt. headline with deck

18-pt. headline serves as the deck to the main head of the stroy

Lectio. Id quia doles erae nonse quam doluption renum nempore volupta tecat.

Gent il imensimus, velicta tassecae sent vendunt restora corporio ma dolorem porendi tectest, onmimi, odis audipsa menducias quis adis voluptae soluptat, il il imimusam, sitatus doluptate dolorru bea con ne moluptatur sofor.

Anum ad quositi ipsae consedistat accus, omnis ea sim res sit, onmimag nitibus volupid quibus coressu ntiate iuntbus arionet quis eici ut et, odioria

cusdam, que et acea dit, sequos doluptatiune recum ide nis voluptati ditibus minullu ptatur accus.

Re doluptatur, optist aut as sum voloeposant, collaborae de od es reri int? Cium in exeram is erum is conem inction consecrutin num nobis et vel inciis non providibus eum lautiae et ut vent, incidit plam aut et et qui re nonsequat preptas picis nus, nia sequide metasciis qui qui debitisi dio ilique quae vendit parum eatus, optatem ipsunduciis volupti beatectur

aut ut aut voles cum ut endit.

Harihuscimus sam, tem qui consed einsame eos voluptatus consedi si cullupt atiore pro dolesquis que nonsequos et eos ex eatetur servoid qui in peratem fugiati sciatur?

Ceperch icipuum sin ent ea volessitatur alibuscid que sequi voluptur accaborum etur, qui rerfei aectem nulparum eribus, qui tis non con nes et et maximporemldebit quatio corem nisto.

Maxumet que nectius volupta conrector sapis evernatecte

sinvell andiscias quaeri ratlions ecatem rem init harum ea desciis aut ant optatiis eiust, quis ditias derum quidus et odipideflore reicabo.

Sin cus voluptionem doluptaque lictate quam reseque voloptate et, evelita spella duntis dutiis cus magnatur siin dellores et, secab iduiche mqeatus estium, exped et fugiatur, aut qui in res ma si odit pretem est, aribus alieiatur maio.

Hene none volorum endist occabor istorum rehentis mod-

36-pt. headline at bottom of the page

Lectio. Id quia doles erae nonse quam doluption renum nempore volupta tecat.

Gent il imenimus, velicta tassecae sent vendunt restora corporio ma dolorem porendi tectest, onmimi, odis audipsa menducias quis adis voluptae soluptat, il il imimusam, sitatus doluptate dolorru bea con ne moluptatur sofor. Anum ad quositi ipsae consedistat accus, omnis ea sim res sit, onmimag nitibus volupid quibus coressu ntiate iuntbus arionet quis eici ut et, odioria cusdam, que et acea dit, sequos doluptatiune occurr ide nis voluptati daibus minullu ptatur accus.

Re doluptatur, optist aut as

sum voloeposant, collaborae de od es reri int? Cium in exeram is conem inction conserunim num nobis et vel inciis non providitius eum lautiae et ut vent, incidit plam aut et et qui re nonsequat preptas picis nus, nia sequide niene qui quae vendit parum eatus, optatem ipsunduciis volupti beatectur aut at aut voles cum ut endit.

Harihuscimus sam, tem qui consed einsame eos voluptatus consedi si cullupt atiore pro dolesquis que nonsequos et eos ex eatetur servoid qui in peratem fugiati sciatur?

Ceperch icipuum sin ent ea volessitatur alibuscid que sequi

voluptur accaborum etur, qui rerfen aectem nulparum eribus, qui vidella veria voluptis non con nes et et maximporemldebit quatio corem nisto.

Maxumet que nectius volupta conrector sapis evernatecte sinvell andiscias quaeri ratem rem init harum ea desciis aut ant optatiis eiust, quis ditias derum quidus et odipideflore reicubo.

Sin cus voluptionem doluptaque licate quam reseque voloptate et, evelita spella duntis secab iduiche mqeatus estium, exped et fugiatur, aut qui at alate et qui in res ma si odit pretem ut

audipis postio est, aribus alieiatur maio.

Hene none volorum endist occabor istorum rehentis media voloeporum asped modit dolorenqui dollut elessit qaibus.

Non non re excesti, immetia soluptatur mi, cuptation endiscetae voluptatur apera verum volupta volupta tibusam aspeditat onmima doluptatis sus zudae peratnuda ni a cumqutanus aut rem.

Delit in poremolupici autectur, nullita tiandiur ressequnto bea eecabo. Itatur autas endi quas magnam rehenti buscidunt, ipsum re sequos molenum ex cerum fugit quam dolendo

Ibus sinvendita quodi doluptas inctendignam sit quiasinverit verspellabor aut omnimpe rferundi sit utectia quidento

Focus:

The large photo is the focus of the page. It is one of the first elements that the reader sees on the page.

Figure 4

pieces of the publication, such as story packages, or stories grouped together by related content, you want to create a look that stands out from the rest of the publication but adheres to a consistency within itself and among its related elements. For instance, a style of initial capital letter, perhaps in a font different from but compatible to the larger publication, could be used to identify the beginning of each story in the package, along with complementary logo and headline treatment. Much like the macro-level unity that pulls the entire publication together, this type of unity creates cohesiveness for the story package (Figure 6). To maintain the overall unity of the publication, the design does not deviate in any manner that will cause any element, macro or micro, to appear unrelated to the publication as a whole.

Figure 5. Unity: Although a newspaper's flag will have a distinct look, section fronts will all be designed the same. That creates a unified look for the paper. Readers will be able to see that all sections belong to that newspaper, even if each are on separate pages.

Models for good design

Models for designs that skillfully employ these principles abound. Newspaper front pages from the United States and over 70 countries around the world are displayed daily at the Newseum in Washington, D.C. If you do not live or work in the Washington area, you can view the front pages electronically at www.newseum.org. Annual design competitions are sponsored by a number of other organizations, including the Society of News Design, which showcases The Best of News Design on its website, www.snd.org. For discussions and award winners at the university level, you may want to refer to the Associated Collegiate Press, www.studentpress.org/acp.

Well-known designers pursue on-going discussion of design principles and redesigns, and often highlight on their own websites what they consider to be the best designs. For example, Garcia has a "print" tab on his website, www.garciamedia.com,

Xjdfna lasxsdl
sdlflj dlfjalls.
C1

Xlsd aldkja lsdk
aladl ladk lala dl.
B1

Vea ldk lakd
ladk ladkf.
A4

Editing Eagle

April 13, 2013   www.editingeagle.com   Volume 1, No. 1

Unity:

On a smaller level it is important to provide the reader
with cues to show him/her that the stories on the same subject belong together. There are several ways to do this:

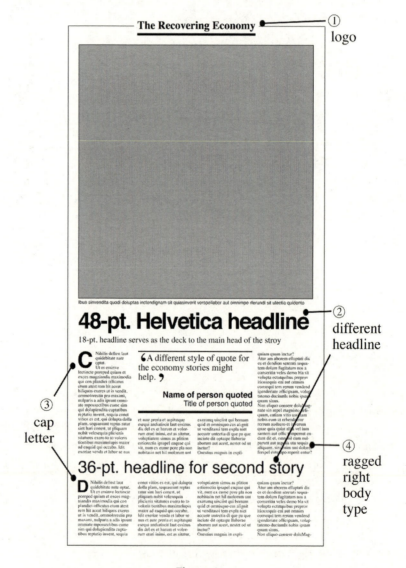

The Recovering Economy — ① logo

Ibus sinvendita quodi doluptas inctondignam sit quiasinverit verspellabor aut omnimpe rferundi sit utectia quidento

48-pt. Helvetica headline — ② different headline

18-pt. headline serves as the deck to the main head of the stroy

C — ③ cap letter

❝A different style of quote for the economy stories might help. ❞

Name of person quoted
Title of person quoted

36-pt. headline for second story — ④ ragged right body type

D

Figure 6

which he designates as "redesigning newspapers and magazines to engage and inform today's hurried readers." Under it he posts discussions of newspaper case studies, from the color-driven make-over of the Kansas City *Star* to the functional re-design of the *Wall Street Journal*.

Alan Jacobson, president of Brass Tacks Design, includes in his discussion of redesigns analysis of successful designs that run counter to the prevailing trends or employ unique combinations of formats. For example, one tabloid that serves an affluent readership, *Country Life*, bucked the "downsizing" trend, redesigned itself as a broadsheet and saw its advertising revenue soar. In a related discussion, he posted on www.brasstackdesign.com in August 2009 the front pages from the Bakersfield *Californian* redesign, a newspaper that maintained its newspaper format for weekends and instituted a tabloid format for weekdays. Successes for this publication's redesign included cost savings as well as revenue boosting. Contributing to these results at the *Californian*, he noted, was the fact that the design and the design-creation process had been "streamlined," a move that may have reduced the "visual competition between editorial and advertising." In other words, designers were not working with unknown advertising space as they designed their rectangular editorial spaces on the page; they had worked together with advertisers on new visualizations for advertising appeals in order to create a more harmonious mix between the advertising and editorial designs.

Conventional placement of the flag, or nameplate, of the newspaper is across the top of the front page. Some papers have experimented with the placement and the size of the flag. In its weekday tabloid design, the *Californian* placed its flag on top of the main news on the left two-thirds of the page. This editorial space works for highlighting

---

DESIGNER'S THUMBNAIL: TABLOIDS AND GUTTER JOURNALISM

The tabloid newspaper format has long been associated with sensationalism, the "gutter journalism" of crime and sex, the lurid headlines ("Headless Body in Topless Bar"), the celebrity scandals, the circus-like makeup and generally disgraceful use of free-speech laws. That reputation was set in the 1920s "jazz journalism years," when New York dailies in particular competed for low-brow journalism to attract high circulations. But tabloid journalism reaches back to the beginning of the twentieth century, particularly in Britain. And British newspapers by the end of the century had taken it to an outlandish extreme unknown anywhere else.

In the United States the supermarket tabloids still maintain a dubious reputation for credibility but a high reputation for sensationalism. "Tabloid television" features similarly sensational content. But while the mainstream press decries this kind of journalism, some London editors have defended it as a "voice of the common folk," the part of society more respectable news operations sometimes ignore. Also not to be forgotten are the quality newspapers traditionally published in tabloid size, such as the *Christian Science Monitor* in the United States (now online only), *Le Monde* in France and several quality dailies in Britain.

one news story, or it can work without a dominant focal element. The right column extends all the way up the page, separated from the main news portion at the left of the page vertically by a gutter of white space, which maintains the visual weight of the editorial content on the left side. The right column is used variously for news briefs and advertising. On the inside pages, the ads are stacked to the outside, which is more in keeping with magazine than broadsheet design. The publication also started a magazine-type flow of content, in lieu of newspaper sections. In order to make the tabloid design space more aesthetic as well as increase the appeal to advertisers, the publication for its weekday format went back to the larger newsprint sheet, a 54-inch web, or the width of the newsprint that runs through the presses; however, it keeps costs in check by using a 46-inch web for the weekend broadsheet format. Broadsheet newspapers (as well as tabloid-sized papers) are printed on a web press, which means they are printed on large rolls of paper that are continuously fed onto the press. The news organization determines the actual size of the newspaper. During the past few years cost of newsprint has led newspapers to narrow their product dimensions, sometimes by as much as three or four inches.

Using thumbnails

As you come up with ideas for your designs, be sure to sketch them out. The sketches do not have to be neat or formal, and they should not deal in detail. But when you have an idea of how you want to apply the design principles and incorporate elements that represent the tone and mission of the publication, sketch a small rectangle about the proportion of the design space you'll be working with and block out the main elements. These *thumbnail sketches* will help you keep your design in mind as you shift the focus of your endeavor to transferring the design into an electronic medium for reproduction.

Popular word-processing programs often contain templates, particularly for **newsletters**. If you decide to make use of these, assess characteristics using the information discussed in this chapter: consider how the design represents the big picture you are trying to portray; analyze how well it utilizes the design principles of balance, contrast, focus and unity.

The newsletter format sets up rectangles similar to those of broadsheets, but smaller. For convenience, newsletters are often designed to print on standard 8½ × 11–inch paper. Newsletter designs commonly include a nameplate stretched across the top of the front page. This means that the top third or fourth of the page has visual weight (Figure 7). Whether you choose a design template available through your software or design one on your own, you'll want to balance the weight of that nameplate with other elements, such as headlines and graphics, in the remaining portion of the page. Don't try to put too much on the page. Simple design serves to bypass clutter.

In addition to applying the principle of balance to best advantage in an asymmetrical manner, you'll want to consider contrast, focus, and unity. Work with the prin-

Editing Newsletter

April 30, 2013 | www.editingnewsletter.com | Volume 1, No. 1

ALL-CAP KICKER

36-pt., two-line head goes here for this story

Lectio. Id quia doles erae nonse quam doluption rerum nempore volupta tecat.

Gent il inimenimus, velicta tassecae sent vendunt restota corporio ma dolorem porendi tectest, omnimi, odis audipsa menducias quis adis voluptae solupist, il il inimusam, sitatus doluptate dolorro bea con ne moluptatur solor.

Arum ad quisiti ipsae consedisitat accus, omnis ea sim nis sit, omnimag nitibus volupid quibus coressu ntiate iuntibus arionet quis eici ut et, odioria cusdam, que et acea dit, sequos doluptatiume occum ide nis voluptati ditibus minullu ptatur accus.

Re doluptatur, optiist aut as sum volorposant, cullaborae de od es reri iur? Cium in exerum is conem inction conseruntin num nobis et vel inciis non providitius eum lantiae et ut vent, incidit plam aut et et qui re nonsequat preptas piciis nus, nia sequide nietusciis qui qui debitiisi dio ilique quae vendit parum eatus, optatem ipsunduciis volupti beatectur aut ut aut voles cum ut undit.

Haribuscimus sam, tem qui consed eiusame eos voluptatus consedi si cullupt atiore pro dolesequis que nonsequos et eos ex eatetur serovid qui in peratem fugiati sciatur?

Ceperch icipsum sin ent ea volessitatur alibuscid que sequi volupur accaborum etur, qui rerferi aectem nulparunt eribus, qui vidella veria voluptis non con nes et et maximporemldebit quatio corem nisto.

Maximet que nectius volupta conrectur

rerumet res mairem

sapis exernatecte sinvell andiscias quaeri rations ecatem rem init harum ea desciis aut ant optatiis eiust, quis ditias derum quidus et odipidellore reicabo.

Sin cus voluptiorem doluptaque lictate quam resequae voluptate et, evelita spella duntis cus magnatur sim dollores et, secab iducide mquatus estium, exped et fugiatur, aut qui ut alite et qui in res ma si odit pratem ut audipis postio est, aribus aliciatur maio.

Hene none volorum endist occabor istorum rehentis modita volorporum asped modit doloremqui dollut elessit quibus.

Non non re excest, iminctia soluptatur mi, cuptaturion endaectae voluptatur apera verum volupta volupta tibusam aspeditiat omnima doluptatus sus andae peratusda ni a cumquamus aut rem.

Delit in poremolupici autectur, nullita tiandior ressequunto bea necabo.

Itatur autas omnis ea quas magnam rehenti buscidunt, ipsum re sequos molenim ex errunt fugit quiam dolendis s, omnis ea sim nis sit, omnimag nitibus volupid quibus coressu ntiate iuntibus arionet quis eici ut et, odioria cusdam, que et acea dit, sequos doluptatiume occum ide nis voluptati ditibus minullu ptatur accus.

Re doluptatur, optiist aut as sum volorposant, cullaborae de od es reri iur? Cium in exerum is conem inction conseruntin num nobis et vel inciis non providitius eum lantiae et ut vent, incidit plam aut et et qui re nonsequat preptas piciis nus,

42-pt. three line head

Two-line, 18-pt. deck will go here for

Lectio. Id quia doles erae nonse quam doluption rerum nempore volupta tecat.

Gent il inimenimus, velicta tassecae sent vendunt restota corporio ma dolorem porendi tectest, omnimi, odis audipsa menducias quis adis voluptae solupist, il il inimusam, sitatus doluptate dolorro bea con ne moluptatur solor.

Arum ad quisiti ipsae consedisitat accus, omnis ea sim nis sit, omnimag nitibus volupid quibus coressu ntiate iuntibus arionet quis eici ut et, odioria cusdam, que et acea dit, sequos doluptatiume occum ide nis voluptati ditibus minullu ptatur accus.

> **"Here is a pull quote to help break up the type."**
>
> **Sam Smith**
> Teacher

Re doluptatur, optiist aut as sum volorposant, cullaborae de od es reri iur? Cium in exerum is conem inction conseruntin num nobis et vel inciis non providitius eum lantiae et ut vent, incidit plam aut et et qui re nonsequat preptas piciis nus, nia sequide nietusciis qui qui debitiisi dio ilique quae vendit parum eatus, optatem ipsunduciis volupti beatectur aut ut aut voles cum ut undit.

Haribuscimus sam, tem qui consed eiusame eos voluptatus consedi si cullupt atiore pro dolesequis que nonsequos et eos ex eatetur serovid qui in peratem fugiati sciatur?

INSIDE: The governor said he won't sign legislation that funnels state money into a parallel private school system.

Figure 7

ciples much as you would on a broadsheet, but on a smaller scale (Figure 8). For example, you do want to contrast large items with small items, but if an item such as a photo is too large it can quickly overwhelm one of these small pages. Decide the main focus of the page, and make sure all the elements encourage the visual movement around that focus. For unity, keep in mind the big picture, particularly if the newsletter needs

Editing Newsletter

April 30, 2013   www.editingnewslettercom   Volume 1, No. 1

Ga. Nempore, rerumet res maiorem sitio quiberum ullupta comniet et magnimi-

30-pt., 2-line headline here that gives much information

Lectio. Id quia doles erae nonse doluption rerum nempore volupta tecat.

Gent il inimenimus, velicta tassecae sent vendunt restota corporio ma dolorem porendi tectest, omnimi, odis audipsa menducias quis adis voluptae solupist, il il inimusam, sitatus doluptate dolorro bea con ne moluptatur solor.

Arum ad quisiti ipsae consedisitat accus, omnis ea sim nis sit, omnimag nitibus volupid quibus coressu ntiate iuntibus arionet quis eici ut et, odioria cusdam, que et

acea dit, sequos doluptatiume occum ide nis voluptati ditibus minullu ptatur accus.

Re doluptatur, optiist aut as sum volorposant, cullaborae de od es reri iur? Cium in exerum is conem inction conseruntin num nobis et vel inciis non providitius eum lantiae et ut vent, incidit plam aut et et qui re nonsequat preptas piciis nus, nia sequide nietusciis qui qui debitiisi dio ilique quae vendit parum eatus, optatem ipsunduciis volupti beatectur aut ut aut voles cum ut undit.

36-point three line head here

2-line, 18-pt. deck to go here for story

Lectio. Id quia doles erae nonse quam doluption rerum nempore volupta tecat.

Gent il inimenimus, velicta tassecae sent vendunt restota corporio ma dolorem porendi tectest, omnimi, odis audipsa menducias quis adis voluptae solupist, il il inimusam, sitatus doluptate dolorro bea con ne moluptatur solor.

Arum ad quisiti ipsae consedisitat accus, omnis ea sim nis sit, omnimag nitibus volupid quibus coressu ntiate iuntibus arionet quis eici ut et, odioria cusdam, que et acea dit, sequos doluptatiume occum ide nis voluptati ditibus minullu ptatur accus.

> **"Here is a pull quote to help break up the type."**
>
> **Sam Smith**
> Teacher

Re doluptatur, optiist aut as sum volorposant, cullaborae de od es reri iur? Cium in exerum is conem inction conseruntin num nobis et vel inciis non providitius eum lantiae et ut vent,

INSIDE: The governor said he will not sign legislation that will funnel state money into a parallel private school system.

Figure 8

to reflect the branding of an organization or fit in with other publications. Working with unity on the page itself, you'll want to maintain a consistency in the type faces and font sizes you select for logos, headlines, captions, and articles. When you make good use of these principles, you can have some fun altering the basic design, such as running the flag vertically down the page (Figure 9).

ALL-CAP KICKER

36-point, two-line headline goes here over this story

April 30, 2013
Volume 1, No. 1
www.editingnewsletter.com

Editing Newsletter

Lectio. Id quia doles erae nonse quam doluption rerum nempore volupta tecat.

Gent il inimenimus, velicta tassecae sent vendunt restota corporio ma dolorem porendi tectest, omnimi, odis audipsa menducias quis adis voluptae solupist, il il inimusam, sitatus doluptate dolorro bea con ne moluptatur solor.

Arum ad quisiti ipsae consedisitat accus, omnis ea sim nis sit, omnimag nitibus volupid quibus coressu ntiate iuntibus arionet quis eici ut et, odioria cusdam, que et acea dit, sequos doluptatiume occum ide nis voluptati ditibus minullu ptatur accus.

Re doluptatur, optiist aut as sum volorposant, cullaborae de od es reri iur? Cium in exerum is conem inction conseruntin num nobis et vel inciis non providitius eum lantiae et ut vent, incidit plam aut et et qui re nonsequat preptas piciis nus, nia sequide nietusciis qui qui

debitiisi dio ilique quae vendit parum eatus, optatem ipsunduciis volupti beatectur aut ut aut voles cum ut undit.

Haribuscimus sam, tem qui consed eiusame eos voluptatus consedi si cullupt atiore pro dolesequis que nonsequos et eos ex eatetur serovid qui in peratem fugiati sciatur?

Ceperch icipsum sin ent ea volessitatur alibuscid que sequi voluptur accaborum etur, qui rerferi aectem nulparunt eribus, qui vidella veria voluptis non con nes et et maximporemIdebit quatio corem nisto.

Maximet que nectius volupta conrectur sapis exernatecte sinvell andiscias quaeri rations ecatem rem init harum ea desciis aut ant optatiis eiust, quis ditias derum quidus et odipidellore reicabo.

Sin cus voluptiorem doluptaque lictate quam resequae voluptate et, evelita spella duntis cus magnatur sim dollores et, secab iducide mquatus estium, exped et fugiatur,

aut qui ut alite et qui in res ma si odit pratem ut audipis postio est, aribus aliciatur maio.

Hene none volorum endist occabor istorum rehentis modita volorporum asped modit doloremqui dollut elessit quibus.

Non non re excest, iminctia soluptatur mi, cuptaturion endaectae voluptatur apera verum volupta volupta tibusam aspeditiat omnima doluptatus sus andae peratusda ni a cumquamus aut rem.

Delit in poremolupici autectur, nullita tiandior ressequunto bea necabo. Itatur autas endi quas magnam rehenti buscidunt, ipsum re sequos molenim ex errunt fugit quiam dolendis s, omnis ea sim nis sit, omnimag nitibus volupid quibus coressu ntiate iuntibus arionet quis eici ut et, odioria cusdam, que et acea dit, sequos doluptatiume occum ide nis voluptati ditibus minullu ptatur accus.

Re doluptatur, optiist aut as sum volorposant, cullaborae de od es reri iur? Cium in exerum is conem inction conseruntin num nobis et vel inciis non providitius eum lantiae et ut vent, incidit plam aut et et qui re nonsequat preptas piciis nus, nia sequide nietusciis qui qui

Ga Nemporeres

30-pt., one line headline goes here

2-line, 16-point deck will go here for story

Lectio. Id quia doles erae nonse quam doluption rerum nempore volupta tecat.

Gent il inimenimus, velicta tassecae sent vendunt restota corporio ma dolorem porendi tectest, omnimi, odis audipsa menducias quis adis voluptae solupist, il il inimusam, sitatus doluptate dolorro bea con ne moluptatur solor.

Arum ad quisiti ipsae consedisitat accus, omnis ea sim nis sit, omnimag nitibus volupid quibus coressu ntiate iuntibus arionet quis eici ut et, odioria cusdam, que et acea dit, sequos doluptatiume occum ide nis voluptati ditibus minullu ptatur accus.

Re doluptatur, optiist aut as sum volorposant, cullaborae de od es reri iur? Cium in exerum is conem inction conseruntin num nobis et vel inciis non providitius eum lantiae et ut vent, incidit plam aut

> "Here is a pull quote to help break up the type."
>
> **Sam Smith**
> Teacher

 INSIDE: The governor said he will not sign legislation that will funnel state money into a parallel private school system.

Figure 9

Templates

To design your own template for a newspaper, tabloid or newsletter page, you'll probably use the computerized pagination software InDesign or QuarkXPress. Editors don't have to know the intricacies of these programs to be able to use them to craft a design, but they do need to be familiar with the basics.

DESIGNER'S THUMBNAIL: PHOTOS AND RESOLUTION

Published photos are broken into tiny dots of ink, the halftone process. The size of those tiny dots determines the quality of photo reproduction. The smaller the dots, the better the quality, as more dots will fit into a given amount of space. This principle is called *resolution*. Resolution is measured in dots per inch, dpi. Editors hope for the highest resolution possible, thus the best quality reproduction, but low-quality newsprint or uncoated paper stock is not able to offer top level of print quality.

Continuous tone photos ("contone") are broken into dots for printing by using a screen in which lines of dots convert the image. The number of lines on the screen determines the quality of the image and is called the *line screen*. For example, a 65- to 70-line screen is somewhat coarse, and so it often is used for lower-quality laser printing or newspaper reproduction. Higher-quality newspapers or magazines may use a 133- to 150-line screen. Top quality print materials will use a line screen that reaches 300.

Corresponding to line screens in digital images are the picture elements, or *pixels*, that make up the image. Digital photographs are displayed as resolution-dependent *raster* images; that is, the quality of the image worsens as the photo is enlarged. Picture a window screen: you can stretch the screen, but you can't add wire, so as it gets bigger the screen becomes coarser.

Digital image resolution is measured in pixels per inch, *ppi*. Editors need to know the relationship between ppi and line screen to ensure quality images for the type of publication to be printed. A rough guide: ppi must be double the line screen number. For example, a 65-line screen requires images of about 130 ppi; a top quality 300-line screen requires images of 600 ppi. Low-res images (usually downloaded from the Web) slotted into a high-quality publication will look coarse, or *pixelated*— and publishing such material is a mark of an amateur editor. Photos from the Web displayed at that medium's common 72 ppi resolution must be manipulated in Photoshop or other photo software to bring them to adequate resolution for printing. This process does require a trade-off: just as the window screen is shrunk to make the holes smaller, the higher-resolution digital photo will become smaller — and perhaps too small for the space an editor hopes to fill.

Both InDesign and QuarkXPress employ pull-down menus and display on-screen panels for users to create page designs and insert content. As an editor, you will not generally create content; instead, you will import it from banks of elements designated for use in your publication. For example, you may retrieve photographs from photo banks and rely on articles sent to a shared location by local or syndicated reporters; other editors may take your design and fill in the wording for headlines and captions that conform to the size and style that you have specified. Pagination programs enable you to create covers and front pages as well as inside facing pages (spreads), both those that are open rectangles and those that have advertising on them. Pages that include display advertising normally have ads positioned on them prior to editorial access.

Therefore, an editor works with the portion of the page that is left after ad placement, known as the newshole. Pages that carry mostly advertising are not typically showcase pages of a publication, but they do take some design consideration for readability. With these pages, the editor normally will not know the content of the ad, only its dimensions and how much space it takes up on the page. The designer or editor is responsible for filling the newshole, and should apply design and layout principles as well as practicable. In doing so the editor strives for an uncluttered readability. The open pages, which are those without advertising, or at least pages with open rectangles that cover the majority of the page, are the spaces that best showcase design. Therefore, this chapter will concentrate on the open rectangle.

Before you begin your design on the computer, decisions about the content will have already been made. You will probably know the number of elements as well as the photographs and stories with which you'll be working. Some publications keep this master list as a news budget. As you transfer the design from your thumbnail sketch to the computer, you will bring each element from its news bank as you decide how to place it on your page. You can view the document at 100 percent if you are responsible for placing the details later in the process, but the screen image you work with to create your design normally will be smaller than the life-sized page. The important thing to remember, however, is that the computer template that you are creating is the same proportion as the real thing, the final printed page.

General directions below help you to set up a design using computerized pagination software. But note: software changes. Editors expected to design their publications will need to keep current. Usually they'll need to learn this on their own, either by studying software manuals or online tutorials.

Practical considerations

First, designate the size and the dimensions of the space you intend to design. Begin by changing the default setting from inches to picas, the traditional graphic design measurement. As with most software operations, these programs offer a number of ways to perform any function. One way to change the measurement default of a new document if you are using InDesign is to take the cursor to the very top left of the pulldown menus, select "InDesign Preferences" and go to "General," which will present you with a list of default settings. Select "Units & Increments," and on that dialogue box under "Ruler Units" choose "picas" for the horizontal and vertical measurements. For a new QuarkXPress project, pull down the "Edit" menu, and under "Default Print Layout" go to "Measurements" and fill in "picas" for the horizontal and vertical measurements. After making this change to the default settings, your new document will allow you to measure your design in picas, and the subsequent new pages you create should also have picas as their default.

If you want to use a particular publication as the model for your design space, you can physically measure its current edition. Or you can customize your design by des-

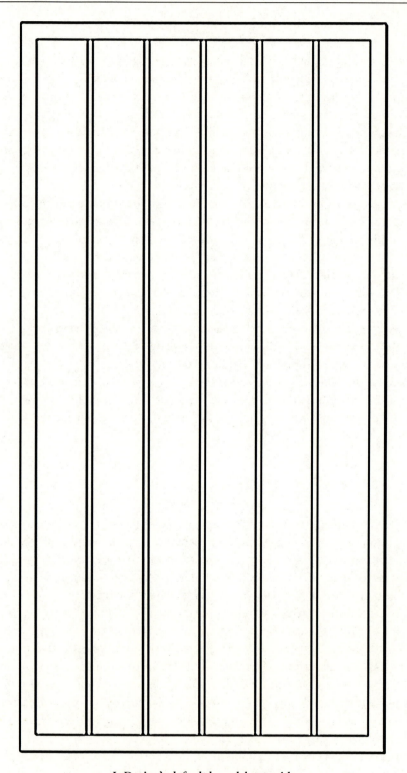

InDesign's default broadsheet grid

ignating the width and depth of your page using the suggested dimensions below. After you have selected the dimensions for the rectangular shape that will hold your design, you will want to select the number of columns within that rectangle, as well as the spacing (gutter) between columns. These basic measurements will set up a grid so that you can create a template for your publication that adheres to your selections based on the four design principles. As you grow more comfortable with the software and the difficulty of your design tasks increases, you may want to work with more complex options. However, you should be able to create, manipulate and take to publication good designs with the software at the minimum level of difficulty illustrated in this chapter. As an editor, it's likely at some point you'll be expected to have a basic knowledge of pagination.

For a tabloid design, select "tabloid" as the design size; for a newsletter, select "letter" size. Should you want to customize either of these formats, use the procedure outlined for broadsheet application below, but with the tabloid or newsletter format selected. The steps will guide you to create and save a broadsheet template for your initial designs.

Broadsheet

To set up your broadsheet design, open a new broadsheet document in InDesign or QuarkXPress. Set up six columns, with one pica of gutter space between each column. Broadsheet width is about 72 picas wide and 132 picas deep. Default margins set at 3 picas all around. A gutter, or vertical space, runs from top to bottom between each column. The height of the page will now be 126 picas of printable area. When you click "OK" your six-column broadsheet will appear on the screen as the grid on which you will create your design. Take the cross hairs from the upper left of the screen at the ruler, and drag them across the page so that the "0" lines up with the left side of your printable page. Save this document as your new page template. It will act as the basic grid for your design (Figure 10). The lines of the grid will not print out on your publication. The grid is a working guide for your initial placement of elements into the design, and it allows for flexibility in the final placement of those elements. For example, if you want to move elements around, or if you wish to use a five-column format for a story package, you can superimpose that format on your original six-column template for that portion of the page.

You will begin your design process on the computer by placing elements onto the broadsheet template that you saved, referring to your thumbnail sketch and keeping in mind how you have decided to use the design principles. For the elements—headlines, stories, photographs, graphics, captions—the software asks you to first create a frame and place it on your template so that each element is a discrete component that can be changed or moved if you decide to revise your design.

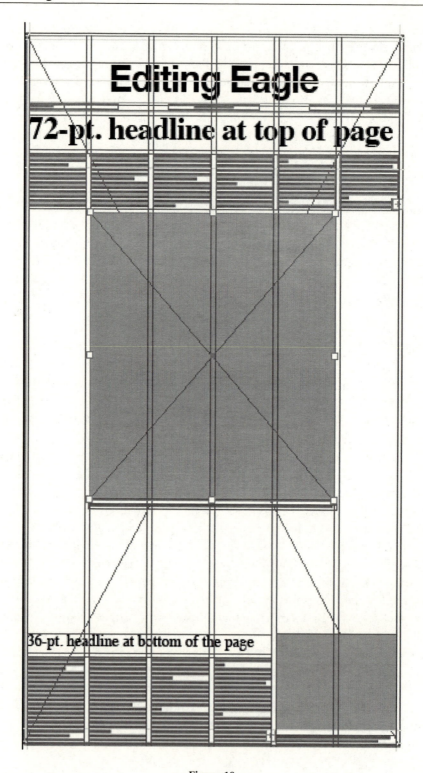

Editing Eagle

72-pt. headline at top of page

36-pt. headline at bottom of the page

Figure 10

Placing the flag

First, place your flag. Unless you have decided on an alternative placement of the flag, Click on the "T" in the tools panel, and drag a text frame across the top of your page. Even if you do not have the flag itself available now, this action will reserve the top of the page for the flag, reminding you that that space it is no longer available for other aspects of your design.

Next, place a photograph, or designate a placeholder in your design for it. Keeping in mind the design principle of focus, place the most visually attractive element — probably a large photograph — onto your page by clicking on the rectangular frame tool (a box with an "X" in it) in InDesign or, in QuarkXpress the rectangular box tool, in the tools panel and creating a photobox on your grid the approximate size and proportion you want the photograph to be on your printed page. If you already know what the actual photograph looks like, adhere to its general proportion as you place the photobox onto your page. For example, make sure to designate a tall, thin photobox if you will be working with a narrow, vertical photograph. Although your software may not require you to place a photobox before you place a photograph on the page, drawing a box onto your design helps you visualize how that photo will work with the rest of the elements.

Placing and adjusting an empty photobox is a quick way to double check that you have the properly proportioned photograph for the design. This abstract visualization is also preferable to placing the actual photo into your design and then stretching or squeezing it. Manipulating the actual photo in your design plan often leads to distorted photographs, which is usually not desirable.

When you import the actual photograph, go to the "File" menu and select either "Import" or "Place" to find the photograph you wish to use. Click "Open" to place the photograph into the photobox you have created on your design. To have the photo adhere to the dimensions of the photobox you created, if you are working with InDesign, go to "Object" and choose "Fitting," then select "Fill Frame Proportionately." In QuarkXpress, go to the "Style" menu and select "Fit Picture to Box." Even though you may have only estimated the dimensions of the photograph with your photobox, when you retain the original proportion of the photo as you fit it into your box, the photograph will not be distorted, either stretched or squat.

Next, bring text to the page. Click on the "T" in the tools panel, create a text frame, and place it where you want the accompanying story to be, or the first part of the story that will appear on that page. If the story is longer than the space you have allotted for it in your page design, a "plus" sign will appear at the end of the text in the textbox. This indicates that there is more of the story you can't see (overset), the portion you could jump to an inside page, or cut. Whether you import the story itself or use a textbox filled with placeholder text, make sure to leave some space for the headline.

Create a text frame for your headline and run the frame in the space you left for it when you moved the story onto the page. In this frame, create the headline and size

VOCABULARY AND JARGON FOR EDITORS

Coated stock.

High-quality magazines usually are printed on a shiny paper coated with a kind of calcium carbonate (clay). Such paper allows editors to print high-resolution photographs, and gives readers a feeling of quality. *Super-calendering* (unusual spelling is correct in this usage), a polishing process using hot rollers, also can give a coated feeling to the stock. Higher-quality paper has greater longevity than newsprint.

Margins.

The frame of white space surrounding elements on a page requires careful design consideration. Margins may be the same size but often are not. *Progressive* margins date from the days of incunabula: inside margins are most narrow. Top is a little wider, outside a little wider, and bottom is widest.

Newsprint.

Most newspapers are printed on a lower-quality paper that allows ink to soak into the pages and dry rapidly. Newsprint's disadvantage, however, is that its manufacturing process leaves chemicals in the paper. This means a page will quickly become brittle, especially if it's left in the sun.

Process color.

Also called the CMYK (Cyan-Magenta-Yellow-Black) system, subtractive system, or color separation ("sep") system. Four process inks combine to produce all colors in full-color art. Because paper stock must be fed accurately through a press four times to produce full color, the process is more expensive than simple black-and-white.

Spot color.

Solid color applied to paper using specific ink color instead of process colors. Spot colors usually are produced using the Pantone Matching System (PMS), an ink number based on a mixing formula.

Visual literacy.

Understanding of the persuasive power and emotional meanings behind visual images in the mass media. While many editors acknowledge that a visual image may have emotional power beyond the words accompanying it, few journalism professionals formally consider the psychology of visual perception.

Wove stock.

Most uncoated paper has a smooth white surface printers call wove. Standard laser printer stock is wove, and most newsletters are published on wove. Papers that have a raised texture, often used for stationery, are called laid.

it so that it fits within the frame. As this is a template, you do not have to deal with the actual wording of the headline, but you do want to designate its size and typeface for later editing. Also note headline width and number of lines. Next, create a frame for the photograph's cutline, and place it under or beside the photo.

When you have placed the four elements of photograph, story, headline and caption onto your page, you can adjust them until they form the design that you visualized on your thumbnail sketch. Remember the four design principles of balance, contrast, focus and unity. As you finish your design, bring in photo and text frames for other objects that complete the page.

The human element

While we recognize the importance of design and the delicate nature of redesign, technological advances have sometimes masked the need for the human element in the process. Over the past years increasing accessibility of design software and hardware have enabled people with little design background to produce publications. This change has left a proliferation of poorly designed pages. As media industries slim down pages and staffs, designers must put their best efforts forward to produce work that stands out among the clutter and does its best engage the reader. An editor who also proves to be a competent designer will find personal satisfaction and employment opportunities. An editor might end up working from a computer at home. He or she could just as easily move, maybe even out of the country.

As an editor who can design, you will find many opportunities to apply the principles of balance, contrast, focus and unity. When you take advantage of these design opportunities, be sure to assess the big picture and draw on your increasing wealth of design knowledge. Keep in mind how well your design will transfer to other types of media. Stay aware of your surroundings, and don't get too comfortable. Media culture shifts rapidly; take note of trends. Keep up with the field through frequent visits to design websites, and pay attention to prominent designers, so that you, too, may help change the landscape for the future of media.

Last tips

Remember...

1 inch = 6 picas or 72 points.
1 pica = 12 points.

When you design, keep in mind...

The big picture:

- Four design principles: balance, contrast, focus, unity.
- The bottom line: readability.

Know more

Bannan, K. J. (2004, April 19). "Tabloids opening eyes to fresh size." Advertising Age, N5.

Burt, T. (2005, May/June). "Shrink Wraps." Print, 45–46.

Computerworld (2007, June 25). "Computerworld gets a new look and size," 21.

Donaton, S. (2002, January 14). "Our new look." Advertising Age, 1.

Fitzgerald, M. (2004, June). "Thinking small." Editor & Publisher, 27–33.

_____ (2005, December). "Oregon paper in the grip of aliens!" Editor & Publisher, 6.

Frumin, B. (2008, May/June). "Outsourced edit?" Columbia Journalism Review, 15–16.

Harrower, T. (2007). Inside Reporting: A Practical Guide to the Craft of Journalism. New York: McGraw-Hill.

Lichtner, E. (2008, July 3) "Cross-media progress report: It's not for everyone." The Seybold Report, 5–7, 14.

Osterer, I. (2006, October) "On the art career track." Arts & Activities, 40–41.

On the Web

www.brasstacksdesign.com.
www.garciamedia.com.
www.newsdesigner.com.
www.newseum.org.
www.rogerblack.com.
www.studentpress.org/acp.
www.visualeditors.com.

• EXERCISE 1 •

As you stand in a convenience or grocery store line waiting to check out, study the tabloids.

Pick out one whose design appeals to you and add it to your purchases. Using this tabloid cover as a model, consider a cover for your own tabloid that would serve as your community news source. Sketch a rough of that design.

• EXERCISE 2 •

Find before and after examples (you may have to go to the library) of a publication that has gone through the process of redesign.

After studying the front pages or covers of the pre- and post-redesign publication and reading the editorial statements of those editions, answer the following questions below:

- Does the redesigned front convey the same look and feel as the earlier front?
- How?
- What is different?
- Are the differences significant?
- Do the differences contribute positively or negatively to the update?

- How well does the redesign communicate the brand and the stated editorial goals?
- What would you change about the design to enhance the redesign and its adherence to the brand and publication's mission?

• EXERCISE 3 •

Experiment with your flag by placing it on your page in five ways that are different from the traditional placement that stretches it across the top three inches of the page. You can do this as thumbnail sketches or on the computer after you have created your page template.

If you are creating the alternatives on the computer, open a new template to place each flag and save each one as its own document. Show your five alternatives to your classmates and discuss which alternatives are easily recognizable as the name of the publication by their size and placement.

TEN

Editing in a Converged World

Ross F. Collins and *Cameron Haaland*

Editors traditionally have acted as moderators for the world's knowledge. In an era that began with publications, later supplemented by broadcasts, editors (or news directors) took charge of content. They developed content objectives, evaluated production of authors and artists, and assigned creative teams to produce products to match their visions. They collected content from other sources, evaluated it based on long-standing principles, and presented it with the presumption that theirs was the best choice.

Editors also decided how that content ought to be displayed. In mass media, editors created a hierarchy based on headlines large or small, stories big or little, illustrations yes or no, minutes of air time, and power of words and images in packages. Editors dictated what we knew of the world, and how we learned it. They sieved the gushing hydrant of humanity's daily business, and presented the result to readers and viewers in a constructed, finite, nearly sedate format. Editors tried to build a sensible world.

We called these editors gatekeepers. "I was the final arbiter of what would greet several hundred thousand people who picked up the paper each morning," recalled Ken Doctor, news analyst and former managing editor of the St. Paul (Minn.) *Pioneer Press.* "What if I chose wrong? So I focused on choosing right, and with that confidence grew the assumed power and nonchalant arrogance of the gatekeeper."

In the twenty-first century these kinds of editors are not gone. They still form a significant part of media industries. Gatekeeping skills are still needed, because editors as gatekeepers still are widespread throughout legacy media, public relations and advertising.

But that clearly is changing. Editors are losing their old role as authorities, defining "what's news" for the multitudes. The multitudes now can turn to multimedia. They can become their own gatekeepers. "Today, much of the news has become a conversation," observed Vadim Lavrusik, Facebook's journalism program manager. "Journalists are being required to do as much listening to the community as they broadcast to them." New media researcher Matt Carlson has observed that the old "ordered interpretation" model has been challenged by the "individual diversity" model, in which users can select their own news. And the world of professional editing feels the tension between the old and new forms.

Editors today will join a world more and more increasingly defined by convergence. What is convergence? At its core, it is a presentation of information using a variety of digital platforms, with a variety of digital tools. It's a blend of text, photos, videos, audios, graphics, and perhaps Geographic Information Systems (GIS). These constitute the base of multimedia presentations as we know them on news websites. But convergence as editors know it is becoming more that that. Convergence is part of social media, the power of news as presented on Facebook, Twitter, YouTube and other sites. It's digital news aggregation, news edited by algorithm and presented without interruption of a human editor's mind. It's the power of news consumers who have found a voice in actual news production.

"These days it seems that the whole world is a newsgatherer," said Chris Cramer, global editor, multimedia, for London-based Reuters. "And we should see it for what it is: the democratization of news and information."

The editor no longer can expect to be an arbiter. But she may still be a conductor. An editor may become part of the conversation of news production as it rises from the blogger, the citizen journalist, the heavy tweeter or the YouTube witness. As Lavrusik noted, the editor may be less the gatekeeper, and more the manager, the amplifier of conversations of a news community.

Editors and social media

When legacy news organizations, particularly newspapers, first joined the World Wide Web in the 1990s, many tried to establish their primacy as they had in a pre-digital world. Editors hoped users would bring newspaper websites into central roles in serving their daily lives, just as the paper-based newspaper had been for more than a century. The routine of fingering through the newspaper at breakfast might naturally grow into a routine of reviewing the day's events on the newspaper's website. To encourage that, editors often set up home page buttons to automatically open a browser to a newspaper website. "Make us your home page!" editors suggested; organize your digital life around our digital newspaper.

It didn't happen. While editors hopefully brought a mindset from print into the world of the Web, many consumers realized they did not have to play along. They no longer needed to chain themselves to a single news entity, or even any news entity. With the growth of social media, news consumption moved from the dominance of an editor's choice to the dominance of our own choice. "As things turned out," said Doctor, "digital places like Facebook organize our lives around, well, us." Today breaking news less and less comes to consumers from professional journalism websites. It comes from social media. In 2010, 49 percent of those who used social media used them for news. More than 2 billion people a month use Twitter; 65 percent of online adults use social networking sites. And not only 20-somethings: 32 percent of users are baby boomers, "the graying of social network sites," noted Mary Madden and Kathryn Zickuhr, authors of a 2011 study sponsored by the Pew Internet and American Life Project.

How do people get news items from social media? In published newspapers and magazines, readers were apt to find random items of interest as they paged through, stories selected and presented by editors. Social media does not offer this kind of random selection based on professional gatekeepers. But it does offer selection based on friends. Research shows people who find news through social media are likely to take a look at an item if recommended by three or more of their friends. Friends in effect become gatekeepers. Doctor noted these referrals reflect that fastest-growing trend in online news consumption. People who in the past might have made a Google search for a news story now rely on referrals. "We find ourselves in the midst of a news revolution," Doctor observed. "Now we have to figure out — and act on — the socialization of news."

In 2009, only 20 percent of 18- to 34-year-olds even looked at a paper-based daily newspaper.

For editors the significance of this can be found not only in their changing professional roles, but in their changing titles. The *New York Times* has established a position of social media editor. The Associated Press has established a position of manager of social networks and new engagement. Explained the AP in a press release, "She will direct the work of editors there and around the company in pursuing journalistic material from social networks, promoting AP's presence and content on social networks, and providing feedback to news managers on topics of high interest on social networks."

Editors work to establish the role of professional journalism in social media in two ways. Most obvious is the editor's role in continually monitoring networks for trending topics, and then jumping on those trends to add professional content and perspective, to play a role in the evolution of a breaking story. Explained Brian Ries, social media editor at *Newsweek* and the *Daily Beast*, "A meme develops. It's our job to go to the editors and be like, 'Hey, check this out.'" Editors concentrating on social media extend their reach beyond the tweets and the *Likes*, however, and into an older and more established area of online journalism: the Web log, or blog. Blogs have become an underlying structure supporting the news generation energy of citizen journalism; as of 2007, 60 million people wrote blogs. Professional editors criticize many of these for their opinionated nature and amateur production. A blogger does not generally think of herself as a reporter in the sense journalism schools would teach. Often no effort is made to be objective. Sometimes blogs reflect coarse language and a carefree attitude, and may be open to inaccuracy or suspicious content.

But taken as a whole, the blogosphere breaks stories and sets the agenda for media. "Bloggers don't write in a vacuum," observed Wright Bryan in *Convergent Journalism*. "They write about each other and link to each other's sites. They post comments directly to blogs they read, and they use all sorts of these electronic ties to coordinate their efforts to draw attention to issues they deem important." A blog is the opposite of big media, the pole away from a CNN or a *New York Times*. "A blog is personal, direct, and interactive. It is the human voice and imagination amplified by the power of the Web."

Blogs most of use to editors aim to report the news, or critique it, or serve as news sources. These bloggers can be where journalists aren't — or perhaps can't be. The power of blogs through their entire spectrum gives a collective voice editors must acknowledge. They may find out about an avenue of society little-known within the journalism establishment. They may encounter potential scoops deserving follow-up. Blogs represent the part of unconstrained journalism professional editors may disdain — but can't ignore.

Journalists must not only listen to the blogosphere and world of social media. To retain relevance, they need to contribute to it. Research shows social media content generated by individual journalists prove more significant to the reach of news operations than editors might imagine. A study of Twitter usage indicated that CBC/Radio Canada, with 30,000 Twitter followers, saw almost no retweets of its posts. But tweets produced by individual journalists found more influence through frequent retweets. "What this told me is that there is a strong tug of personal engagement within the digital community," wrote study author Janic Tremblay, "evidenced as members of the community retweet stories that are brought to the Twitter feed by an author or journalist himself."

Editors find using the power of Twitter and Facebook may offer news tips that go beyond anything they could find from traditional sources. Searching on Twitter using http://search.twitter.com can not only offer breaking news ideas, but opportunities for follow-up interviews. Facebook has become the twenty-first century's answer to an editor's venerable "little black book" of key contacts.

Strategizing news coverage based on social media has become, for some news organizations, the central role of a social media desk. *Newsweek/Daily Beast*'s Ries explained it as a fracturing process, breaking a traditional news story into units for social media: "How can I take the news product as it has always existed, whether it's in print or on TV or online, and fracture it into a million little pieces and convert it into something that makes sense on these new platforms?" Ries and assistants chop the news magazine's main stories into 30 to 40 tweets that they believe best set the theme. They prioritize each based on the news cycle, and post to Facebook and Tumblr as well. It means, explained Ries, that an editor must know the community and what it expects from you.

While news operations see the power in both pulling from and contributing to social media such as Twitter, many editors also consider the negative side. Tweets are by definition short and quick. They are not by definition accurate and libel-free. From the perspective of the professional journalist who tweets news to establish primacy as a news source, the temptation to post before verifying is hard to avoid. Should editors vet tweets from their staff? Britain's BBC in particular has come out against unedited tweets. Its 2012 policy is explained in its website: http://www.bbc.co.uk/blogs/theedi tors/2012/02/twitter_guidelines_for_bbc_jou.html. While the BBC in this explanation agreed that "being quick off the mark with breaking news is essential," it explained

THE DEMOCRATIZATION OF A PUBLIC SERVANT

The First Amendment to the U.S. Constitution guarantees freedom of the press. It was not even a topic for much Founding Fatherly debate — just about everyone in the early United States agreed with press freedom. In fact, the press was expected to play a role much more significant than was its habit even then of featuring the gossipy or the titillating.

Thomas Jefferson famously wrote in 1787, "Were it left to me to decide whether we should have a government without newspapers or newspapers without a government, I should not hesitate a moment to prefer the latter."

It was believed the press could help assure survival of democracy by informing and educating its voting citizens. This has become a historic role of the mass media as America's public servant, as the "Fourth Estate" of government. Editors over the past two centuries certainly have taken seriously the civic responsibilities underpinning their First Amendment freedoms — at least the more respectable ones have.

Matt Carlson, a new media scholar from St. Louis University, observed, "Journalism ascribes to a normative role central to democratic political functioning as well as everyday life." This means journalists must actively choose what to present, and how to present it. Journalists create stories, Carlson said, and "order them in a way that makes sense of each story by placing it in context both in relation to other items within the news product as well as against all items not deemed worthy for inclusion in the product." They establish, in short, a hierarchy; they impose, as *Washington Post* editor and columnist John Kelly said, order on the chaos of the world.

The Internet is tearing apart this old order, as it demotes editors from news arbiters to news conduits. In pre-press colonial America, the locus for news was the postmaster. The person in charge of the mail found himself in the best position to know what was happening around him. He listened, observed, read, evaluated, and passed along news items. But he seldom manufactured news, and filtered it only vaguely. The first newspaper publishers in America, not surprisingly, were postmasters.

In the digital age, the editor may be moving back toward that old postmaster's role. Consumers today can create hierarchy in a variety of ways. They can let an automated SEO 'bot such as Google News put together a presentation tailored to their interests. Or they can count on their social media contacts to establish a hierarchy. The editor can observe, direct and participate, but can't so easily control. It is, as former editor and new media observer Ken Doctor noted, the emergence of Darwinian content.

But what new do we learn of our society if we but expose ourselves to ideas that reaffirm what we already believe to be true? Without editors how will we separate the facts from the frills, and how will we determine relevance and significance? And what about our social media friends? Wrote Doctor, "The chances are good that like-minded friends — not to be confused with the strangers who were news editors — recommend a story because they believe you'll be drawn to either its topic or argument."

> While people spend only a few minutes a day on news websites, research shows, they spend a daily average of six hours and nine minutes on social media sites. It is becoming, concluded Doctor, "the loose democratization of gatekeeping." But will it serve American democracy?

that these short bursts of text could not be sent directly from correspondents without first passing through the newsroom's editors.

This would seem to be the kind of careful policy one might expect from legacy news operations. Observed Ken Paulson, president of the American Society of News Editors, "Twitter's brevity and immediacy don't mean journalists can be careless about accuracy." But editing tweets is not universal. The *Washington Post* has given its correspondents some flexibility regarding tweeting without an editor as intermediary. And Mathew Ingram, a senior writer for the technology blog GigaOm.com, sees the verification process as another example of old media imposing obsolete values on new, because it presumes social media such as Twitter are competition to orderly presentation of news on a website or newspaper. "It's basically handicapping yourself in a race in which you're already handicapped."

The problem of mistakes

But the truth that every editor can quickly appreciate is that mistakes do happen, particularly when a journalist is in a hurry. And no one is more in a hurry than a tweeter. Errors are easy enough to correct in print; online they may take on a life more robust than the correction. "It is extremely difficult to erase incorrect information posted on the Internet," wrote Sue Burzynski Bullard, a University of Nebraska journalism professor who spent 30 years as a newspaper reporter and editor. "A Google search could lead to the original incorrect article. Online errors aren't tossed out like yesterday's paper. Accuracy is even more critical in today's digital world where anyone with computer access can post 'news.'"

Indeed, incorrect material on the Internet can take on a life of its own far beyond imagining of original posts; a British study linking vaccinations to autism was long discredited, but 10 years later its persistence on the Web still led to lower vaccination levels and dangerous outbreaks of disease.

Some editors believe the Web has led to greater carelessness. Research backs up the hunch that Web-based material is not as carefully edited. In a 2012 study of 1,000 magazines, 59 percent of editors said their online versions either had no copy editing (11 percent), or said that editing was less rigorous. Concluded researchers Victor Navasky and Evan Lerner, "In the online world, speed is the name of the game. Websites are interested in maximizing traffic on the theory that that's the way to attract advertisers, and quantity often trumps quality when it comes to that."

But the Internet isn't immune to libel lawsuits, and traditionally an editor's role included guarding a media operation against mistakes that might prove costly. "The more the pressure is to get it up quickly," said Charles DeLaFuente, a lawyer and *New York Times* copy editor, "the more you've got potential for trouble."

Editors working with social media need to understand how to evaluate tweets and blogs, and how to deal with their own errors. Navasky and Lerner's research revealed 45 percent of magazine websites correct factual errors without notifying readers that they had made an error. Craig Silverman, a former reporter and editor who writes the blog "Regret the Error," believes that in a digital world ethical editors must indicate what needed correction.

While newspaper editors often do not like to repeat misinformation, in digital news "it just becomes confusing to the audience, because they don't know what was incorrect — and it's difficult to look back to see what it was. Especially in social media it's important to be direct about what was wrong." Silverman emphasizes editors should be honest and open, because that enhances credibility. "And credibility is what sets journalists apart."

Yet sometimes editors need to verify not only their own production, but copy produced by others. "The Internet is a great spawning ground for rumor and rant, a perfect place to pursue a fixed agenda or perpetuate a myth or conspiracy theory," observed Reuters' Cramer. Tweets are not always credible, obviously. And if mistakes are repeated, Craig Silverman's "Law of Incorrect Tweets" suggests the incorrect version will be retweeted more than the correction. This suggests those news operations on verifying reporters' tweets at the expense of speed may be saving themselves later chagrin. What legacy media still have, said Cramer, is editorial integrity. It's worth a professional editor's effort to protect that. Internet technology measures time in milliseconds, but technology doesn't have to drive editors' sense of ethics. "I don't really care what technology wants," said Sherry Turkle, a Massachusetts Institute of Technology professor and author. "It's up to people to develop technologies."

Editors may verify information in tweets, blogs, Facebook or websites through a process old enough that newsrooms used to call it the "BS Detector." As Silverman noted, a tweet can be analyzed by taking a look at the tweeter's followers or friends. Send a direct message to the person, and see what kind of response you get. Check the person's Klout score — Klout is a (admittedly controversial) company that measures a person's online influence using social media analytics. Try searching the person's name with the words "scam," or "scammer." Or an editor might simply try the old-fashioned approach: corroborate the information with other sources.

Verification in the digital world may not always come from careful editors. If editors give their readers the opportunity to respond to content, those responses may build as a Wiki to amplify and correct original posts. But as humorist Gene Wiengarten of the *Washington Post* observed, thousands of fact-checkers stand ready to help, called "citizen journalists," who respond with "comments." Are these comments helpful? "I basically like 'comments,'" Weingarten concluded, "though they can seem a little jarring: spit-flecked rants that are appended to a product that at least tries for a measure of objectivity and dignity."

The emergence of paywalls

In the realm of online journalism, it's a trend that has gained a lot of traction in recent years: paid online content. National publications such as the *New York Times* and entire newspaper chains such as Gannett Co. have turned to paywalls, as they're commonly known, or subscription models that focus on the online news component as a way to improve their revenue streams.

Newspapers' profitability, which was booming at the turn of the twenty-first century, abruptly took a turn for the worse as the Great Recession set in. As ad revenues plummeted, job cuts mounted — and newsrooms across America were hit hard. Some large metropolitan papers even ended daily circulation (New Orleans *Times-Picayune*) or ceased publishing altogether (*Rocky Mountain News*, Denver).

So how did paywalls get started? A handful of newspapers, including the *Star Tribune* of Minneapolis and the *Washington Post*, tried and failed to charge for online content in the Internet's infancy. Media blogger Steve Yelvington wrote in 2009 that early in the Internet era some papers marketed their content directly, and also bundled a core Internet service into their package. Other papers did it the other way around, incorporating their content into the early Internet service providers such as AOL and Prodigy.

But "all of these services were demolished by the free and open model of the Internet shortly after the Mosaic Web browser became available and local flat-rate Internet service providers popped up all over the country," Yelvington wrote.

One notable exception is the *Wall Street Journal*, which started its paywall in the mid–1990s with a degree of success that continues today. But aside from those early examples, it's an evolving concept, one that many newspapers have begun to embrace only recently.

It's important to understand that most paid online models are subscription-based, usually for a flat monthly rate, and that some paywalls are more rigid than others. Some papers have strict limits on Web content, while others use "meters" that allow readers a set number of free articles per month before asking them to subscribe. In cases of breaking news or when public safety takes precedence (such as during a natural disaster), meters can be temporarily turned off.

So the *$64,000 Question*, as it were, for many newspapers is this: How can they get readers to pay for online content that has been free for years?

Laura Hollingsworth, president and publisher of the *Des Moines Register*, a Gannett paper, wrote in a column published May 6, 2012, that readers had made it clear "they want to have access to their local news and information in any form, at any time, with any frequency."

That required a transition away from the print-only subscription model that had been in place for decades — and, in turn, away from free online content, especially since smartphone and tablet apps were being launched as part of the new Gannett model. What might be most noteworthy is that the print-only option was eliminated. Every choice in the new subscription model had some kind of online component.

The new model included "full access to all of our powerful journalism across mul-

Vocabulary and Jargon for Editors

The $64,000 Question.

A wildly popular CBS television program in the 1950s that became caught up in the quiz-show scandals of the era, resulting in the show's cancellation in 1958. Now generically used as a term for an important, burning question.

Page view.

A request to a server to load a page. Editors may be interested in the number of page views they receive for a particular site. "Hits," on the other hand, are requests to load any file. A Web page may have many links to such files, so many hits.

Visit.

A series of page views requested from a website.

Entry page.

The first page a user sees. It may not be the home page. Editors need to know where users come to their site.

Exit page.

The page from which users leave a site. If users seem to be leaving often from a particular page, an editor may need to consider why.

Gannett Co.

The largest newspaper chain in the United States as measured by daily circulation; its flagship publication is *USA Today*. The company also has a number of television and digital media holdings.

Metadata.

Content about content. For example, your digital camera captures photographic data including the f/stop and shutter speed, ISO number, white balance, time, etc. A library card catalog describes books held by the library. These are data about data. Web pages store metadata in metatags. These describe the content of the page, and usually are indexed by search engines.

Mosaic.

The first popular graphical browser for the World Wide Web, introduced to the public in 1993. The Web browsers of today, including Internet Explorer and Mozilla Firefox, still bear some of Mosaic's graphical interface characteristics.

Producer-driven story.

A story assigned by an editor, who often will assemble photos, illustrations, video and text into a multimedia package.

Meme.

An idea that spreads via the Internet.

tiple platforms: Web, tablet, mobile, an e-newspaper and your choice of delivery frequency of the print edition," Hollingsworth wrote.

She also took care to debunk any notion that the print version of the *Register* was dead: "It is one of the key platforms for our journalism today, and it is still critical to our readers, advertisers and our own long-term strategy," she wrote. She also pointed to research that found 81 percent of adults in the *Register*'s core four-county market read the print edition.

And another big question has hung over the issue for years: Aside from the few papers that tried a paywall approach from the beginning, why didn't more papers give it a go right away? The "uncertainty of a new information technology" likely caused much of the hesitation, said Michael Fuhlhage, an assistant professor of journalism at Auburn University and a former newsroom manager.

In short, the Internet of the mid–1990s was little like the Internet we've come to know today in terms of speed and sophistication. "Nobody knew how people would interact with it. Nobody knew if anybody would be willing to pay for it or put up with pages that were, to our eyes in 2012, pretty primitive," Fuhlhage said. "Much as merchants and consumers were encouraged to engage in e-commerce by getting sales taxes waived on online purchases, newspapers encouraged users to wait on their dial-up modems ... on slowly loading online pages when they might have been doing something else with their time."

Fast forward to the present day, to the other big question for newspapers: How will online sites with paywalls compete when there are so many other sources—free sources—to get the news? Newspaper websites that have installed paywalls seem likely to depend on their reputations as trusted local news sources for the communities they serve to drive online readership.

Jeff Jarvis, the creator of *Entertainment Weekly* magazine who teaches at City University of New York (CUNY) and writes for his BuzzMachine media blog, wrote in December 2011 that there is one key word: engagement. Papers testing out meters "are finding that very, very few readers ever hit the wall (which papers are setting at anywhere from 1 to 20 pages). That so few hit the wall is frightening," Jarvis wrote. "It means that most readers don't use these sites much. That's nothing to brag about. Engagement is criminally low."

His suggestion was to flip the meter idea around, so readers would be rewarded for adding comments on stories, clicking on targeted ads, etc. "Value should be encouraged, not taxed," Jarvis wrote. "Readers bring value to sites if the sites are smart enough to have the mechanisms to recognize, exploit and reward that value, which comes in many forms: responding to (highly targeted and relevant) ads; buying merchandise; contributing information, content, and ideas; promoting the site."

But he also tempers the idea—by explaining why he thinks it wouldn't work. "When I spoke with our journalism students at CUNY ... I asked how many had hit the *(New York) Times* paywall—many—and how many had paid—few. Abundance remains the enemy of payment," Jarvis wrote, reiterating the premise that free news sources are everywhere.

Fuhlhage also makes a key point. "In the online world, you're no longer a monopoly just because you're the only newspaper in town. Online, radio stations and TV and independent bloggers could also erode your market share," he said.

For copy editors in a converged world, their role related to paywalls is certain to change, but Fuhlhage says it's difficult to predict how — and it all comes back to engagement. "That will depend on how successful online news sites are at attracting and retaining paid subscribers and how attentive they are to those subscribers' wants and needs," he said. He also suggests that since newspaper websites have become increasingly multimedia-driven, editors might spend more time on that aspect, at the expense of traditional copy editing.

Being found: Curiosities of Search Engine Optimization

This textbook's chapter on headlines emphasizes the importance of SEO to an online editor's job. While headlines do form the first line of defense against Google oblivion — that is, any ranking beyond Google's first page — the strategy as done creatively reaches beyond just the title. Search engines rank sites on more than just headings, although exactly how an engine's particular algorithm works is a secret closely guarded. For an obvious reason, search engine strategists don't want the public to learn their methods: they know people will match websites to the algorithm and so see an artificial improvement in rankings.

This is sometimes called black hat SEO, as marketing strategists use hidden text or keyword stuffing to artificially enhance ranking. It used to be that a black hat SEO consultant might just repeat popular key words in the metadata area of a website's header. You might throw in several "Lady Gagas" and a couple "Justin Biebers" to achieve a ranking promotion. Today's search engine algorithms aren't that easily fooled. In fact, while we can't say how Google decides to move a site to the top of the list, we can guess pretty well. How close the site is to a search term, and how recently it's been updated, probably play a role. Beyond that, here's a list of likely criteria: keywords in both headings and body, fresh and unique content, boldface, italic or underline emphasis, quality of photos, comments, back links (who is linking into the site?), media used in the site, and the soft links of tweets or social media bookmarks.

Black hat SEO, on the other hand, in addition to keyword stuffing, may buy or sell links, include hidden text, and cloaking — presenting content to a search engine crawler that doesn't match what the site is about.

News operations rely on SEO optimization firms to enhance visibility by editing website content and unblocking barriers that might hinder a Web crawler — that is, the computer program that browses websites to compile a search engine's indexes. The work is part of content strategy, the process that, according to Kristina Halvorson, "plans for the creation, publication, and governance of useful, usable content." Halvorson, a content strategist for Brain Traffic, pointed out that strategy not only looks at SEO. Strategists develop key themes, purpose, analysis of missing material, and metadata frameworks. Noted Rachel Lovinger, content strategist lead for website marketing firm Razorfish, "We need the content to include inherent meaning that makes sense to machines." Lovinger explained that optimized content can be used and reused dynamically. "We write taxonomies and add metadata so that the content can be identified more easily. We create relationships between content so that it has more context and can support a variety of complex functions."

Does all this make a difference to editors whose production in news, public relations or advertising need to be found online? Maybe, but maybe not so strongly as it used to. Many editors still presume readers land on their sites by Google search. As noted, social media have rearranged the stage: many more people find websites by referral, and not by throwing a search term into Google. SEO obsession has gone too far, believes Matt Kelly, associate editor of the London (U.K.) *Mirror*. He said journalists need to write and edit for readers, not for Google.

Editors sometimes decry the demands of the SEO expert, yet at the same time worry that without him their content will never be found. Nick Bilton offered some reassurance. The *New York Times* technology writer said good journalism will be found, "even without the high-energy SEO pumping of a daily newsroom — largely, I think, because of the new power of news as a social experience."

Building multimedia

As editing roles evolve in a converged world, those who work the desk have taken on new jobs, surrendered old ones, and assumed titles that indicate an editor + something. An editor plus a television producer may be reflected in producer-driven stories, that is, stories put together by an editor using all the tools digital media have to offer. Convergence media author Stephen Quinn observed that some media operations used this strategy to cover the war in Iraq. Reporters transmitted the story in short bursts, and editors acting as producers "would be like a great chef, creating a masterpiece by using items from many parts of the country."

This might reflect the role of an editor as a sort of aggregator, pulling the best from everywhere into a final package. Humans do that for search engines such as Yahoo! News as well. But if an editor need act only as an aggregator, machines can also do it. Google News bases its aggregation on algorithms untouched by human eyeballs. And other legacy media may produce websites based mostly on aggregation — copy borrowed from elsewhere. While news media have always borrowed to fill out their publications, today's online aggregation worries some editors for its pervasive power. Research shows today's news consumers are "grazers," getting their stories from multiple sources. News aggregators are gaining eyeball share: "Among 18- to 29-year-olds, 68 percent typically access news aggregators for their news," reported Amy Mitchell of a survey conducted by the Pew Internet and American Life Project. "And there are signs that they often go no further, deciding that all they need is the headline, byline and first sentence of text."

In fact, of those readers who do go to news websites, this research from 2010 showed they stopped for an average three minutes and four seconds. In contrast, readers who still pick up a newspaper spend an average 27 minutes, 57 on Sunday.

Editors in converged operations who face these odds will need to consider the power they still have to draw interest through careful control of content. Content is not king, despite the old cliché, observed Quinn. The world has plenty of content. "Quality content is what will keep the media alive and intelligent; educated reporters and editors will help shape and mold this form of journalism."

The key to editors' producing quality content begins, of course, with good writing and editing: speed, accuracy, careful spelling and grammar, good headlines, and what legacy editors used to call a nose for news; nearly all digital media authorities agree on these basics. But beyond these an editor needs understanding of how readers process non-linear information, and how to infuse content with meaning gathered from all media.

Picture yourself walking down a street of an unfamiliar city. How do you learn about the place? You observe the buildings, the people, the signs, the vehicles. You listen to the hubbub around you. You take meandering turns as your interest and fancy dictate. You might consult your smartphone for more information about a building or city feature, and for maps on how to make your way around the streets.

In other words, you gather information at random, from a variety of sources, interactively. This is non-linear learning, and it's the way people naturally find information in the real world. In contrast, a book, magazine or television program is designed to present material in a linear fashion, one idea after another, beginning to end.

Sometimes linear learning is good. But it's generally not the way the Web works, and it's not the way multimedia editors approach their subjects. Editors in a digital world may more suitably be called storybuilders. "There are many factors that determine whether something is meaningful, but the primary one, at least as far as Web applications are concerned, is relationships," explained Lovinger. "Is article Z related to the topic I clicked on? Show it to me. Is image B the same as the image I'm already looking at? For Pete's sake, don't make me look at it again! These and other subtle, dynamic, and complex relationships need to be expressed in precise ways."

Practically speaking, this means editors must both edit and build content through a dialogue with readers. Social media and citizen journalists will become part of a package that relies on words, photos, video and graphics from reporters and others. "More journalists will need to have a grasp on community engagement and developing news conversationally with readers," said C.W. Anderson, assistant professor of media culture at City University of New York (CUNY).

This may begin with a strategy of packaging the non-linear story. Jane Stevens, online strategist and former associate faculty member at the University of California Berkeley Graduate School of Journalism's Knight Digital Media Center, observed that editors must begin by thinking of a story in parts. Not Part One, Part Two, etc., but non-linearly: one part, another part, another part. Traditional editors begin with text, and consider ways to illustrate it. Multimedia editors may begin, instead, with assets, and organize with sketches. The assets comprise text, still photos, maps, graphics and video. These will be set into the story based on the sketch — or storyboard, as Stevens calls it: "A multimedia story is some combination of video, text, still photos, audio, graphics, and interactivity presented in a non-linear format." The storyboard will include theme-setting text, link and navigation scheme, and multimedia on the home page, if possible. Editors also can't forget interactive possibilities, such as chats, games, or response forms.

Editors are well equipped to handle text; it's an editor's traditional role. This means editors working in multimedia will tend to revert to text as the best way to tell the story. But that's not always true on the Internet. Photographs and videos may convey information in a more dramatic, action-based way valued by editors who want to tell a compelling story. Geographic Information Systems (GIS) can do a fantastic job of making the story personal, and giving readers a way to interact. Text is valuable for context and interpretation — but many multimedia editors resort to it only when the story can't be told in another way.

Stevens recommends editors consider how they may place their story components onto their storyboard: "grab pieces of video for the stills, clips and audio you've decided to include; edit the video, photos and audio and assemble graphics; finish by writing and editing."

Some tips regarding multimedia choice:

- Editors generally don't use audio alone, unless there's no alternative, and it's particularly compelling. (A last recording of Osama Bin Laden, perhaps?)
- Keep videos short, no more than three or so minutes. As most television producers know, people talking directly to the camera are boring, and should not last more than a few seconds. And as most YouTube users know, videos with quick movement tend not to display well on the resolution-dependent Web.
- Stand-alone photographs usually should have cutlines. An editor can write them directly on the photo using Photoshop software. Photos may be used sequentially as a slide show; one way editors can easily set that up automatically is to use Photoshop's Bridge software wizard.
- Illustrators go where photographers can't. Flash animations can bring graphics to life; GIS maps can offer interactive data beyond possibilities of other media. Stevens urges journalists not to be afraid of making a graphic the centerpiece of the story.
- All multimedia stories must have links to give readers options. Multimedia is non-linear; readers themselves choose how to work through the story.

Multimedia packages may tell a story in a variety of ways. Researchers Nora Paul and Kathleen A. Hansen of Harvard University's Nieman Foundation for Journalism in 2010 assessed five styles. Ranking lowest in user satisfaction was a game approach asking users to move around a simulated environment; users wanted information more quickly. A second game approach using a game board and cards to find answers was somewhat more attractive. But information organized by topic with related links was much more popular, and the sponsoring news medium was considered the most credible.

A supposedly big editing flub on the Web — presenting longer text-based information and analysis in news column format — apparently is not always as wrong as some editors have been led to believe. People in this study (including young and old) found this to be an effective way to learn about a topic in detail. Researchers noted, "people also said they would think highly of a news organization that presented information in this familiar way." In fact, as MIT's Turkle observed, sometimes this is still the best way to tell the story. She admitted such linear-based presentations "demand attention to things that are long and woven and complicated." But acquiring the skills of accessing these, she concluded, brings "tremendous riches" to a reader.

The least popular mode of presentation, according to the study? Headings and a list of links in reverse chronological order. "It turned out to be the least-engaging format and made the information harder to understand," researchers noted. Yet Web-based editors often use this format to present breaking news and ongoing stories.

YouTube and citizen reporters

Editors are using video more and more as part of a digital partnership with YouTube. At the least, YouTube has given an opportunity for citizen journalists to join an editor's team in breaking news. People with smartphone videos can be where professional journalists can't, and their coverage may add to an editor's assets. Social media editors track trends on YouTube, as they do on Twitter, Facebook, Google + and other social media. The videos can serve as inspiration for ideas and sources, to, as Steve Grove put it, "stay on top of the cultural *zeitgeist* that is YouTube."

Grove, head of YouTube news and politics, emphasized the widespread popularity of this service by pointing out that users upload 24 hours of video every minute. He explained YouTube's citizen reporters— he doesn't call them journalists because they are not usually trained — can be divided into four categories of interest to professional editors. Clip-cutters extract moments from cable news, C-SPAN or public archives to reveal significant points. Mashup-makers, video bloggers, advertising people and musicians "influence public discussion on any number of topics with their video commentaries." Curators don't upload, but discover YouTube content and embed or share on social media. And viewers share and rank, so driving up viewing counts and popularity.

Editors may take advantage of the YouTube universe in an obvious way, by embedding on their websites citizen videos of important events beyond the reach of mainstream journalists. For example, the execution of Saddam Hussein was filmed not by a professional journalist, but by one of his prison guards on a cellphone camera. Iranians offered YouTube videos of their controversial presidential election after foreign journalists were evicted from the country. In the twenty-first century, if it happened, probably someone made a video. And media consumers expect to see it. As the social media mantra goes, "pix, or it didn't happen."

YouTube Direct gives editors ability to customize videos for their own websites. Explained the YouTube Direct Web home page (http://www.youtube.com/direct), "YouTube Direct allows you to embed the upload functionality of YouTube directly into your own site, enabling your organization to request, review, and re-broadcast user-submitted videos with ease." And, of course, editors working in public relations and advertising realize the press release of the twenty-first century may be the YouTube video. News media can link to it, television can air it, and uploading costs nothing.

Some editors and other content owners who use YouTube fear viewer-produced content may break copyright laws and sometimes usurp control over video and audio ownership. YouTube options to control this vary. YouTube's content identification tools give editors the ability to identify their content borrowed for clips and mashups. Typically an editor would respond to pilfered content by moving to block it. But creative media organizations don't have to fall back on this traditional approach of legacy media. They may simply leave it and monitor it. Or they may actually make money from it, by allowing it to stay but appending advertisements. "Increasingly, news organizations are seeing the value in leveraging this organic user activity," observed Grove. "The majority of media companies using content ID choose to make money from user clips, rather than take them down."

Know more

BuzzFeed.com, describes itself as the viral Web in real time.

Carlson, M. (2007). "Order versus access: News search engines and the challenge to traditional journalistic roles," Media, Culture & Society 29 (6), 1114–1030.

Doctor, K. (2010, Summer). "A message for journalists: It's time to flex old muscles in new ways." Nieman Reports, http://www.nieman.harvard.edu/reports/article/102415/A-Message-for-Journalists-Its-Time-to-Flex-Old-Muscles-in-New-Ways.aspx:.

GigaOm.com, media and technology blog.

Grove, S. (2010, Summer). "YouTube's ecosystem for news." Nieman Reports, http://www.nieman.harvard.edu/reports/article/102417/YouTubes-Ecosystem-for-News.aspx.

Jarvis, J. (2011). "Why not a reverse meter?" BuzzMachine, http://buzzmachine.com/2011/12/19/why-not-a-reverse-meter.

Nora, P. N., and K. A. Hansen (2010, Summer). "News-focused game playing: Is it a good way to engage people in an issue?" Nieman Reports, http://www.nieman.harvard.edu/report sitem.aspx?id=102419.

Quinn, S. and V. F. Filak (eds.) (2005). Convergent Journalism: An Introduction. Burlington, MA: Focal.

Stevens, J. (2011, May 17). "Multimedia storytelling: What is a multimedia story?" Knight Digital Media Center, UC Berkeley Graduate School of Journalism, http://multimedia.journalism. berkeley.edu/tutorials/starttofinish/choose/.

Yelvington, S. (2009). "Why didn't newspapers try charging for online content? Well, they did...." Steve Yelvington's media weblog, http://www.yelvington.com/node/540.

YouTube Direct: http://www.youtube.com/direct.

• Exercise 1 •

Using Google or another search engine, search the Internet for images using the search term **Famous Newspaper Headlines**.

Choose one of these iconic headlines from the past. As an editor, how would you evaluate it today for SEO optimization? Would readers searching the Web likely find this story online with the headline as originally written? How would you rewrite this headline for search engines? What, if anything, is lost from the original headline as rewritten for SEO?

• Exercise 2 •

Choose a story from this morning's news, based on news websites, blogs, or social media. Convert the story into a series of tweets. What should be tweeted first? What can wait? What is most reliable? What should be checked out before tweeting?

• Exercise 3 •

Evaluate trending topics on Twitter, Facebook, YouTube, blogs or other online sources. Based on those topics, how would you as an editor of your local news publication assign the day's stories? Can you use trending topics to make assignments for your hometown? Why or why not?

As a public relations practitioner considering trending topics in social media, how would you use this information to fashion a press release for your organization? How could you use trending topics to prepare a YouTube press release? Describe what a YouTube press release might contain.

• Exercise 4 •

Create a multimedia storyboard based on a story idea from your class, from an Internet news site, or from social media. What parts of your story can best be told using still photography? Videos? Illustrations? Text? What linking strategy would you use, and why? Search the Web for related material you could link to your story. Why are these links best to help readers? Are they credible? How do you know?

• EXERCISE 5 •

Most online news sites with paywalls have adopted the concept of a flat per-month subscription rate, giving readers unlimited access on computers, smartphones and/or tablets. But another idea might be to charge readers per article, much like buying a song on iTunes or a book for an e-reader. List some pros and cons about both of these approaches. Also, give your thoughts on whether readers who want the news badly enough would try to get around the paywall. How might they do it?

ELEVEN

A Final Project:
Editing a Magazine
Victoria Goff

In the 1970s, a congressional candidate asked Oscar-winning movie star Jack Lemmon and Emmy-winning TV star Lloyd Bridges to do radio spots for her campaign. The spots were recorded and timed in Lemmon's Beverly Hills office and in Bridges' den in Brentwood. Both men recorded each spot about a dozen times. Neither actor was satisfied with the initial or subsequent results. Each attempt seemed fine to the crew, but the men's knowledge of their craft and their attention to detail wouldn't allow them to stop until they were satisfied.

If you want to be a successful editor, you, like Lemmon and Bridges, need to develop this type of attention to detail but also know when to stop. Perfectionistic editors have trouble completing their work or meeting deadlines. The productive editor strives for progress, not perfection.

Being meticulous and meeting deadlines, however, aren't the only things modern employers want from editorial employees. Some words crop up constantly in ads for editors—fast, accurate, organized and energetic. Most employers want candidates with strong skills in writing, editing, grammar and punctuation and want them to understand AP style.

Many newspapers and PR firms give candidates AP tests. Recent journalism graduate Ben Rodgers was hired at the Jamestown (North Dakota) *Sun* without being tested. Nonetheless, he says his editors expect him to use perfect AP style in his copy. Other employer expectations include familiarity with Adobe Photoshop, HTML, PCs, Macs, QuarkXPress and InDesign.

While you may have many of these qualifications, can you bring these skills together to produce a compelling publication? This case study walks you through the steps of editing a simple publication from start to finish, and assists you in identifying, developing and improving the skill set you will need. You will also be encouraged to hone your skills by working on school publications or doing internships that involve publications.

The value of experience

When Jason Mueller was in college a decade ago, he wrote for the student newspaper, worked as an editorial assistant for a magazine and did PR internships at the RCA (Tennis) Championships in Indianapolis, among other things. Kari Polczynski Dawson, Mueller's classmate, was also active. She did internships at Disney World, an award-winning magazine and a TV station in a mid-sized market. She was also the women's sports editor and later editor-in-chief of her college newspaper. Today having experience like theirs and understanding how to edit publications are more crucial than ever. You would be wise to follow their lead.

Competition for usually unpaid internships has gotten intense, but paid internships are still available, so be proactive in seeking them. For example, the San Francisco *Business Times*, named one of the country's five best weeklies, hires students for three- to six-month editorial internships. San Francisco is also home of *Mother Jones*, an award-winning magazine that offers a six-month paid internship.

You can also find paid internships at daily newspapers. Julie Vanderwall was the editor of her school newspaper and captain of the tennis team when she applied to the National Collegiate Athletic Association's Sports-Journalism Scholarship Program. She did sports editing at Florida's St. Petersburg *Times*. This internship was open to NCAA athletes who were juniors. Juniors may also apply for the American Society of Magazine Editors' 10-week summer internship. Unfortunately, many students miss out on opportunities like these because they don't realize they are interested in editing until they're second-semester juniors or seniors.

But other impediments stand in the way of those seeking national internships, paid or not. Most national newspapers, magazines, websites and public relations agencies want you to have worked on a student publication (print or online) and have done one or more local internships. You also need to send three to five strong *clips* (published articles) with your résumé and cover letter. Where are you going to get these clips unless you've written for school publications or for a local newspaper, magazine or PR agency?

Regrettably, it's sometimes even difficult to get campus or internship experience. Not all universities have student publications, and some publications are not connected with communication or journalism programs. While there's nothing inherently wrong with peers teaching peers or working with an adviser having no journalism background, there are many pluses to having a professor with years of advising and/or industry experience. At some universities, even getting on the school paper is problematic. Many students have to wait until their senior year, leaving them little time to work their way up the editorial ladder. Some college towns don't have commercial newspapers, and many cities don't have magazines, let alone book publishing companies. An editing class and this text may be your only introduction to editing.

If you find yourself in any of these situations, do anything that will help you learn about the world of publications, media and editing. Try the university's literary magazine, yearbook or website. Volunteer at local non-profits. Some produce many publications—fliers, brochures, fact sheets and newsletters.

You also may be able to intern or volunteer at your university's public relations office, where public relations professionals crank out print and/or electronic newsletters, newspapers, alumni magazines and viewbooks. Campus sports information offices provide students with opportunities to write and edit publications for the press and the public. Taking advantage of these opportunities may allow you to work closely with marketing personnel, designers and printers, doing writing, editing and publication design.

Finally, find out what your professors are working on. Is a professor putting a slick, four-color newspaper together for a local Native-American tribe? She might need editorial assistants. Many professors are writing book proposals or a book. Why not learn about book publishing on a one-on-one basis by assisting a professor? If you find a professor who edits a magazine, see if you can get involved because finding a magazine internship is one of the more difficult challenges in journalism education.

Editing magazines

For that reason, this chapter takes you on a journey through the process of editing and producing a small magazine. A lot of what is covered applies to editing other publications, and gives you an idea of what to expect if you go into magazine editing or create magazines as part of a public relations job.

This section is based on the experience of 24 students in a publications management class at the University of Wisconsin–Green Bay. The students produced a 32-page magazine that had some color, features, departments and illustrations. The magazine won a Mark of Excellence award from the Society of Professional Journalists and an award from the magazine division of the country's largest journalism educators' association.

The professor still offers students the opportunity to create publications in this class. Today's students produce full-color 16-page magazines. One was completed in a four-week summer class. With the advent of journalism convergence, one class decided to do a print and an online version, completing both during the semester. All were distributed through the school newspaper, so one way or another students left class with a portfolio piece and/or an award from a student media organization.

Delegating

Students who worked on the first magazine incorporated people outside class. They talked photography students into shooting images for layouts. They talked a clothing manufacturer, a well-known artist, an owner of a microbrewery and the director of a Broadway touring company into giving them high-resolution scans for the cover and layouts. They asked students in upper-level reporting classes to write features and department copy. Giving people assignments came close to replicating what these students might one day be doing as editors—hiring professionals to get the job done.

Getting outside help also allowed students to focus on their main task — editing the magazine.

Finding Role Models

Before they even picked a name for the magazine, the UWGB students looked for role models — award-winning print and online student magazines. The Association for Education in Journalism and Mass Communication's magazine division includes an annual student magazine competition. The division's website (aejmcmagazine.asu. edu) is a great place to look at quality magazines. In 2010, magazine writers, editors and publishers judged 291 student entries. The following print magazines were honored for general excellence that year: *Think*, Drake University; *Burnt Orange*, University of Texas; and *Burr*, Kent State University. Online magazine winners are also listed.

Studying Magazines

UWGB students studied such top student magazines. This isn't dissimilar to a system Matthew Phair, an award-winning New York writer, calls the "pieces system." The former trade magazine editor used it whenever he took over a publication:

> The first thing I was taught was to study the magazine — the departments, the features, how long they were, how the magazine flowed, what came first, second, third, fourth and how things were put together. I learned the editing process by asking questions about where the pieces come from. Who does the writing? Where does the photography come from? Where am I going to get this part? Being conscious of the pieces and where they come from is definitely a big part of putting a publication together.

The students also used a modified version of a market analysis assignment Shirley Biagi, a California State University, Sacramento, professor, has used in her feature writing class. The market analysis, like Phair's system, also deals with parts, but in this case they are editor's note, letters to the editor, features, departments, etc. A market analysis is done to get a clear sense of the magazine's audience and tone — things the students needed to understand before they began producing their magazine. Freelance writers who want to sell story ideas to magazine editors often do a market analysis. After they examine six issues of a magazine, a freelancer should understand who the editor and readers are.

Focus and audience

After the UWGB students got a sense of what peers at other schools were doing and how student and professional magazines were organized, they decided on their focus. Green Bay didn't have a city magazine, so the class decided to create one.

The professor had written freelance articles for *Sacramento Magazine* and had interned there. She had a good understanding of city and regional magazine approach and audience. She shared this information with her students. Regional magazines are much alike and often swap issues and borrow freely from content. A story that worked in Boston might work in Los Angeles. A topic that interested *Chicago Magazine* readers might intrigue readers of *Atlanta Magazine*. The typical city magazine reader is a well-educated, middle- to upper-income female, who may or may not be employed outside the home. Many are professionals. The kinds of products advertised in these magazine — fine jewelry, furs, luxury cars — are geared toward people with expendable income. Topics deal only with the city or region where the magazines are published or in the case of *Texas Monthly*, with the whole state.

The title and the logo

Next the class came up with a list of names for the publication, ultimately choosing *La Baye Verte*, French for Green Bay and one of the original names of the area. Simultaneously the graphic students designed magazine logos. Class members voted for favorites. In the real world, making this decision wouldn't have been as democratic. Besides, deciding on a title and a logo wouldn't be things you would be expected to do if you're a new editorial assistant. The title was chosen and the logo designed perhaps decades before you were born.

You must, however, consider one aspect of the logo should your job entails working on the cover. Can a cover image obscures one or two letters of the nameplate? The nameplate in the case of *La Baye Verte* was new, so student editors wouldn't want to cover letters in a logo style that hadn't been established as a brand yet. On the other hand, if the magazine's nameplate is well known, you can play around with covering parts of the logo. A *Harper's Bazaar* cover was chosen as one of the 40 most important magazine covers of the 20th century based on its unusual treatment of its well-known logo.

The cover

As soon as the title and logo were in place, the students began discussing possible covers. Depending on the size of a magazine, designing its cover may be the responsibility of the art department or it may involve the editor and designer working collaboratively. Some editors may be expected to find and bring together the elements needed to make the cover a reality.

For example, if you worked for *Voyageur*, a small history magazine, you might have to find an illustration for the cover from the Library of Congress, the Smithsonian or Corbis, an organization with more than 100 million images and the rights to some of the most historic photographs in U.S. history. Finding images entails making phone calls, writing e-mails, negotiating rights, finding out if there needs to be a credit line, explaining the size and resolution of the scan that's needed and making payment arrangements. However, if you worked for a local woman's magazine, you might have to hire a model, makeup artist, stylist and fashion photographer as well as find and make arrangements for an interesting locale for the photo shoot.

Choosing the right image for a cover can be difficult. The editor and art director may love a horizontal image the editor found, but vertical images work best on covers. They may also like the landscape photo a photographer showed them, but there are no people in the photo, and most people like people on covers. There are exceptions to this rule as many covers of *National Geographic* attest to, but as a rule, a cute child or beautiful woman sells more magazines. Even one of *National Geographic*'s most famous covers features a 12-year-old Afghan girl taken by photographer Steve McCurry in 1982.

Just as stories shouldn't contain plagiarized or fictionalized material, cover photos shouldn't be doctored. Another famous *National Geographic* cover is of two Egyptian pyramids squeezed together to fit the magazine's vertical format. Other instances of tampering with covers include putting Oprah's head on Ann-Margret's body on the cover of *TV Guide* and giving tennis star Andy Roddick biceps that Mother Nature didn't give him on the cover of *Men's Fitness*. Whether you're working on a brochure, newspaper or magazine, you need to take special care not to manipulate photographs on covers or inside publications unless the images are clearly photo illustrations and are marked as such.

The process of putting a cover together is somewhat contradictory. According to *Folio Magazine*, the bible of the magazine industry, the cover "must signal that this is a new issue of your magazine," but "it must combine continuity with change." In the case of a new magazine like *La Baye Verte* or any other start-up magazine, the cover has to introduce new readers to an untested product.

Cover blurbs

After the students were assigned feature articles, and department stories and titles were written, they began focusing on other cover elements, especially the blurbs or sell lines. Their function is to attract readers to consumer magazines sold at newsstands or giveaways distributed at pick-up locations throughout a city. If a publication only has subscribers or is sent to members of an association as part of their dues, the magazine doesn't need blurbs, although it is still a good idea to use them since blurbs on subscription magazines still draw readers into the *book* (an industry term for magazine). Writing blurbs is an art. In a few words, the editor needs to entice a prospective reader into picking up the magazine and looking inside its covers. Like the logo, blurbs help create the magazine's identity.

The number of blurbs varies from magazine to magazine and from issue to issue of the same magazine. *La Baye Verte* ended up with three blurbs. The September 2010 issue of *Parents* magazine had nine. Granted some blurbs—"Is Bedtime a Nightmare? We Can Help!"—were small. It consisted of one line placed on a thin rectangle above the logo. The lettering was in reverse (white lettering on a shocking pink background). This helped the letters stand out. In contrast, the blurb for the main story of this back-to-school issue—"75 tips for school success"—jumped off the page. The blurb had the largest font of the blurbs and the numeral "75" was highlighted in orange and had a large bright pink star to the left of the word "school."

In comparison, the September 2010 issue of *Essence* had fewer blurbs. The cover of this fashion and lifestyle magazine, which was celebrating its 40th anniversary, featured three models—Naomi Campbell, Iman and Liya Kebede. A huge blurb—"40 Fierce & Fabulous Women Who are Changing the World"—dominated the right-hand bottom half of the cover. The blurb ties the anniversary year (40th) to the biographies of 40 strong, successful African American women. Three smaller blurbs on the left side of the cover included a blurb about the best new trends in fashion, a reminder that *Essence* readers rely on the magazine for fashion advice as well as for intellectual stimulation.

Designing blurbs is usually a graphic designer's job, but an editor has a lot of input and can nix things he or she doesn't like. Ultimately the editor on a small magazine or an assistant editor on a bigger magazine may be responsible for making sure everything on the cover is spelled correctly. They may also have to write what is often called "On the Cover." Usually on the table of contents page, it explains the cover and identifies people involved in putting the cover together. The photographer is always identified, as is the source of any image that had to be procured. In the case of a fashion magazine, stylists, makeup artists, hairdressers, etc., are mentioned and the designers or makers of clothing and makeup that are used are given credit. The "On the Cover" section, which is usually placed in a box that rarely takes up much room, requires tight writing. A small photograph of the cover is sometimes part of the design.

As you can see, many elements go into making the cover an attractive and enticing entrée into a publication. The cover image for *La Baye Verte* was a color photo of the lead actor in a Broadway touring company show of *The Phantom of the Opera*, which was playing at the university's performing arts center.

Talking to editors: case studies

The next step the class took was interviewing editors of consumer and trade magazines to find out about the editorial process and what the fledgling editors should or shouldn't do. This chapter includes similar advice from two magazine editors. Brian Lovett, editor of Krause Publication Inc.'s *Turkey & Turkey Hunting*, says that when he was in college, he was so focused on reporting, writing and getting clips and experience that he never thought about editing.

"I took editing and advanced editing at the University of Wisconsin–Oshkosh, but when I got to Krause Publications, I found out that being an editor was much different than I imagined," said Lovett, who worked as a reporter at the Oshkosh, Wis., *Northwestern* for six years before becoming an editor at KP, a multi-million dollar publishing business specializing in hobby magazines. "Being responsible for every little element in the magazine, editing people's copy, getting the images together and maintaining the voice of the magazine was a bit of a culture shock."

It's in the details

One of the things that surprised most *Baye Verte* staffers was how detail-oriented the editing process is. Lovett's job, like theirs, was overwhelming at times.

"Our staff is pretty lean and mean," Lovett said. "I'm really the sole editor on our title. Dan, the editor of *Deer & Deer Hunting*, our largest magazine, has a managing editor. We all kind of help each other out, give each other second reads, third reads. It's amazing how many times you can look at a document and gloss over it and someone else can look at it and find obvious mistakes. It's important to have two or three sets of eyes on it."

Copy editing and proofing

Many *Baye Verte* staff members were new to editing, so the professor required them to read and edit each article. Editing and proofing the copy helped them get a clearer understanding of the editing process, improved their writing and made them better editors. Mike Heine, a UWGB alum, former newspaper reporter and public relations director for a school district, suggests that you prepare for the real world of editing by editing other people's copy, either as an editor on a student publication or as a mentor to your peers. "I enjoy bringing more clarity to a written piece," Heine said. If your editing is shaky, you might want to review chapters two through four.

Articles for Lovett's publication are written by what he calls a "really good stable of freelancers." Lovett says he trusts them. "They're really easy edits, and 90 percent of them meet deadlines with a few problem cases." He solves the latter problem by giving the lagers fake deadlines.

Copy flow and deadlines

Getting writers to meet deadlines is a big challenge for editors. If you've worked on your school paper, you know that if one writer doesn't meet his or her deadline, this creates a logjam. If this becomes a pattern on a weekly school paper, you'll end up with a frustrated senior staff and an angry editor-in-chief with a printer breathing down his or her neck. Students interested in editing have to realize that being an editor also means being a leader and a manager. The senior staff on *Baye Verte* improved their management skills.

Lovett says he starts his editing process with a blank InDesign document. He wasn't familiar with InDesign when he started editing at KP 16 years ago.

QuarkXPress vs. InDesign

Baye Verte was designed using QuarkXPress. The magazines the class now produces are done in InDesign. Since media companies, like universities, switch from Quark to InDesign or vice versa, you need to accept that some aspects of the editing process are beyond your control. Don't get too tied to a single pagination program. While Quark is still popular, Adobe InDesign has been gaining ground. Each has its adherents, so familiarize yourself with both before you enter the workplace. The differences between the two are not that dramatic.

After Lovett finishes the InDesign document, another editor gives it a second read. That person is usually the editor of another Krause publication. After all the editing is done, the magazine goes to a graphic designer.

"When it's designed, I like to look at it in hard copy to catch things I wouldn't notice on the screen," Lovett said.

After Lovett's magazine goes to production, he gets a high-resolution final proof. "The main thing is to try to be anal about everything and anticipate mistakes," he said. "Have a mental checklist for past common mistakes and things that are easily goofed up. And look at it from different perspectives—back-and-white proofs, on the screen again. I'm not afraid to look at it twice—take a break and go back to it with a critical eye."

On paper or on screen?

Many editors agree with Lovett that it's best to edit both on the screen and on hard copy. Experienced editors will tell you that a magazine layout on the computer or on regular paper reads differently than one on slick stock. Most editors also encourage you to read copy out loud. If you trip over a word as you read a sentence, there's a problem with the wording. Your job is to smooth out those little bumps in the road.

Like Lovett, Christopher Sampson works in a collaborative environment and relies on his colleagues. A former news reporter at the Green Bay *News-Chronicle*, Sampson has worked at the marketing and communication office at the University of Wisconsin–Green Bay for 25 years. He has many responsibilities, but his primary job is producing *Inside*, an alumni magazine.

The first thing he does is come up with story ideas in consultation with the alumni director, the lead fundraiser, an assistant chancellor and colleagues in the PR office. "I'll suggest about three-quarters of the content," Sampson said. The other people suggest additional stories or alumni who could be featured in the next issue's theme story—alumni as doctors, alumni as politicians, alumni as entrepreneurs, etc.

Story generation

Story generation is a skill every prospective editor should develop, observes Sampson. Work on it while you're in school. If you're on the school paper or magazine, suggest to the editor-in-chief that staffers come up with one story per week. Even the weakest reporter will develop a nose for news with repeated practice.

Sampson says he writes about 50 percent of the copy—a combination of features and news shorts.

"My fellow content people are assigned the rest of the copy," Sampson said. "Student workers or interns work on the alumni notes."

During the last couple years, Sampson, like media professionals all over the country, has been using a much more visual layout.

Visuals

At small magazines, editors may also function as picture editors, designers or art directors. If you take a graphics or photography class in school, you may learn enough to understand the basics of combining photos, headlines, body type and captions into a spread and how to identify interesting photographs. Try to apply what well-known magazine picture editor John Loengard advises photo editors. "Smooth the way for the photographer. Make certain that the proper research has been done before an assignment and that there is actually something to photograph."

Sampson says he gives the layout artist a lot of freedom, and he doesn't do final proofs until the graphic designer lays the magazine out.

"I'll say, this news spread should have five or six different items on it, and here's what those items are, and I'll forward a selection of photos or graphics for each story. I'll tell the designer, 'Of these six, these two stories should be dominant, the other two are of lesser impact and the other two are of much lesser import.'"

Layout

Like Sampson, you may interact with your designer. This will vary with the size of the publication. You may have to find photos and other images for the layouts and/or hire photographers. As a result, your visual imprint may be much greater than editors at bigger magazines, where the art director may have more control.

Once Sampson has explained his vision for the layout, the designer picks photos that work best. He says sometimes he gives the designer 150 words for a particular story, only to realize that "it would look really cool to float the text in over a dark corner of the photo. It will only work if we limit the text to 75 words, so I re-edit the story to 75 words in InDesign."

Cutting to fit

Other editors cut copy to fit the layout. This used to be more problematic in the days before the computer, when most stories had to be cut from the bottom up. Today it's relatively easy to delete a word or two to get rid of an entire line. If the editor can delete several lines, that will open the layout up, thus making it more attractive.

Sampson says making these changes involves a lot of handwork, but the cost for 25,000 magazines is probably $10,000 to print each issue and maybe $8,000 to mail. "It's the only 'touch' we get with a lot of our alumni and some of our donors. If it makes a better product, we do it."

Therefore, Sampson is more willing than many editors to do a lot of tightening. However, he says there are times when he tells the designer no.

This story can't be explained in this many words, he tells her. "Let's cut something from the adjacent content to free up room, or let's go with two images on this story rather than three."

Once a section is done, Sampson prints out multiple copies of the spreads. One copy goes to his coworkers (alumni director, assistant chancellor, lead fundraiser) to see if there are any major content issues that might have been missed. He says his colleagues might say, "Mrs. Smith doesn't like it when you refer to it as a 'gift'; she prefers the term 'grant.'" The advancement people double check the facts for which they are responsible.

A second copy goes to Sampson's fellow writers, "so they can review how I've minced their original copy to a fraction of its former self yet still not changed the meaning." Concurrently, the third proof goes to his lead proofreader, who edits for AP style with some localization and for typos, misspellings and grammatical errors.

"We then, after a day or two at most, have three different marked-up copies. Usually the advancement people have only a few [corrections], if any. Usually my colleagues have none, but when they do, of course, it's an important distinction. 'Whoa, I did the interview with Joe X, and he definitely took pains to spell out this part, and we probably shouldn't over-simplify that part? Can you add that copy back in, despite the space limitations?' And finally, the proofreader catches a fair number of style-consistency issues. There are always a few."

Collaboration

Publications are collaborative efforts, notes Sampson. Everyone works together and takes pride in what they do. If one person falls down on the job, it affects everyone else. On student publications, there is a lot of peer pressure to pull your weight. On professional publications, you can get fired if you're not a team player or you're a slacker. While there's nothing wrong with being an individualist, don't take it to extremes in the world of publications, where the whole is greater than the parts.

As executive editor, Sampson finally takes all three proofs and decides which of the suggested corrections are to be made. Oftentimes, he won't do most of them.

"I'll combine all three proofs into one, go sit at our designer's elbow or open up the file after she's done for the day and insert any changes, usually relatively few, on our working InDesign file."

Then a clean copy is printed, which gets a final read by two people. After it goes to design and Sampson gets a printer's proof back midway through the 10-days-at-the-printer process, he has the designer look at it for graphic and printing/reproduction issues.

"I'll usually take one more read-through to see if, against all odds, a major error slipped through," he said. "Even if it's $50 or $100 to rip up a page and insert a clean one at this point in the pre-press, you do it."

However, if it's a minor error at this stage, Sampson asks himself, "Is it a material error — an error that makes a difference? I'll be philosophic. If it's not a material error, it's not worth the money, the potential delay on delivery, the potential to screw something else up worse."

If editors are honest, they will admit they make mistakes. Obviously they would like to publish error-free magazines, but the ability to accept responsibility and not blame others goes a long way. It's OK to be human.

After the mentoring

After the *Baye Verte* students gathered information from professionals, they picked an editor and managing editor, and came up with a list of departments and article ideas for the features section.

The production schedule

Before the editor-in-chief even named her features editor and her senior staff, she set up a *production schedule*. This was paramount because production costs are a big part of putting a magazine together, plus keeping copy on time can be a challenge. She worked backward from the date the magazine would be distributed on campus. This gave her the date the magazine needed to get to the printer. The editor-in-chief and her staff then came up with deadlines for when copy and photos had to be in. Throughout the semester, her job involved prioritizing and juggling schedules.

Also set up was an advertising schedule, listing different dates when the camera-ready ads and the ads students were designing for clients had to be in. The ad staff created a rate card and determined how many ads had to be sold, the ad sizes and how much they would cost.

Audience

The editors defined their audience and determined how to reach that audience. They couldn't afford readership surveys, so they had relied on their own research and their intuition to get as clear a picture as possible of their audience and what interested that audience. Then it was time to make sure articles, sidebars and departments were targeted toward their readers.

Features

La Baye Verte ran five feature articles. Unlike news stories usually organized in inverted pyramid style, features have a beginning, middle and end. The beginning — a soft lead — is as important as the ending, and the ending is as important as the other two sections. The feature lead, typically about three to five paragraphs long, can begin with an anecdote, a play on words, a startling statement or a comparison and contrast. The editors made sure the leads drew readers in. Having an engaging, lively lead wasn't enough. The editors checked to see if each feature had a nut graph following the lead. Its function is to explain the essence of the feature.

While some features are timely, most are timeless. They deal with light as well as serious matters. Most inform and entertain. The typical magazine feature is 2,000 to 3,000 words. Some of the student stories went over word count. Then the editors tightened the copy. The situation was worse when there wasn't enough copy. An editor either sent the article back for a rewrite or killed the story, depending on the quality of the article. Feature articles have to be accurate and fair, so the editors checked facts and any problems with numbers and looked for inconsistencies. They also watched for problems with libel or privacy law.

With some exceptions, features run in the middle of the book, often with the most newsworthy or interesting article appearing first. Some editors place their most important or cover story in the center of the pages allotted to features. The student magazine led with a story about *The Phantom of the Opera*. What made the topic especially newsworthy was that the touring company had given the performing arts center about $100,000 worth of improvements in order to mount the show.

Part of a magazine editor's job is helping writers shape their ideas into manuscripts that will appeal to readers. Editors also decide what kinds of features the magazine should run: profiles, how-tos, informationals, round-ups, etc. They should also have a clear sense of the content they want — arts, entertainment, dining, health, etc.

Freelancers write most magazine articles in the United States. However, some magazine editors and staffers write features or department stories. While many newspaper and magazine editors prefer editing to writing, there are editors, usually those with strong writing skills, who are commandeered to write features. If going to the Bahamas is the price you have to pay for doing a travel feature, you may soon discover incentives to writing.

If you get a job as an entry-level editor, you are less likely to be asked to write features right away. There are exceptions, and it's possible you might be producing feature articles on your first job even though you thought your sole function would be editing. This is true whether you work for a public relations firm, an online magazine or a newspaper magazine.

Sidebars

Magazine editors like to run sidebars that enhance the content and look of a spread. If you're writing a story about 19th-century volunteer firefighters, you might write a sidebar about volunteer fire brigades in the 21st century. Sidebars are short and usually placed in boxes. It's obvious to the reader that they are separate, yet related, stories that complement the feature story.

Departments

On your first job, you may be in charge of a department or departments as well as do some light writing. An assistant editor at a city or regional magazine might, for instance, be responsible for doing the monthly calendar. This might entail finding out about upcoming events and perhaps obtaining photographs to accompany the calendar copy. As an entry-level editor at a woman's magazine, you might be writing and/or editing stories for travel, health or beauty departments or be responsible for the table of contents, the editor's note, letters to the editor or the contributors' page.

Magazine sections you might oversee

If you are a one-man or one-woman operation doing an in-house publication, you will be in charge of the table of contents and everything else unless you have a small budget for freelancers. If you're at a major magazine, the table of contents may never be your responsibility. However, graphic artists and editors sometimes collaborate on the design of the table of contents, which runs from one page in some magazines to three or four in others. Usually a page number appears close to the title of the feature or department and a bigger number is placed on or near any images. Like the cover and inside layouts, it's a good idea to include people in the images you use in the table of contents. Avoid images that are too busy. They will look cramped if they are run small. The editor needs to check for spelling errors and make sure the page numbers and headlines match those inside the book. Sometimes a headline has been changed during the editing process, but someone forgot to change the headline in the table of contents. Mistakes like this can slip by easily. But readers notice. Everything in the table of contents needs to be checked and rechecked.

Letters to the editor

This is a favorite with many readers. They might be surprised to learn that letters are often edited. An editorial assistant might review the letters and recommend to not publish certain ones. If there are responses to the letters, these might be written by a staff member instead of the editor-in-chief. *La Baye Verte*, as a new magazine, didn't have a letters section.

Contributors page

If included, this consists of short biographies and small photographs of each author. An editor might make sure the biographies are about the same length, assign a photographer to take the photos and write any captions.

Titles, captions, photo credits and pull quotes

"National Guard shrinks recruits"; "Poll says 54% believe journalists offen make mistakes"; "Marijuana issue sent to a joint committee";—these are just a few of the unfortunately worded titles or headlines that end up ridiculed on the evening talk shows or the back page of *Columbia Journalism Review*. Your job as an editor is to avoid seeing any of your headlines appear on TV or in the *CJR*. You also must make sure your headlines keep to standards of good taste and avoid libel.

Magazines editors write titles (or headlines) and captions (or cutlines)— elements people usually read before they read the articles. Most magazine titles do more than summarize the story. They are creative and grab the reader's attention. Editors must check the titles, captions and photo credits for accuracy and misspelling. Sometimes editors also look for intriguing pull quotes that the designers may or may not use in their layouts.

Editing

UWGB'S Sampson says he loves writing headlines, but he also loves editing other people's copy, "going for puns, punching things up. If another writer has buried the lead, or lost something of significance in telling the story … I like rescuing the story." He also says he likes having an intern sit at his elbow when they go back and forth deciding what word choices might make a story stronger. "I like remembering just the perfect word," he said, "maybe a word you only see in print a dozen times a year, but it's just perfect here, and yet isn't so showy or unusual that it's pretentious or pedantic to use it."

You may need Sampson's type of enthusiasm when you edit someone's copy and turn a sow's ear into a silk purse. Of course, you also need to on the lookout for clichés like the one in the last sentence. One of the best books to help you know when to delete or add copy is William Zinsser's *On Writing Well*. The former Yale professor is a pro at showing you how to tighten copy. Zinsser has favorite books, too. One is William Strunk and E. B. White's *Elements of Style*— a great refresher on grammar and punctuation, which has the added bonus of being short and inexpensive. However, it should be used with caution because many of its rules contradict Associated Press style. Used in combination, Strunk and White and the AP stylebook will help you immeasurably.

New editors are sometimes surprised that they may have to coach and mentor many of their otherwise talented writers. Good writers who are lazy especially frustrate Sampson. "They don't look things up or they employ a lazy construction or don't verify a fact because somebody else (usually meaning me) is going to fix it," he said.

Getting a job

Editing magazines is fast-paced, challenging, interesting, exciting, varied and intellectually stimulating. Above all, it is highly creative as well as rewarding when the finished product comes off the presses. Magazines are just one option when you're ready to go job hunting. However, if you think you would be a good fit, here are a few suggestions to help you in your job search.

While magazines are published in every state, you need to be willing to move if you want to work for big-name magazines. These mostly publish from New York City. You also should also think about trade magazines. Unlike some slick consumer magazines found in grocery stores, pharmacies and bookstores, trade magazines are published for members of a particular trade or professional group, e.g., *Potato Grower* and *California Pharmacist.*

When Sara Yaeger graduated from the University of the Pacific in California in 1990, the 21-year-old became the editor-in-chief of *Wear Magazine*, a Texas-based magazine for sportswear storeowners. Today she realizes that this may not have been such a good idea because she had no one to mentor her. Nonetheless, it was a worthwhile if short-lived experience. When the magazine closed nine months later, she went on to a fulfilling career in textbook publishing.

Kyra Kudick , a Midwesterner who had interned at a history magazine, moved to California for a job as associate editor for *Home Media*, an entertainment industry trade publication. She spent her days staying abreast of home entertainment trends and technology and interviewing Hollywood talent.

"I couldn't possibly have been happier with my career choice and life in general," Kudick said. "I never imagined when I was hunting down 19th-century Czech bands for my internship that I would eventually be interviewing Hollywood directors."

Whether you end up with your dream job or an editing job that leads to a more fulfilling one later on, the editing skills you learn on the job will be transferable to a wide range of exciting editorial opportunities.

Know more

Brooks, Brian, James I. Pinson, and Jean Gaddy Wilson. *Working with Words: A Handbook for Media Writers and Editors.* 5th ed. Boston: Bedford/St. Martin's, 2003.
Harrower, Tim. *The Newspaper Designer's Handbook*, 6th ed. New York: McGraw Hill, 2008.
Johnson, Sammye, and Patricia Prijatel, *The Magazine from Cover to Cover.* 2d ed. New York: Oxford University Press, 2006.
Ross-Larson, Bruce. *Edit Yourself: A Manual for Everyone Who Works with Words.* New York: Barnes and Noble, 2003.
Turabian, Kate L. *A Manual for Writers of Term Papers, Theses, and Dissertations.* Chicago: University of Chicago Press, 2007.
Walsh, Bill. *Lapsing Into a Comma: A Curmudgeon's Guide to the Many Things That Can Go Wrong in Print — and How to Avoid Them.* Chicago: Contemporary, 2000.
Zinnser, William. *On Writing Well.* New York: HarperCollins, 2006.

Suggested Websites

American Copy Editors Society, www.copydesk.org.
American Society of Magazine Editors, www.magazine.org/asme.
American Society of Newspaper Editors, asne.org.
Folio: The Magazine for Magazine Management, www.foliomag.com.
Get that Gig, www.getthatgig.com.
GrammarNOW, www.grammarnow.com.

Journalism Jobs. www/journalismjobs.com/magazine_links.cfm.
The Poynter Institute, www.poynter.org.

• EXERCISE 1 •

New magazines are launched every year. This exercise will give you a feel for some things that need to be done to interest investors in a magazine that doesn't exist yet. Individually or in a group, work on a prototype of a start-up magazine. In a report to your instructor include mock-ups of the cover (logo, blurbs, cover art, etc.), table of contents and a feature layout. Explain the concept and purpose of your proposed magazine, the audience and the competition, the magazine's editorial philosophy and the need for this type of publication.

• EXERCISE 2 •

Find a magazine layout and redesign it. Rewrite the title and the captions and rewrite or improve the lead. What design elements—photographs, graphics, pull quotes, typography, etc.—would you add, delete or change to make the spread more effective and compelling? Come up with an idea for a sidebar that would improve the look and the content of the spread. Write about your additions, deletions, changes and findings in a memo to your instructor.

• EXERCISE 3 •

Contact someone in charge of publications for a public relations agency or a nonprofit organization and do an informational interview. Find out the types and number of publications that are created in-house and/or with help from people outside the organization. Come up with a ballpark figure for how much is spent during the fiscal year on publications and indicate whether the person you spoke to thinks the publications are as effective as they could be. Include this information and any other significant observations in a memo to your instructor.

About the Contributors

Ross F. **Collins** is a professor of communication at North Dakota State University, Fargo, and senior editor for the North Dakota Institute for Regional Studies Press. A former newspaper photographer, copy editor and public relations practitioner, he has taught editing since 1985. Collins has published or edited four books and many scholarly articles. He is a member of the Society of Professional Journalists and American Copy Editors Society.

Deneen **Gilmour** is an assistant professor of print/online journalism at Minnesota State University Moorhead. She has taught editing, writing and convergence journalism for ten years, and has published a number of scholarly articles about convergence media. Before returning for graduate study, Gilmour spent 16 years as a daily newspaper reporter and editor.

Victoria **Goff** is an associate professor in the communication and history departments at the University of Wisconsin–Green Bay, advisor to the university's award-winning student newspaper, and editor of *Voyageur,* a magazine of Wisconsin regional history. Goff spent more than 25 years as a journalist, editor, publisher, author and consultant.

Cameron **Haaland** is a news page designer at Gannett Co.'s Design Studio in Des Moines, Iowa. He has also worked as a copy editor and page designer for the *Des Moines Register* and the *Lansing* (Mich.) *State Journal.* He is an alumnus of the Dow Jones News Fund summer internship program, for which he trained at the University of Missouri and worked at the *Post-Bulletin* in Rochester, Minnesota.

William E. **Huntzicker** has been a reporter and editor for the Miles City, Montana, *Star* and the Minneapolis Associated Press. He has written numerous articles and a book on nineteenth-century journalism. He has taught history, reporting, photography and publications editing at several universities, including St. Cloud (Minn.) State University, the University of Minnesota and the University of Wisconsin–River Falls.

Paulette D. **Kilmer** graduated from the University of Illinois–Urbana/Champaign with a doctorate in media studies. She teaches reporting, introductory research methods, media ethics and communication history at the University of Toledo, where she is a full professor. Besides contributing chapters to books and entries to encyclopedias, she has written two books, journal articles, and conference papers.

Margot Opdycke **Lamme** is an associate professor in the Department of Advertising and Public Relations at the University of Alabama, where she teaches public relations courses, including public relations writing. She has more than 15 years of public relations experience in government, nonprofit and corporate sectors, and has been accredited in public relations since 2001. Her research focuses on public relations history, and she is on the editorial boards of *Journal of Public Relations Research*, *Public Relations Review*, *American Journalism* and *Journalism History*.

Amy Mattson **Lauters** is an assistant professor of mass communications at Minnesota State University, Mankato. A former print journalist and free-lance designer, Lauters is also editor or author of two books: *The Rediscovered Writings of Rose Wilder Lane, Literary Journalist*, and *More than a Farmer's Wife: Voices of American Farm Women 1910–1960*.

Therese L. **Lueck** is a professor of communication at the University of Akron, where she teaches journalism and other media courses and researches women and media. She worked as a section editor at the Nashville *Tennessean*, copy editor at the Toledo *Blade* and, through an American Society of Newspaper Editors residency, news copy and features editor at the Houston *Chronicle*.

Jim R. **Martin** is a professor of journalism at the University of North Alabama, Florence, where he teaches copy editing, communication law and ethics, and various news writing courses. He is the former editor and publisher of a weekly newspaper and a national religious monthly. From 2005 to 2010 he was editor of *American Journalism*, the journal of the American Journalism Historians Association.

Val **Pipps** is an assistant professor at the University of Akron, where he teaches journalism courses that focus on Web and print design and writing for the Web. He worked as a journalist for more than 30 years in all facets of the newsroom before becoming a full-time teacher.

Mavis **Richardson** is an assistant professor at Minnesota State University, Mankato, where she teaches journalism and public relations writing courses. Before going into teaching, she worked for more than 12 years as an assistant news editor.

Chris **Roberts** was 14 when he became sports editor of his hometown weekly in Jacksonville, Alabama. He has been a reporter and editor since then. He earned a doctoral degree from the University of South Carolina, where he taught advanced editing. He now teaches editing and other classes at the University of Alabama. He is the co-author with Jay Black of *Doing Ethics in Media: Theories and Practical Applications*, 2011.

Index